The Yale
Architectural Journal

**Perspecta 35—
Building Codes**

The MIT Press
Cambridge, Massachusetts
London, England

Editorial Statement

Winy Maas: Interview

Perspecta
The Yale Architectural Journal
is published in the United States of
America by the Yale School of
Architecture and distributed by
The MIT Press
Massachusetts Institute of Technology
Cambridge, Massachusetts 02142
http://mitpress.mit.edu

© 2004 Perspecta. The Yale
　　　Architectural Journal, Inc.
　　　and Yale University
All rights reserved.
No part of this book may be reproduced in any form by any electronic
or mechanical means (including
photo-copying, recording, or
information storage and retrieval)
without permission in writing from
the publisher.

ISBN 0-262-58245-7
ISSN 0079-0958

Send editorial correspondence to:
Perspecta, Yale School of Architecture
180 York Street
New Haven, CT 06520

Printed and bound in the Netherlands
by Lecturis, Eindhoven

Editor
Elijah Huge

Co-editor
Stephanie Tuerk

Faculty advisor
Lauren Kogod

Consulting editors
Bimal Mendis
Michael Osman
Adam Ruedig
Matthew Seidel
Lisa Tilney

Design concept
Min Choi and Albert Lee

Layout and typography
Min Choi

Contributors
Sources of Illustrations
Acknowledgements

4

8 **Antoine Picon**
The Ghost of Architecture: The Project and Its Codification

< Jerold S. Kayden
Understanding the "Code" of Codes

20 **Daniel Sherer**
Le Corbusier's Discovery of Palladio in 1922 and the Modernist Transformation of the Classical Code

< Andrés Duany
Notes Towards a Reason to Code

40 **Peter Eisenman**
Digital Scrambler: From Index to Codex

< Michael Sorkin
Entering the Building

54

62 **Edward Eigen**
The Housing of Entropy: On Schrödinger's Code-Script

< Alexander Garvin
Regulating in the Public Interest

74 **Karl Chu**
Metaphysics of Genetic Architecture and Computation

< William McDonough
Principles, Practices and Sustainable Design —
Toward a New Context for Building Codes

< Rob Imrie
The Corporealization of Codes, Rules,
and the Conduct of Architects

98 **Sylvia Lavin**
What Color is it Now?

112 **Jonathan Massey**
New Necessities: Modernist Aesthetic Discipline

< Bruce J. Spiewak
Current Developments for Building Codes:
Perspectives of a Code-Consulting Architect

< Phillip G. Bernstein
Digital Representation and Process Change
in the Building Industry

134 **Felicity D. Scott**
When Systems Fail: Arthur Drexler and the Postmodern Turn

< Edward Mitchell
Fear Factors

156

Editorial Statement

More than ever before, architecture is bounded, shaped, and directed by codes. As systematic structures of organization and regulation, they set the terms for architecture's amenability to an ever-widening web of internal and external forces. Nevertheless, codes generally—and building codes specifically—are frequently dismissed as onerous requirements to be met and inhibitions to the free undertaking of design. This myopia overlooks the reality that codes are neither neutral nor objective documents. Physically ambiguous, yet charged with political, social, and formal intent, codes operate as the architecture of architecture, creating its preconditions and shaping its production. As they continue to exert such power, architecture cannot remain uninterested in the production of codes, nor disengaged from their directives.

The title *Building Codes* invites misinterpretation. Much like the journal's topic, it is an invitation haunted by echoes of post-structuralism, and one whose paradoxical alchemy of uncertainty and predictability reflects the sort of merger from which codes themselves are inevitably built. More importantly, the title is an invitation to recognize that codes, like architecture, are constructed conditions, assembled with authorial and authoritative intent, yet open to the vagaries of use. Though the term "codes" may carry intonations of a linguistic model, it has long been prevalent in law, genetics, cryptography, and management, where there is a shared notion of codes as possessing a systematically structural quality. Architecture's own history abounds with codes, from abstract models such as Vitruvius's systems of mathematical proportions and Le Corbusier's *Modulor* to comprehensive conceptions of site-specific urbanism, from the London Building Acts of 1667 and 1707 to Michael Sorkin's *Local Code* (1995). In addition to this historic presence, the contemporary pervasiveness of the term in architectural contexts could be situated relative to the discipline's current fascination with developments in the sciences on the one hand—mathematics and biology in particular—and the ongoing encroachment of legal, political, and economic directives on the other.

Traditionally, in architecture as in other fields, codes have been treated as a tool of choice for the imposition or explication of order. It is therefore hardly surprising that in the years following his architectural elaborations for the Panopticon, and until his death, Jeremy Bentham turned his attention largely to codes. Specifically, he sought to maximize their inherent capacity to act as immaterial mediators between individual articulation and collective unity through what he termed a Pannomion:

a single code that would be "all-comprehensive," built on a "perpetually interwoven rationale." Recently republished by Oxford University Press, Bentham's "Writings on Codification, Law, and Education" from the 1810s and 1820s made clear his intentions. Echoing the goals of the Panopticon, yet unencumbered by its material constraints, the Pannomion was proffered as a complete system of regulation to be implemented as law.

In the two hundred years since Bentham's pursuit of an immutable, code-induced order—a pursuit that has proven as illusory as it was ambitious—codes have become ubiquitous, but also surprisingly diverse in their scopes, methods of implementation, and effects. The range of interpretations and positions presented in this issue of *Perspecta* is telling both in its exposure of the extensive historical relationships between codes and architecture, and in its framing of the proliferation of codes implicated in contemporary architectural practice and thought. What emerges is not a vision of codes as merely calcified and calcifying systems, marked by parameters whose sole purpose is proscriptive, but rather an array of codes which are both defining and indeterminate, momentarily fixed, yet historically malleable. While the questions put to the journal's authors focused on the place of codes in architecture, the questions raised by their texts are more concerned with the role of architecture in relation to the many codes, and ideas of code, that affect it. How does architecture codify its boundaries, and how should those boundaries be mediated? Is there room for social, political, or economic agency in architecture, and how might their terms be negotiated? What role could architectural production play in shaping —through tactful engagement with the codes that intersect it—the systems behind these codes? Such questions are as expansive, and as unavoidable, as the possibilities of codes themselves.

Perspecta 35: Building Codes contains two distinct collections of texts. Occasionally converging, they represent responses to solicitations for professional perspectives and scholarly research. Eight shorter pieces, written by Andrés Duany, Michael Sorkin, Phil Bernstein, Bruce Spiewak, William McDonough, Robert Imrie, Jerold Kayden, and Alexander Garvin, explicitly address the contemporary role of codes in the practice of architecture. Commenting on issues raised in their particular areas of expertise, these authors cover topics ranging from the use of parametric modeling software to the distinctions between publicly and privately administered design codes. In response, Ed Mitchell frames this "portfolio" of short texts by ruminating on the extent to which regulatory codes are a response to publicly shared fears.

The second collection of texts consists of eight essays and an interview which address broader issues within the history of architectural codes. These can be read as a series of complementary pairs. Introducing codes as agents of architecture's historical crises and continuities, Antoine Picon and Daniel Sherer show how codes have occupied a parallel history to architecture whose past continues to return, exerting its influence on the discipline and its production.

The pairing of Winy Maas and Peter Eisenman provides the greatest contrast: between an architect who situates his work within political, economic, and social regulatory forces ostensibly outside architecture and considers those external forces formative, and one who focuses instead on an internal logic of architectural coding while offering a rereading of a series of historical projects set in light of these internal codes.

Edward Eigen and Karl Chu examine relationships between architectural codes and those in the sciences. Eigen reflects on the scientific and personal writings of Erwin Schrödinger, the twentieth-century physicist, and draws out the psychological and metaphoric relationships that entangle biological codes, architectural space, and personal identity. Chu focuses on current developments in biology and computation to revise architecture's own coding while offering a critique of contemporary strategies in architectural production.

Sylvia Lavin and Jonathan Massey present codes as mediators between subjective meaning and universal signification. Lavin muses on the potential of color's contemporary and contemporizing affectivity—in contrast to historical attempts at codifying color—while Massey examines codes of ornamentation in the context of historical developments in class-based aesthetic regulation. Collectively, they draw attention to codes in both regulatory and communicative capacities.

In the issue's final essay, Felicity Scott turns her attention to architecture's transitions during the sixties and seventies as seen, interpreted, and presented by Arthur Drexler. Commenting on the current implications of these transitions, Scott's examination of the curator's tenure at MOMA serves as a concluding and cautionary tale.

Elijah Huge
New Haven, April 2004

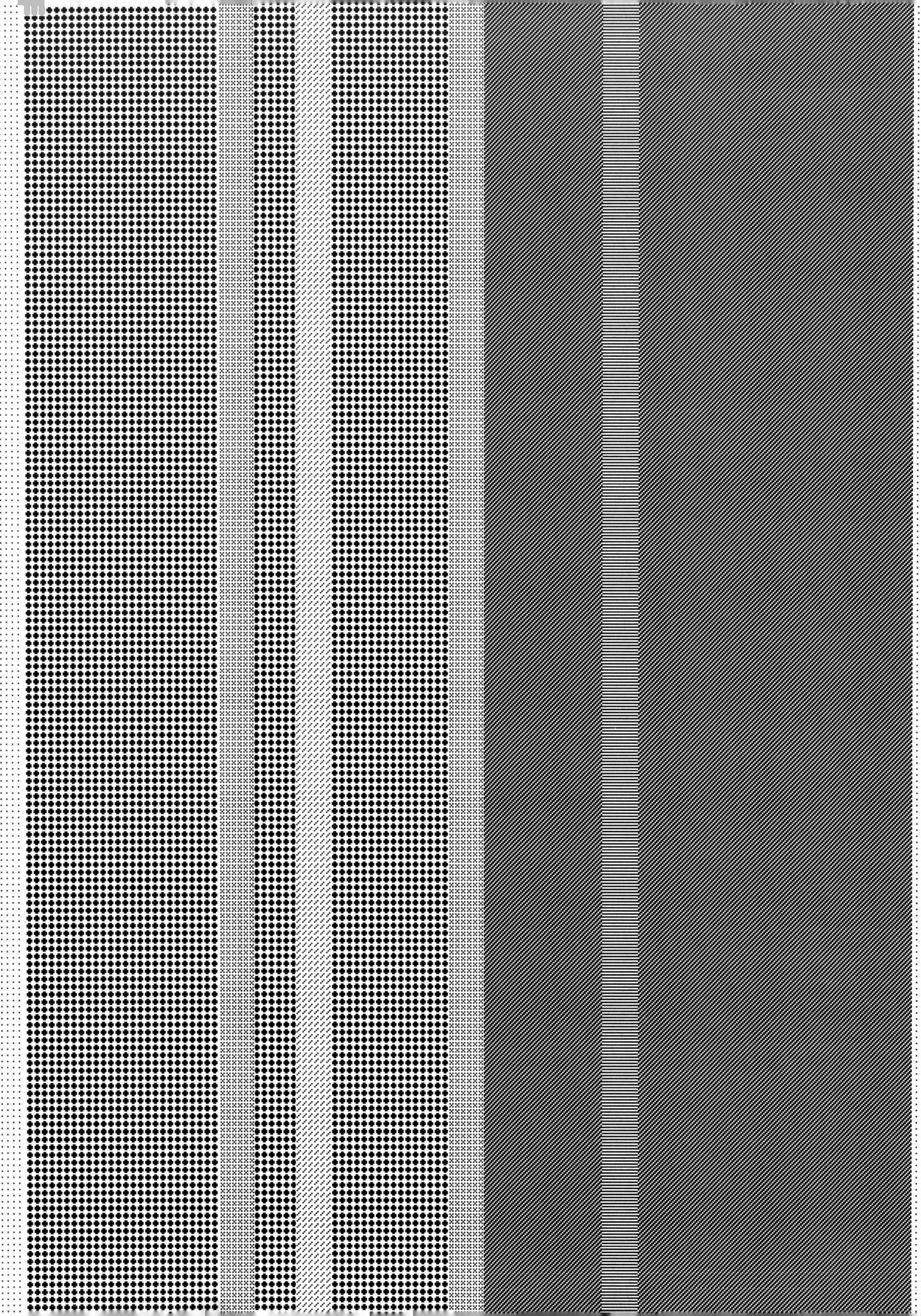

Antoine Picon
Translated by Emmanuel J. Petit and Lucia Allais

The Ghost of Architecture

1 On this subject, see, for example, Alina Payne, *The Architectural Treatise in the Italian Renaissance: Architectural Invention, Ornament, and Literary Culture* (Cambridge: Cambridge University Press, 1999).
2 See Antoine Picon, *French Architects and Engineers in the Age of Enlightenment* (Cambridge: Cambridge University Press, 1992).
3 Kenneth Frampton, *Studies in Tectonic Culture: The Poetics of Construction in Nineteenth and Twentieth Century Architecture* (Cambridge, Mass.: MIT Press, 1995).
4 Thomas S. Kuhn, *The Structure of Scientific Revolutions* (Chicago: University of Chicago Press, 1962).

A haunted discipline
There is no art without rules to codify its practice. This truism has been consistently reaffirmed from antiquity to the present, and it rings particularly true for architecture. Whether to withstand the constraints of physicality, or to respond to the needs of patrons, buildings must obey an entire set of prescriptions that are as social as they are technological. From the Vitruvian orders to the various norms that frame contemporary practice, architecture has never been without rules.

In artistic terms, these rules cannot be dissociated from their transgression—the set of deviations that allow designers to give their work a mark of distinction. Even within the tradition of Vitruvian orders and proportions, room was always found for artistic license, whose infidelities are more or less pronounced depending on the architect.[1] Today's designers take similar liberties with dominant aesthetic codes, willfully transgressing even technological directives for the sake of a desired architectural quality.

Rules and licenses have varied considerably over time; this essay proposes to examine two moments of transition between an old and a new system of codification. The first moment lies at the threshold between the eighteenth and nineteenth centuries, when the Vitruvian principles that architects had endorsed since the Renaissance were brought into question. We live in the second moment, when a digital revolution confronts architecture as much as other artistic and technological practices, from photography to film. While it would be difficult to assess the full implications of a phenomenon as it is unfolding, we may attempt to discern some of its most significant characteristics.

Unprecedented liberties arise during periods of

The Project and Its Codification

transition, much to the displeasure of the guardians of instated tradition. In early-1770s France, a certain Jacques-François Blondel served as an ardent defender of the classical tradition. Blondel could not find words strong enough to fustigate the work of Claude Nicolas Ledoux, whose departures from this tradition strayed well beyond the limits of what had been viewed as permissible.[2] Today, it is not difficult to discern an echo of Blondel's position in Kenneth Frampton's critiques of digital architecture, particularly in his reproach that dematerialization is antithetical to the "poetics of construction" he has deemed fundamental to Modern Architecture.[3]

Yet the freedom afforded by a crisis of architectural codes cannot last forever. New codes emerge to replace those lost, and new licenses to soften these codes also begin to appear. Such new codes are never coincidental. Directly or indirectly, they shape the identification of the elements that constitute the discipline of architecture at a given moment and in a given context. As we shall see, the questioning of the Vitruvian orders and proportions, and the corresponding emergence of composition and type as the guiding principles for French architectural practice, correspond to a centering of the discipline around the question of *project* at the turn of the nineteenth century. The current diffusion of digital culture in architecture will undoubtedly produce a similar shift, and it is in the context of this shift that our contemporary understanding of the architectural project must be interrogated.

Although the codification of architecture is directly related to its disciplinary definition, rules and codes do not systematically address what appears to be essential to the discipline. Once the foundational era of the Renaissance came to a close, the Vitruvian tradition itself granted only distracted attention to the question of orders and proportions. This question was not a central issue until the end of the seventeenth century, when it resurfaced in the debate between Claude Perrault and Blondel, which marked the beginning of the crisis that would ultimately empty the teachings of Vitruvius of their content. Similarly, Jean-Nicolas-Louis Durand's efforts to articulate rules for architectural composition constitute only a transitional phase in the early nineteenth century, after which French architecture found itself more preoccupied with stylistic questions and problems of technological standardization than with the continuation of Durand's efforts. In fact, putting aside these periods of rupture, efforts at architectural codification often seem peripheral to what constitutes the core of the discipline.

Here it is difficult not to think of the vision of history that Thomas Kuhn developed in the early sixties, wherein the history of science is defined by paradigm shifts and their associated revolutions.[4] These shifts, condensed in time and intensely polemical, were, according to Kuhn, to be followed by longer and calmer periods during which research would shun fundamental questions in favor of segmental explorations of one or another principle.

The analogy is tempting. Yet it would be reductive to use a theory like Kuhn's to make sense of the history of the architectural discipline and its succession of codes—be it only because architectural and scientific communities operate so differently. However, the comparison does reveal the prominent role of tradition in both domains. Much like science, architecture seems to function as a succession of traditions that become discontinuous during periods of crisis. From this perspective it becomes futile to search for a timeless definition of the discipline of architecture founded on values or codes that remain unchanged. The history of architecture, then, becomes that of its values, its codes, and their transformations over time, transformations at times so radical that little remains of the architectural truths from an era once a revolution has ended it. Clearly what we call architecture today has little to do with what, say, François Mansart would have judged relevant to architectural theory and practice.

One should not be completely seduced by the intellectual appeal of this discontinuist model. Some projects from the past continue to speak to us; some could even serve as a guide for contemporary practice. Mansart and Francesco Borromini may be remote figures by now, but their architectures—of French Classicism and Roman Baroque—still have much to teach us. Past and present have an uncanny way of short-circuiting one another. The fragments out of which architectural history is made continue to adhere to one another, and though some of the seams are distended, every so often architects are tempted to don the Harlequin's costume this patchwork comprises.

Certainly we could attribute the persistence of past traditions to the existence of a disembodied spirit of architecture that hovers over an ocean of forgetfulness, fishing out certain epochs and certain works—that of Karl Friedrich Schinkel, for example, for the sake of his ties to Ludwig Mies van der Rohe[5]—and casting back others. Even without subscribing to such imagery (an idealist one, to say the least) the astonishing capacity of formal systems to survive their own deaths is nonetheless noteworthy. Although they are attached to distinct historical traditions, the codes and rules of architectures past haunt the present like the shadows that populate the Elysian Fields of Greek myth, capable on occasion of addressing the living and conveying to them some part of their experience. Though we have long since abandoned the Vitruvian creed, we continue to respond to questions of orders and proportions, to the eurythmy of certain compositions, and even to the artistic licenses that architects like Giulio Romano granted themselves. Similarly, having long since repudiated the nineteenth century's obsessions with style, we continue to refer to the notion of architectural style when the need arises. Codes and rules are not simply confined to the successive architectural traditions that they constitute. Beyond their deaths they continue to exert their power, lending our rereadings of the past a contemporary flavor. It is only because architecture is haunted by shadows and ghosts, who drift from room to room murmuring old stories into

[5] Cf. Terence Riley and Barry Bergdoll (eds.), *Mies in Berlin* (New York: Museum of Modern Art, 2001).
[6] René Ouvrard, *Architecture harmonique, ou application de la doctrine des proportions de la musique à l'architecture* (Paris: R. J. B. De La Caille, 1679).
[7] The authors of the *Logique* drew particular contrast between natural signs and signs instituted by people.
[8] On the debate of Perrault and Blondel one may consult, for example, Wolfgang Herrmann, *The Theory of Claude Perrault* (London: A. Zwemmer, 1973); Alberto Pérez-Gomez, *Architecture and the Crisis of Modern Science* (Cambridge, Mass.: MIT Press, 1983); Antoine Picon, *Claude Perrault, 1613–1688, ou La Curiosité d'un classique* (Paris: Picard, 1989); Alberto Pérez-Gomez, "Introduction to Claude Perrault," in Claude Perrault, *Ordonnance for the Five Kinds of Columns after the Method of the Ancients*, trans. Indra Kagis McEwen (Santa Monica: Getty Center for the History of Art and the Humanities, 1993), 1–44.
[9] Denis Diderot, *Thoughts on the Interpretation of Nature, and other Philosophical Works* (Manchester: Clinamen Press, 1999), 38.
[10] Cf. Anne Debarre-Blanchard and Monique Eleb-Vidal, *Architectures de la vie privée: Maisons et mentalités XVIIᵉ–XIXᵉ siècles* (Brussels: Archives d'Architecture Moderne, 1989).

the ears of their occupants, that its successive traditions project the appearance of disciplinary unity.

If one accepts this hypothesis, the question splits: What will remain of architecture as we know it after the digital revolution? Which aspects of this revolution will prove to have a decisive effect? In this respect, the issue of materiality presents less pressing questions than does the privileged status that the project has come to hold.

The crisis of the Vitruvian tradition and the attempts to codify the project

The notion of project is not an invention of the late eighteenth century. It emerged during the Renaissance alongside the modern distinction between the builder occupied by a trade and the architect preoccupied with an idea. Both the Italian *disegno* and the French *dessein* refer to the existence of a creative conception that precedes execution—a conception that simultaneously carries humanist connotations and encompasses technological knowledge.

This could be the end of the story, except that it is not clear that the architecture of the fifteenth and sixteenth centuries defined itself primarily around the *projective* process of design. In their Renaissance reinterpretation, the Vitruvian orders addressed architectural objects in their ability to manifest the regularity of the cosmos rather than in the various steps of their creation. In other words, the built object was given critical weight, whereas the process of its design remained hidden. This emphasis on the building over the design manipulations is particularly apparent in the case of France, where the privileged status that numerous treatises accorded Vignola's system of proportions testified to a desire for simplification in the design process. Indeed, it was to this ambition for simplicity that Perrault would, in turn, bring his own supplementary touches.

The theoretical counterpart to the success of Vignola's system came in the form of a repeated affirmation of the analogy between architectural and musical proportions. Having been frequently rehearsed since its Pythagorean origins, this theme was given a new paroxystic expression in the middle of the seventeenth century in René Ouvrard's *Architecture harmonique* of 1679.[6] Ouvrard's proportions were not instruments for projecting; rather, they were measures by which to sanction those exemplary buildings whose dimensions conform to rules of harmony. Such rules of measure had nothing to do with the effective procedures involved in conceiving buildings.

Around the same time Perrault argued for an almost combinatory simplicity in defense of his own system of proportions—which was more radical even than Vignola's. But in his debates with Blondel the process of design became a secondary issue, eclipsed as it was by questions of taste and convention. Indeed, what Perrault sought in his caustic *Ordonnance for the Five Kinds of Columns after the Method of the Ancients*, published in 1683, was the normalization of taste, or rather its *institution*, in the sense of the term institution borrowed from the authors of the *Logique de Port-Royal*.[7] Blondel, in turn, would rely on Ouvrard to reject this conception of a socialized architectural beauty, in his effort to reinvest orders and proportions with a naturalist and cosmic authority. It has been noted that this confrontation constitutes one of the earliest signs of a weakening in the Vitruvian theoretical framework.[8] Still, the project and its possible codification were addressed only peripherally. It was not until the second half of the eighteenth century that it became a central issue within architectural debate.

The motives surrounding this emergence of the project are too complex to dwell upon here. On a basic level, they have to do with the growing importance of the imperative of utility, as well as a desire for the predictability and control that characterize much of Enlightenment culture. "The idea of 'usefulness' sets boundaries on everything. The criterion of usefulness is about to place limits on geometry, & in a few centuries from now, it will do the same for experimental science,"[9] wrote Diderot in his *Thoughts on the Interpretation of Nature* of 1754. Understood in the rather general sense that the eighteenth-century elites gave it, utility was part and parcel of a desire for predictability. It is important to remember that it was within this context that modern economic science was born.

From an architectural point of view, a whole series of external phenomena foreshadowed the prioritization of utility and its effects. The first stems from a growing interest in questions relating to program and distribution. In fact Jacques-François Blondel[10] himself had cast distribution as one of the principal branches of architecture. Programming spaces, questioning their interrelationships, and organizing them into functionally satisfactory sequences provided a way to address both the administrative needs of institutions and the aspirations of a ruling class who was discovering the virtues of domestic privacy. Public buildings began to be specialized and organized according to specific needs, while the residences of enlightened nobility came to be comprised of rooms with clearly defined uses, whose interrelation was materialized by the connective space of the corridor.

Along with this heightened attention to program and distribution, one must also account for the desire to control the cost and quality of construction more effectively. The debates that surrounded the erection of Soufflot's Abbey Sainte-Geneviève, now the Pantheon, are particularly revealing of the questions that arose around the establishment of rules to ensure the solidity of buildings.[11] Though a famous example, it is by no means an exception. In Paris and the provinces alike, less notorious polemics around questions of construction multiplied throughout the second half of the eighteenth century.[12] This evolution toward a more rigorous control of the building process also unfolded in other domains; for example, techniques for quantifying construction and estimating the expenditure of resources began to surpass the level of precision previously afforded by Pierre Bullet, whose 1691 *Architecture practique* had served as the authoritative manual on the subject. Toward the end of the century, measurement derived from use and convention would be replaced by measurement founded in geometry, resulting in much more reliable techniques of estimation.

Measured against these new stakes, the inadequacies of the theoretical and regulatory framework inherited from Vitruvius soon became evident. New foundations were needed if architecture was to be more than merely useful and provident. Architecture would also have to "speak" to the mind and senses.[13] To preserve its status as an artistic practice aligned with the fundamental values of society, its utility could not be only physical; it also had to be moral. To these challenges one must also add the growing rivalry between architecture and engineering, and the corresponding threat that architecture might be subsumed as merely a branch of the conquering new art of the engineer.

As a cultural production, architecture followed the general movement of a century that spanned from Locke and Condillac to Kant and German Idealism, which is to say, from a diversification of experiences to their progressive re-concentration into a transcendental subject who, alone, gives them meaning. So it is that French architectural thought between the years 1770 and 1790 would come to lend an increasingly determinant importance to what happens in the mind of the architect, and to the primarily intellectual nature of the operations that he practices.

Before Durand's *Précis*, Boullée's *Essai sur l'art* was perhaps the clearest expression of this shift. It is in this perspective that his famous introductory statement should be read:

What is architecture? Shall I join Vitruvius in

---

11 See Michael Petzet, *Soufflots Sainte-Geneviève und der französische Kirchenbau des 18. Jahrhunderts* (Berlin: W. de Gruyter, 1961); and *Le Panthéon, symbole des révolutions* (Paris: Caisse Nationale des Monuments Historiques et des Sites and Picard, 1989).

12 See, in the case of Nantes, G. Bienvenu, "L'Affaire de la plate-bande du grand escalier du palais de la Chambre des Comptes de Bretagne: Expertise et pratique de chantier à Nantes au XVIIIe siècle" (D.E.A. dissertation, Université de Paris I – Sorbonne, 1996).

13 Cf. Anthony Vidler, *The Writing of the Walls: Architectural Theory in the Late Enlightenment* (Princeton: Princeton Architectural Press, 1987).

14 E.-L. Boullée, *Architecture. Essai sur l'art*; present translation is from the English edition, *Boullée's Treatise on Architecture*, ed. Helen Rosenau (London: A. Tiranti, 1953), 46.

15 Read in this context Werner Szambien, "Notes sur le recueil d'architecture privée de Boullée (1792–1796)," in *Gazette des Beaux-Arts* (March 1981), 111–24.

16 Cf. Jean-Marie Pérouse de Montclos, *Étienne-Louis Boullée, 1728–1799: De l'architecture classique à l'architecture révolutionnaire* (Paris: Arts et Métiers Graphiques, 1969).

17 See Monique Mosser and Daniel Rabreau, "L'Académie Royale et l'enseignement de l'architecture au XVIIIème siècle," in *Archives d'Architecture Moderne*, 25 (1983): 47–67; and Jean-Marie Pérouse de Montclos, *Les Prix de Rome: Concours de l'Académie Royale d'Architecture au XVIIIe siècle* (Paris: Berger-Levrault and Ecole Nationale Supérieure des Beaux-Arts, 1984).

18 Manfredo Tafuri, *Architecture and Utopia: Design and Capitalist Development*, trans. Barbara Luigia La Penta (Cambridge, Mass.: MIT Press, 1976 [Bari, 1973]).

Fig. 1 Plans and section of the various versions proposed by Soufflot for the dome of Sainte-Geneviève. The engraving is supposed to provide graphic evidence against the stability of the dome finally proposed by Soufflot. Pierre Patte, *Mémoire sur la construction de la coupole projetée pour courroner la nouvelle église de Sainte-Geneviève à Paris*, 1770

Fig. 2 Étienne-Louis Boullée, design for a cenotaph in the Egyptian manner, 1784

defining it as the art of building? Indeed, no, for there is a flagrant error in this definition. In order to execute, it is first necessary to conceive. Our earliest ancestors built their huts only when they had a picture of them in their minds. It is this product of the mind, this process of creation that constitutes architecture.[14]

While writing these introductory lines, Boullée also reflected on the principles of what would become *composition* in the work of his former student Durand.[15] From his study of simple bodies and their analogy to sensations, to his reflection on composition, Durand's writings and drawings sketch out a definitive theory of the project, though this theory stops short of becoming normative.

In the 1780s, this budding theory found a most fertile ground in the school of the Académie Royale d'Architecture, where Boullée could be counted among the most influential professors.[16] Under his tutelage, which typically involved programs as ambitious as those envisioned in *L'Essai sur l'art*, the student projects developed at the academy are also clearly defined by their exploration of compositional techniques.[17]

One could demonstrate that the shift in the definition of the architectural discipline—from the tension between the rules of order and proportion and the canon of notable buildings, toward a theory and a practice equally centered on the project—extends well beyond the borders of the French cultural territory. The work of Piranesi bears the mark of this same kind of displacement, as do English and American references to Palladio, who had been one of the few authors of sixteenth-century treatises actually to formulate explicit hypotheses on the design process, by serializing his villa projects. Manfredo Tafuri had already traced the line from Piranesi through Jeffersonian Paladianism in *Architecture and Utopia*. Echoing Tafuri's argument, we must underscore the appearance of a fundamental contradiction between an architectural discipline fully contained, so to speak, in the head of the architect, and one with pretensions of purpose and utility for a growing number of citizens.[18] Though the notion of "genius"—that faculty to be profoundly oneself all the while following a universal inspiration—would serve as the ideological justification for this strange pretension, the balance between the project of the Architect and the project as a political and social "Utopia," again to borrow Tafuri's terms, nevertheless remained fragile at best.

Could it be to overcome this fragility that Jean-Nicolas-Louis Durand sought to strip Boullée's legacy of anything that might, in any way, recall the inspired genius of the architect? In his *Précis of the Lessons of Architecture* delivered at the École Polytechnique from 1802–1805, everything is re-ordered to codify the architectural project into a practice based on the distinction between a building's elements and the process of its composition.[19] The elements, beginning with the architectural orders, are standardized even more radically than had been proposed by Claude Perrault. Composition is subject to a similarly extreme codification. In this scheme, Durand begins by analyzing the different functions of the building to be designed. A system of axes, in turn, allows for these functions to be organized in relation to one another. The standardized vocabulary of architectural elements then leads the project stage by stage toward its final form. This codification of the various stages of the design process may have allowed architecture to achieve rigor comparable to the science of the engineers, but the "poetry of art" so dear to Boullée had also thereby been banished from Durand's conception of architecture. In his introduction to the *Précis*, Durand even went so far as to state that aesthetic pleasure ought not to be part of the architect's objectives.

[19] On Durand, see Werner Szambien, *Jean-Nicolas-Louis Durand, 1760–1834: De l'imitation à la norme* (Paris: Picard, 1984); S. Villari, *J. N. L. Durand (1760–1834): Art and Science of Architecture*, trans. Eli Gottlieb (New York: Rizzoli, 1990 [Rome, 1987]); and Antoine Picon, "From 'Poetry of Art' to Method: The Theory of Jean-Nicolas-Louis Durand," introduction to Jean-Nicolas-Louis Durand, *Précis of the Lectures on Architecture*, trans. David Britt (Los Angeles: Getty Research Institute, 2000), 1–68.

[20] Léonce Reynaud, *Traité d'architecture: Contenant des notions générales sur les principes de la construction et sur l'histoire de l'art* (Paris: Carilian-Gœury and Victor Dalmont, 1850–8). About the teachings of Reynaud and his treaty, read Fernand de Dartein, *M. Léonce Reynaud: Sa vie et ses oeuvres par l'un de ses élèves* (Paris: Dunod, 1885); and Vincent Guigueno and Antoine Picon, "Entre rationalisme et éclectisme: L'Enseignement d'architecture de Léonce Reynaud," in *Bulletin de la Société des Amis de la Bibliothèque de l'École Polytechnique*, 16 (December 1996), 12–19.

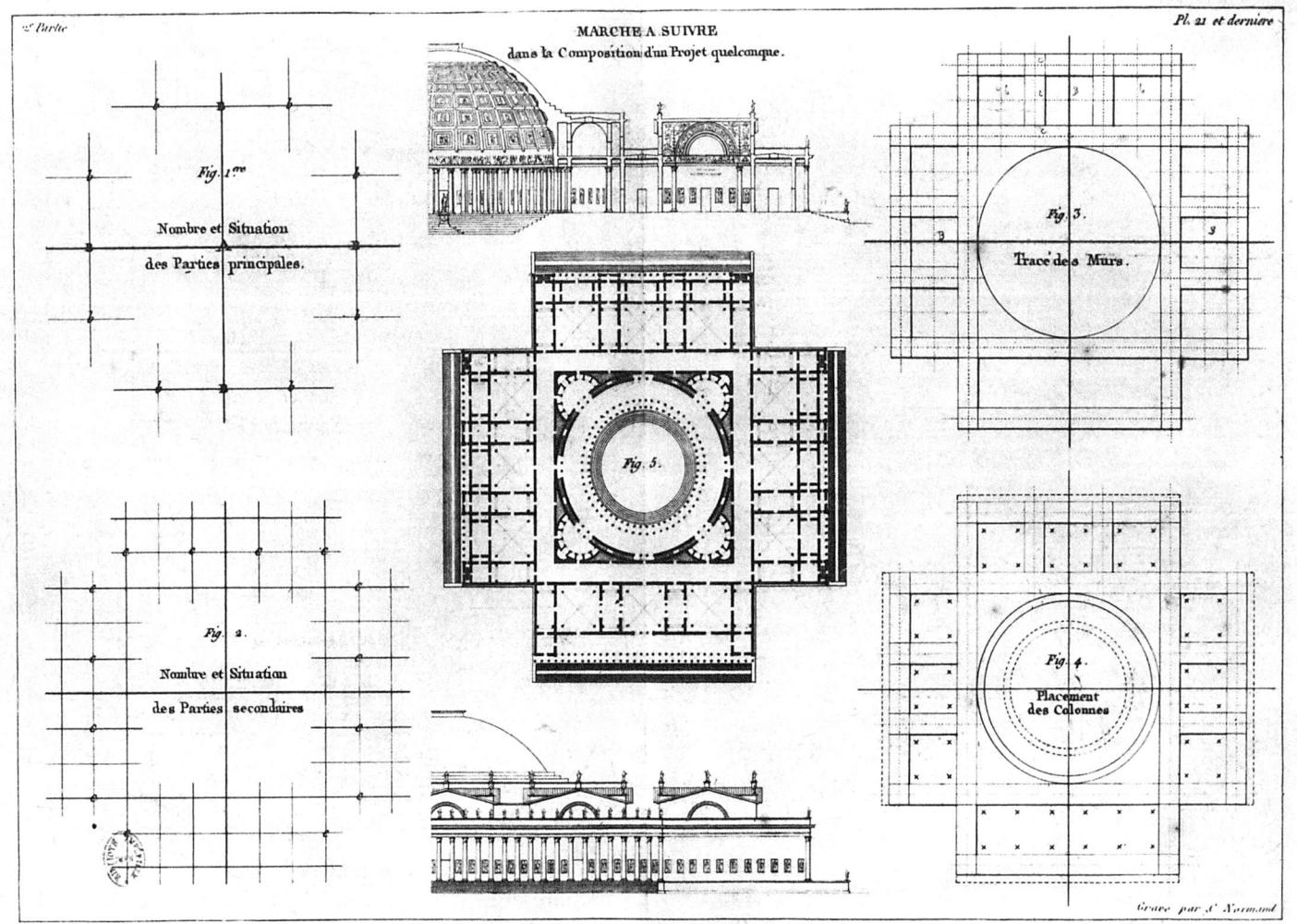

This effort to make architecture subject solely to the imperatives of social and political utility reveals a utopianism in Durand's work, an echo of the revolutionary dream that most commentaries on Durand have overlooked.

Despite the kinship that unites it with the compositional techniques developed throughout the nineteenth century at the École des Beaux-Arts, Durand's attempt was in many respects an isolated endeavor. It is as if, once the architectural discipline had been re-centered around the project, this project's actual codification lost all importance. The nineteenth century would be preoccupied less with extending the trajectory laid out by Durand than with historical styles, their definition, and the norms that would allow new techniques to be adapted to the architectural climate. The *Traité d'architecture* by Léonce Reynaud, who succeeded Durand as the chair of architecture at the École Polytechnique, is revealing in this respect.[20] Its pages are filled with illuminating elaborations on Gothic architecture and the Lombard style, with dimensioning systems updated with the latest material resistance studies, with reflections on heating and ventilation, but with very little of value concerning the rules and norms of the project itself.

It is troubling to realize that this practice would continue to occupy a central position in the definition of the architectural discipline, even through the advent of the Modern Movement, without any effort to subject the codes of this practice to the kind of ambitious investigative scrutiny deployed by Durand. Like a panoptic device whose ever-empty center nevertheless controls its periphery, the Modern Movement passionately pursued standards of all sorts without ever really codifying the very kernel of its own preoccupations. By contrast, the collapse of the Vitruvian tradition did not correspond solely to a transformation of the founding values of architecture. It was also evidenced in the discipline's adoption of an internal economy that was radically different than before. While there were multiple attempts by fifteenth- and sixteenth-century architects to codify the orders and proportions, their distant successors managed only to remain unsettlingly silent about the project and its methods. To be sure, questions concerning the orders lost much of their importance in the

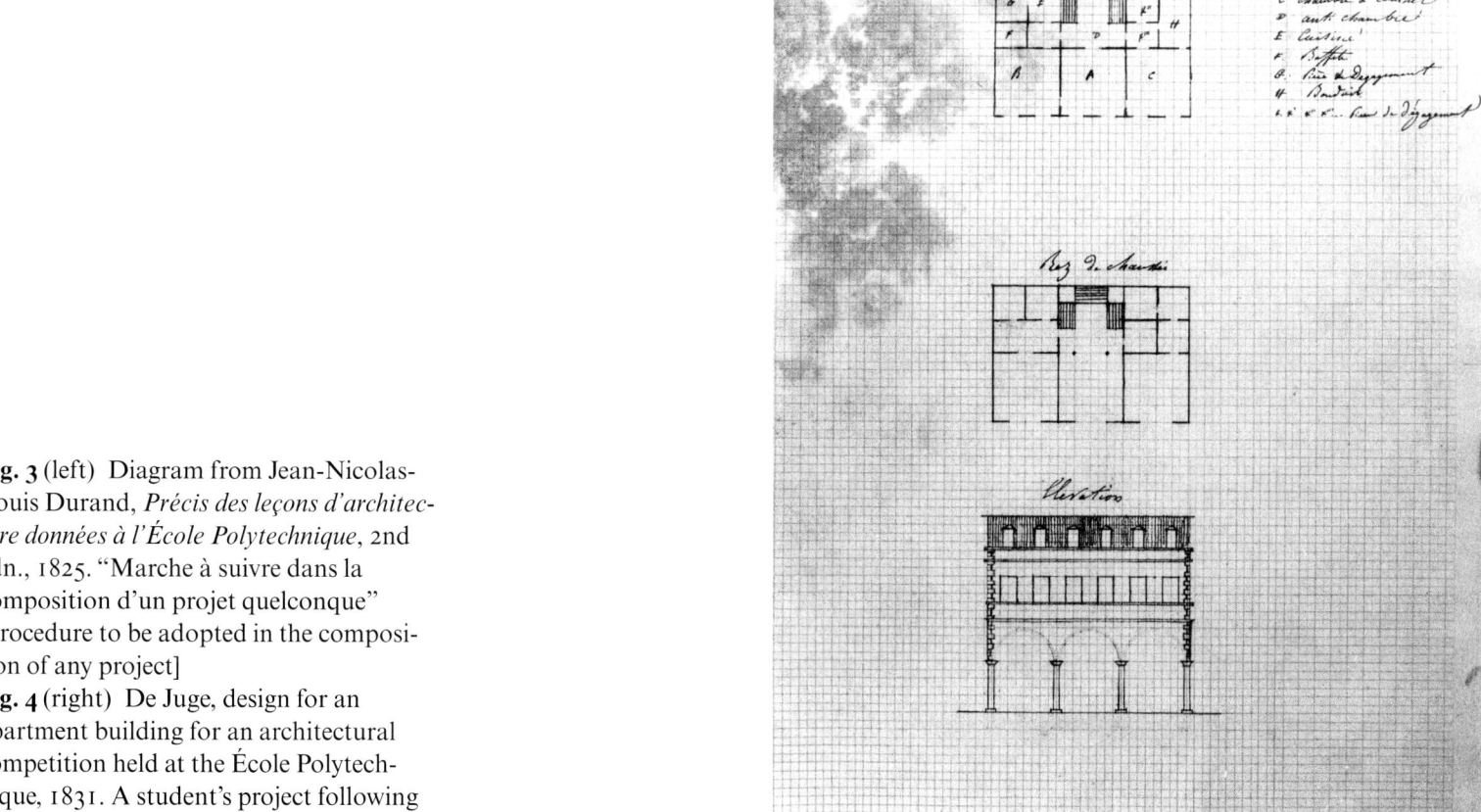

Fig. 3 (left) Diagram from Jean-Nicolas-Louis Durand, *Précis des leçons d'architecture données à l'École Polytechnique*, 2nd edn., 1825. "Marche à suivre dans la composition d'un projet quelconque" [Procedure to be adopted in the composition of any project]

Fig. 4 (right) De Juge, design for an apartment building for an architectural competition held at the École Polytechnique, 1831. A student's project following Durand's method

Mannerist and Baroque periods. Still, their codes remained prominent and were ritually reaffirmed at the beginning of treatises. The situation that subsequently prevailed undermined this clarity, as the rules and codes of architecture were deployed only at a respectable distance from what could be said to constitute its center. Durand's isolated voice did not suffice as a countermeasure, especially when one considers all that he chose to abandon in devoting himself to the investigation of the rules of architectural composition. With its abundance of manifestos and essays, of *œuvres complètes* and critical reviews, the architecture of the nineteenth and twentieth centuries is like the proverbial big talker—who consistently fails to reveal anything of substance about himself.

Post- or Super-modernity?
In thinking about the present, anthropologist Marc Augé may well have formulated an essential question: are we actually living in post-modernity, or rather in a paroxysmal form of modernity?[21] Post- or Super-modernity? A good many things hinge on the answer to this question. Is digital culture truly of a different nature than the industrial culture of a modernity that has reached maturity? Does the computer usher us into a new world, or has it simply extended the processes of communication's intensification, processes already at work at least since the end of the nineteenth century?[22] The answer to this latter question is far from obvious. Indeed, the information society as we know it has its roots in the technologies of extensive documentation developed by governments and large corporations to manage, respectively, their social policies and their clientele.

For now, we seem to be confronted with a kind of super-regime of communication. Supermodernity seems to be our fate, while we wait for quantitative changes to give way to a comparable leap in quality. Not all revolutions immediately trigger the kinds of epistemological shifts described by Michel Foucault in *The Order of Things* and *The Archaeology of Knowledge*.[23] It is striking to realize that, while we wait for the advent of the global village promised by some, the Internet tends to accentuate, rather than absorb, the developmental disparities between cities, regions, and countries.

In terms of architecture, one could, by the same token, suppose that the central position occupied by the project in the definition of the discipline will not be questioned in the immediate future. The use of the computer seems rather to reinforce the privileged status of the project. What is likely to change, instead, is the blur that surrounds this constitutive practice of architecture. Indeed, several factors point toward a

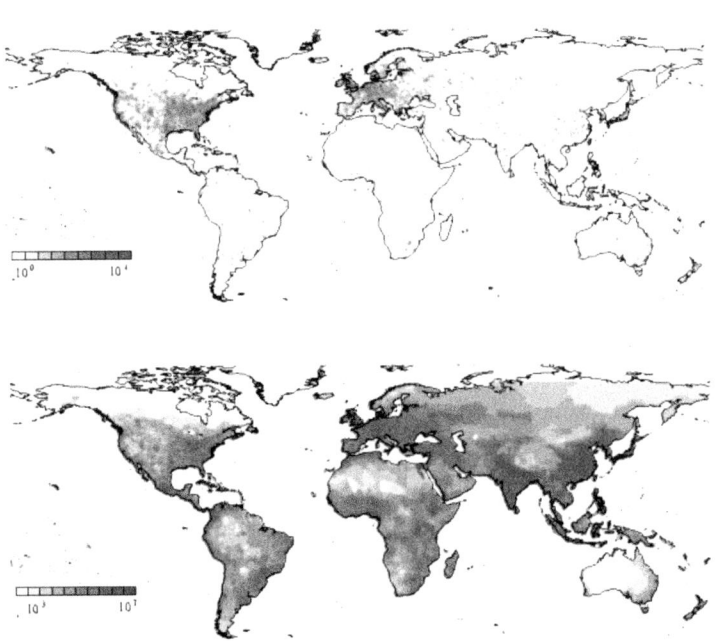

Fig. 5 World maps showing the density of Internet routers (above) and the actual population (below)

21 Marc Augé, *Non-Lieux: Introduction à une anthropologie de la surmodernité* (Paris: Le Seuil, 1992). See, also, by the same author, *Pour une anthropologie des mondes contemporains* (Paris: Aubier, 1994).
22 See, for example, Armand Mattelart, *L'Invention de la communication* (Paris: La Découverte, 1994).
23 Michel Foucault, *Les Mots et les choses: Une archéologie des sciences humaines* (Paris: Gallimard, 1966); Michel Foucault, *L'Archéologie du savoir* (Paris: Gallimard, 1969).
24 See, for example, Greg Lynn, *Animate Form* (New York: Princeton Architectural Press, 1998).
25 Cf. Antoine Picon (ed.), *L'Art de l'ingénieur: Constructeur, entrepreneur, inventeur* (Paris: Editions du Centre Georges Pompidou and Le Moniteur, 1997).

structuring of the processes of design, if not to their codification.

The first of these factors lies in the fundamentally procedural character of the computer. The computer imposes rules onto its user. The structure of a particular design software constitutes an additional constraint. In contrast with the traditional tools of the architect, graphic programs implicitly suggest to the user certain types of geometric solutions. In order to avoid being locked up in a set of codes and rules foreign to the practice of architecture, it becomes essential to be able to prescribe a certain number of constraints to the machine and to the software. The formulation of such instructions requires a greater clarity about the strategies and the stakes of the project than before.

On a perhaps more fundamental level, the computer theoretically allows for the limitless generation of fluid geometries. Since parameters can be continually adjusted, the decision to stop the process at such and such a stage of geometric transformation becomes absolutely essential. When manipulation becomes so easy that it can cycle indefinitely, even without the direction of the designer since machines can "run" all by themselves, the decisions actually made by this designer emerge thoroughly reinforced. Here again, this reinforcement plays in favor of a codification of the procedures of design more advanced than ever before. It is striking that most of those who try to theorize digital architecture only ever talk about those procedures and the way they are affected by the use of the computer. The most innovative aspect of Greg Lynn's writings lies not so much in the philosophic references, from Leibniz to Deleuze, that he mobilizes in support of his argument, but rather in the light that he sheds on what the manipulation of fluid geometries means, concretely.[24]

The question of admissible licenses is also at stake in the context of this multiplication of formal propositions that are so disarming to the critic. What to say about the "blobs," the spaghettis and the other *mille-feuilles* that digital architecture so tirelessly produces? It may well be that in such a context, the criteria for judgment are displaced, from an evaluation of the *form* toward an assessment of the motivations that underlie the *process* of its birth. Hasn't engineering long offered an example of a discipline where forms are meaningful only in reference to the decisions of which they bear the mark?[25] Such a transformation again implies an increased transparency in the process of design.

To these somewhat internal factors are added the problems posed by architecture's interaction with other disciplines and other practices. One would expect that the digitization of projects should allow for improved interaction between the architect and the structural designer, between the architect and the mechanical engineer, and even between the architect and the materials fabricator, since it has become possible to specify with increasing accuracy the properties of the materials that will be used. It is difficult to see how these multiple interfaces could facilitate smooth interaction if the project were to remain a "black box," accessible to

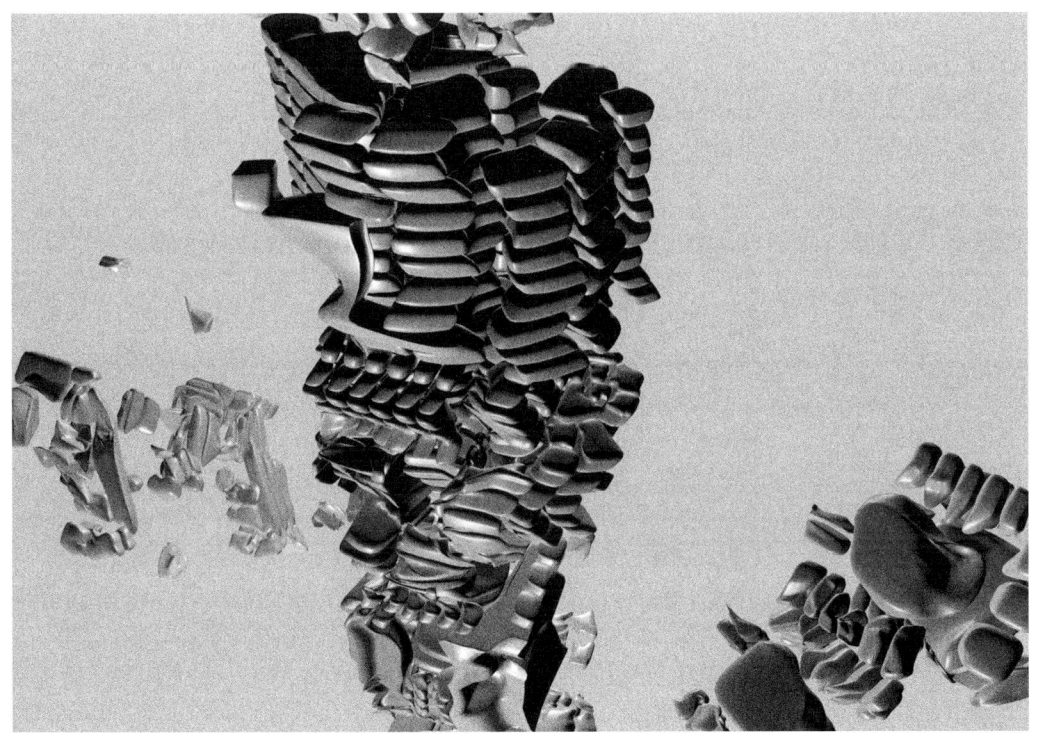

Fig. 6 Kolatan/MacDonald Studio, Resi/Rise (Vertical Mode), 1999. "The Resi/Rise is not so much a building as a matrix of 'lots' taking the shape of so many independent pods. Taking up the whole volume offered by New York's 'zoning laws,' the form of the tower incorporates the site's local restrictions. The organization of the pods among themselves carries on the urban analogy. Individual choice and 'collective' performance merge in a complex and flexible system linking the parts and the whole together."

non-architects only after the architect has fixed its principal parameters.

Without its protective opacity, can the project retain the absolute sovereignty that we grant it today? The real revolution—the change of the *episteme*, the entry into post-modernity—could well be the outcome of this process of clarification whose premises are only beginning to reveal themselves.

These premises stem from the role increasingly played by certain aspects of architecture previously considered secondary: such as the working of surfaces, and questions of texture and light generally. Whereas the Modern Movement had emphasized the three-dimensionality of its projects, most contemporary approaches seem to operate on a kind of two-dimensionality. The importance given to notions and themes like platform and interface point in the same direction. Architecture as a socle, architecture as threshold or as screen: these attitudes appear in project after project, to deploy the effects of walls, according to a logic that is more reminiscent of writing than of the sculptural plasticity of volumes that modernism has accustomed us to. In this context, it is not difficult to understand the renewed interest in the tectonic theory of Gottfried Semper, which allowed a simultaneous understanding of architecture and of ornamental writing, of the project and the wall. The success of Frampton's *Studies in Tectonic Culture*, in which Semper holds a significant place, could well contribute to this evolution, even as the book endeavors to denounce its dangers. It would not be the first time that a treatise of theory and history worked against the intentions of its author.

Far from acting as abstractions, writings and walls seek to engage humanity in its corporeal dimension. A new sense of materiality seems to have been called upon to articulate new possibilities for interfacing between man and machine, and new elaborations of materials through computer-assisted fabrication.[26] This new materiality often goes hand in hand with an eagerness to conform to the laws of the economy, rather than rejecting them as the modernist avant-gardes had done. Is this not the claim of the principals of UN Studio and the members of MVRDV alike?[27] Both the former's acceptance of the fashion system, and the latter's Koolhaasian apology of density, point in the same

---

26 See, among others, Toshiko Mori (ed.), *Immaterial/Ultramaterial: Architecture, Design, and Materials* (Cambridge, Mass.: Harvard Design School in association with George Braziller, 2002).
27 Cf. Winy Maas, Jacob van Rijs and Richard Koek (eds.), *Farmax: Excursions on Density* (Rotterdam: 010 Publishers, 1994); and Ben van Berkel and Caroline Bos, *Move* (Amsterdam: UN Studio and Goose Press, 1999).
28 Cf. D. Rouillard, "Radical Architettura," in *Tschumi: Une architecture en projet* (Paris: Editions du Centre Georges Pompidou and Le Fresnoy, 1993), 89–112.
29 See Ron Witte (ed.), *Toyo Ito: Sendai Mediatheque* (Munich: Prestel, 2002).

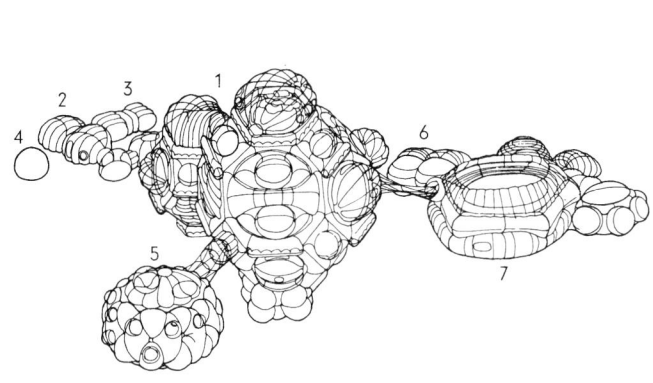
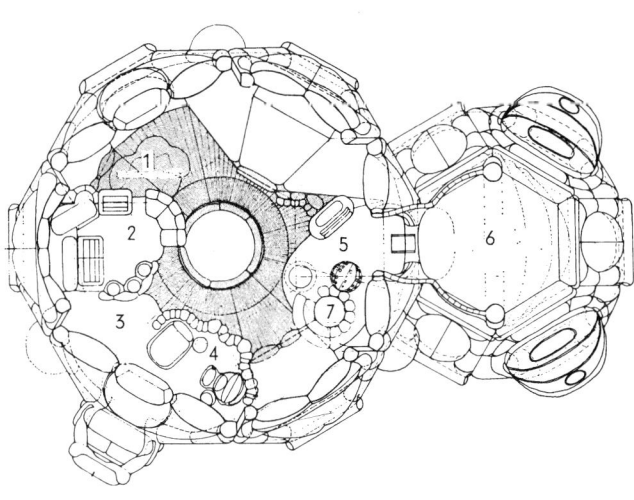

Fig. 7 Jean-Paul Jungmann (with Utopie), Dyodan (pneumatic residential cells), 1967. A flexible cellular system intended to allow for an extensive variety of configurations and additions.

Left:
1. main house; 2. children; 3. playroom; 4. guest-room; 5. conservatory; 6. winter-garden; 7. swimming-pool

Right:
1. rest-room; 2. library; 3. top bedroom; 4. bathroom; 5. studio; 6. terrace; 7. living room

direction: an acceptance of the existing order of things, inequalities and tensions included. It is as if the political and social ideals that accompanied the emergence of the modern condition—ideals whose *ambiguity* Manfredo Tafuri denounced—had been definitively rejected in favor of a search for economic and programmatic efficiency. In this respect it is symptomatic to observe the pervasive rejection by architects of utopian ambitions, as if one had to forget an unresolved past for the sake of a more realist present. Nor does this prevent designers like Rem Koolhaas or Bernard Tschumi from recycling techniques drawn from the "radical" projects of the early seventies.[28] Once marked by utopian thinking, these techniques are now made to work in the service of tangible goals, in accordance with the logic of globalization.

Contrary to what is often claimed, it is not the risk of dematerialization that looms over contemporary architecture, but rather the loss of all political and social bearings, in a world where devotion to programmatic and economic efficiency is king. In such a world, architecture no longer seems equipped to engage anything more than the physical individual and the consumer: the body and the credit card. In discussing his Sendai Mediatheque, Toyo Ito willingly acknowledges the doubling of the subject into a physical identity and a virtual one, in contact with materials but also with the flows of information that structure the world.[29] This duality should be questioned, imprinted as it is with a kind of cultural otherworldliness, for these information flows belong to the broader domain of merchandise, in the same way as most cultural goods, from the book to the DVD. The real doubling of the subject is more likely a reflection of the split between the body and purchasing power than that of the famous line between the real and the virtual that is so often invoked, whether in celebration or lament. The users of Sendai are certainly not an exception to the rule, their physical bodies and their purchasing powers being equally courted by providers of all sorts of services. The political and social utopia that accompanied the emergence of the modern condition for the project seem desperately absent from the manipulations that arise from digital culture today.

Should one be alarmed by their absence? Architecture, as we said, is much like a haunted house, and the ghosts of modernity have not yet had their final word. Even as their power seems about to vanish with the development of computer-aided design, they whisper in the ears of whoever will listen to old stories of projects that might be inseparably aesthetic, political, and social.

Daniel Sherer

Le Corbusier's Discovery of Palladio in 1922 and the Modernist Transformation of the Classical Code

For Kenneth Frampton

1 Colin Rowe, "The Mathematics of the Ideal Villa," in *The Mathematics of the Ideal Villa and Other Essays* (Cambridge, Mass.: MIT Press, 1995 [1947]), 1–28. The comparison was taken up again in "Mannerism and Modern Architecture I," published in the same volume, 29–58. For assessments of Rowe's method, see Paolo Berdini, "Introduzione," to the Italian translation which appeared under the title *La matematica della villa ideale e altri scritti* (Bologna, 1984), 2–25; Joan Ockman, "Form without Utopia: Contextualizing Colin Rowe," *Journal of the Society of Architectural Historians*, 57:4 (1998), 448–56; George Baird, "Oppositions in the Thought of Colin Rowe," *Assemblage*, 33 (1997), 22–35; the monographic issue of *Any*, 7/8 (1994) dedicated to Rowe; Daniel Sherer, "Architecture in the Labyrinth: Theory and Criticism in the United States: *Oppositions, Assemblage, Any* (1973–1999)," *Zodiac*, 20 (1999), 46–7.

2 It is of course true that even in the Renaissance the classical language was never fully recuperated, if only because from the outset it was never fully recuperable. In this connection Manfredo Tafuri has observed that "imitation of antique models oscillated between two extremes. On the one hand, aware of the irretrievability of a longed-for ideal, the mimetic canon was forced to rely on artifice and fiction. On the other, it did not renounce the attempt to transcend the model." See Manfredo Tafuri, "A Search for Paradigms: Project, Truth, Artifice," *Assemblage*, 28 (Cambridge, Mass.: MIT Press, 1995), 56.

In his famous essay of 1947, "The Mathematics of the Ideal Villa," Colin Rowe first proposed a striking formal comparison between Le Corbusier and Palladio which, despite the passage of over half a century, still shapes perceptions of both.[1] Indeed, this parallel has played such a pivotal role in defining formalist criticism in architecture that it can be said to exemplify the essential aims of this approach. Prompting methodological reflection on formalism's guiding assumptions and characteristic preferences, this analogy tends to emphasize what is privileged, and what is omitted, when specific boundaries are drawn, boundaries that direct the reading to problems of proportion, visuality, and aesthetic perception. And since the relationship between architecture's formal and non-formal attributes typically involves the mediation of some specific corpus of rules, Rowe's formalist strategy, which does not address this important theme except incidentally, clearly limits itself in this sense. On the other hand, this limitation just as clearly works in its favor, as Rowe's method, having focused on the internal logic of form, can now act as a spur to re-examine all that it excludes. One way to investigate what has been left out by Rowe as a result of the inherent logic of his method is to try to give an account of the norms and constitutive codes of classicism and modernism, both on their own terms and as they change over time. Taking this shift from *form* to *norm* as its starting point, the new reading of Le Corbusier's reception of Palladio outlined in the following pages attempts to provide a complement to Rowe's by extending it in ways that were barred by its strictly formal criteria.

First, some preliminary questions concerning the logic of the norm and its corollary, the inevitability of the exception, must be explored. For centuries architecture has oscillated between a need for rule and theories and practices of license. In architecture as in other fields, norms are caught up in dialectical relationships with ideas that resist them. In fact, prior to any normative claim, the exception cannot be recognized as such: in the absence of a rule to break, the exception is not exceptional. And yet, even before the enunciation of the theoretical *a priori*, the exception indicates the presence of a problem which, once resolved, leads to a solution that can be generalized, and which thus attains the prescriptive status of what one should do in such cases. Norms, then, are rules which arise out of problems that previously went unnoticed—predicaments that await, and in a certain sense induce, the very normative procedures, stipulations and discourses which aim to set them aright. From this it is clear that *what makes an architectural norm possible is that which violates it in advance, even before it can be codified.* Thus, the classical code (like the modernist one which came after it) can be understood as a system of representation which elicited exceptions that proved to be as decisive as the norms they defied.

In the late seventeenth century, however, when Perrault's critique of Vitruvius revealed the full extent of the crisis that affected the classical code, not only architectural norms, but also every theory or practice that resisted them, lost a fixed point of reference that was never completely recovered.[2] The real proving ground of this process was not the era of philosophical "rationalism," however, but that of technological rationalization. This phase coincided with the so-called First Industrial Revolution that was already underway by 1800: a point when standardization, the new modality assumed by the norm, displaced the metaphysical presuppositions of the classical language. Modern architecture was one result of this process. Even as classicism managed to develop new ways of dealing with the anomalies it ceaselessly generated, the ultimate exception to its logic—industrial standardization— eventually gave rise to modernism itself: a force able to challenge, assimilate, and recast the norms of the classical tradition after having dispensed with its external conventions. It is therefore reductive, although at first sight quite tempting, to assert that classicism lost any claim to universality once industrial standardization became universal. In reality the problem is more complex: exceptions elicited by the classical language undermined it from within, effectively facilitating the emergence of modernism. Thus, even when the classical legacy was condemned by the exponents of the "tradition of the new" as sterile or superseded, it could still operate as a *variable* and *internal* norm for the modern.

This hypothesis is not all that surprising given the important revision in our understanding of the origins of modernism which has occurred since Rowe. Among other things, this revision has thrown into question traditional accounts of radical discontinuity in the polemical discourse of modern architects. For although the advent of modernism is typically thought of as a clean break with the classical tradition, a norm-based reading sensitive to the role performed by the exception in elaborating a "middle way" between continuity and rupture indicates, yet again, the mythical status of this view. In so doing, this approach underscores modernism's implicit ties not only to the normative attempt to establish a new code, but also to the classical norms it presumably overcame. That these ties are bonds of inversion—dialectical continuities—only serves to bring out the inherent logic of modernism's underlying normative procedures. This reading is thoroughly historical, even if it takes its essential orientation from epistemological considerations: as such, it focuses on those points in the genesis of codes linking antithetical universes of discourse.

Le Corbusier's reception of Palladio is just such a turning point. To understand its significance we are obliged to consider a *carnet de voyage* whose existence was unknown to Rowe when the "Mathematics of the Ideal Villa" was written. Published for the first time by Stanislaus von Moos in 1996, this sketchbook, the so-called *Album La Roche*, documents a trip that the young architect took to Venice and Vicenza with his friend and patron Raoul La Roche in 1922, before returning to Paris the following year to work on the Maisons La Roche-Jeanneret, partly for the same client.[3] This *carnet* contains the only evidence uncovered to date which proves that Le Corbusier had detailed, first-hand knowledge of Palladio's architecture. Close analysis of its contents can help redefine the crucial, yet still largely unexplored role Palladio played in Le Corbusier's production in the early 1920s, at a point in his development when he could be said to have accomplished the transition from premodern to modern.[4] From these initial considerations one can argue that Le Corbusier elaborated a fundamental aspect of his modernist strategy—the systematic inversion of classical norms—partly as the result of a dialogue with Palladio that was more extensive than Rowe's formalist criticism has led us to believe.

Before analyzing Le Corbusier's reception of Palladio it is necessary to clarify his relationship with the classical legacy. The first decisive encounter between Le Corbusier and the antique took place in 1911, when the young architect visited the ruins of Pompeii and then travelled to Greece to study the Acropolis. The Hellenic finale of this journey (by any account a major turning point in his formation) is documented by a photograph of the eighteen-year old Charles-Edouard Jeanneret standing in front of the Parthenon. It is revealing to compare this image with another which appeared in *Vers une architecture* in 1923 juxtaposing the latest Delages and Humber motorcars with the Periclean monument (Fig. 1).[5] This visual analogy of ancient and modern underscores an important dimension of Le Corbusier's theoretical project in the 1920s: its consistent appeal to rational norms and standards.[6] This strategy of transhistorical comparison aligned the normative principles animating

---

3 Le Corbusier, *Album La Roche*, ed. Stanislaus von Moos, 2 vols. (Milan and Paris: Fondation Le Corbusier, 1996); cf. von Moos, "La Leçon de Venise," in Benedetto Gravagnuolo (ed.), *Le Corbusier e l'Antico: Viaggi nel Mediterraneo* (Naples: Electa Napoli, 1997), 87ff. The album was a new year's gift for La Roche, intended to underscore the close bond the architect felt with his client and friend. For an acknowledgement of the intellectual and aesthetic importance of the trip for La Roche, linking it explicitly to the gift, see La Roche's letter of 4 January 1925 addressed to the architect cited in von Moos, *Album La Roche*, I. 8. On Le Corbusier and La Roche, see Ulrike Jehle-Schulte Strathaus (ed.), *Le Corbusier und Raoul La Roche: Architekt und Maler, Bauherr und Sammler*. Exhibition catalogue, Architekturmuseum Basel, July–August 1987; Jacques Sbriglio, *Les Villas La Roche-Jeanneret* (Basel, Boston, and Berlin, 1970), 59ff.

4 It is striking to note that in another context, without expressly referring to Le Corbusier, Rowe dated the point of emergence of modern architecture to 1922–23, a decision that may indicate that he had the Maisons La Roche-Jeanneret in mind, especially since this project took shape in these years and is generally regarded as the first truly modern work of Le Corbusier's architecture: "By my own standards, the words 'modern architecture' refer to a strategy of building which erupted circa 1922–23, and its characteristic physical gestures are exceptionally easy to summarize." Colin Rowe, *The Architecture of Good Intentions: Towards a Possible Retrospect* (London: Academy Editions, 1994), 16.

5 Le Corbusier, *Towards a New Architecture*, trans. Frederick Etchells (London: J. Rodker, 1931), chapter 2, esp. 124ff.

6 See, on the theme of standardization in Le Corbusier's theory and practice in the 1920s, Winfried Nerdinger, "Standard et type: Le Corbusier et Allemagne, 1920–1927," in Stanislaus von Moos (ed.), *L'Esprit Nouveau: Le Corbusier et l'industrie 1920–1925* (Strasbourg: Les Musées de la Ville de Strasbourg, 1987); von Moos, "Standard und Elite: Le Corbusier, die Industrie, und die Esprit Nouveau," in Tillman Buddensieg and Henning Rogge (eds.), *Die nützlichen Künste* (Berlin: Quadriga Verlag, 1981), 306–23; Kenneth Frampton, *Le Corbusier: Architect and Visionary* (London: Thames & Hudson, 2001), chapter 2.

7 Le Corbusier, *Towards a New Architecture*, 123.

8 Michel Foucault, Introduction to Georges Canguilhem, *The Normal and the Pathological* (New York: Zone Books, 1991), 16.

9 Le Corbusier, *Towards a New Architecture*, 7–8. On this passage, the observations in R. Gabetti and C. Olmo, *Le Corbusier and L'Esprit Nouveau* (Turin, 1972), 186, still retain all of their cogency. On the relation of classic and modern in Le Corbusier the bibliography is vast: only a few basic indications can be given here. See Giuliano Gresleri, "Il silenzio delle pietre, le parole dei 'numeri', il solitudine, il 'deflagrante ricordo,'" and Mogens Krustrup, "Il luogo di tutte le misure," both in Gravagnuolo, *Le Corbusier e l'Antico*, 71–84 and 35–43; Alan Colquhoun, "The Significance of Le Corbusier" in *Modernity and the Classical Tradition: Architectural Essays, 1980–1987* (Cambridge, Mass.: MIT Press, 1994), 163–70 and "Displacement of Concepts in Le Corbusier," *Essays in Architectural Criticism: Modern Architecture and Historical Change* (Cambridge, Mass.: MIT Press, 1995), 51–66; F. Passanti, "Architecture: Proportion, Classicism, and Other Issues," in Stanislaus von Moos and Arthur Ruegg (eds.), *Le Corbusier before Le Corbusier: Applied Arts, Architecture, Painting, and Photography, 1907–1922* (New Haven: Yale University Press, 2002), 69–98; Manfredo Tafuri, "'Machine et memoire': The City in the Work of Le Corbusier," in H. Allen Brooks (ed.), *Le Corbusier* (Princeton: Princeton University Press, 1987), 208; Kenneth Frampton, *Le Corbusier: Architect and Visionary*, 15, 77–9. On Le Corbusier's reading of the Parthenon, see now *Le Corbusier before Le Corbusier*, 182–5, esp. 184; Krustrup, "Il luogo di tutte le misure," 35–43; Giorgio Ciucci, "Le Corbusier e il Partenone," in *Le Corbusier: Il linguaggio delle pietre* (Venice: Cataloghi Marsilio, 1988), 59ff; Kenneth Silver, *Esprit de Corps: The Art of the Parisian Avant-Garde and the First World War 1914–25* (Princeton: Princeton University Press, 1989), 376–7 (I owe this reference to the kindness of Mary McLeod); Paul Venable Turner, *La Formation de Le Corbusier: Idéalisme et Mouvement Moderne* (Paris: Macula, 1987), 104–10.

Fig. 1 Spread of *Towards a New Architecture* [Vers une architecture] (1923), showing modern automobiles compared with the Parthenon

classical buildings with the new standards guiding the modern universe of precision. For this reason he could observe: "The Parthenon is a product of selection applied to an established standard. Already for a century the Greek temple had been standardized in all its parts."[7]

This analogy suggests that the elective affinity which Le Corbusier perceived between classical principles and modern technology presupposes, to adapt a phrase of Michel Foucault, an essential *norm-process* traversing the entire history of architecture.[8] This process, cutting obliquely across a divergent series of codes, designates a unitary phenomenon whose significance eludes the conventional categories of Classic, Modern, Baroque, Mannerist, and so on. For Le Corbusier, then, it was not simply a matter of arguing that the advent of modernity had put an end to the "styles." Instead, his aim was to show that the "styles" do not really count, but the norms which implicitly govern them do. This idea was strengthened by his insight that normative principles have a different historical periodicity, a more profound relation to the regularities of architectural discourse, than any stylistic codification. Le Corbusier thus used the normative thematic disclosed by ancient architecture to denounce the Ecole des Beaux Arts, which saw itself as the classical tradition's only legitimate heir. When Le Corbusier announces, for instance, in the introduction to *Vers une architecture*, that "les styles sont une mensonge," the polemic is persuasive not only because it mobilizes a pre-existing critique of academic ideology, but also because it is used to further an argument uniting the ideals of a nascent modernism with the normative principles of ancient architecture.[9] By adopting this complex stance, which might be called an anti-historicist historicism, Le Corbusier cannily outflanked the claims of Beaux-Arts classicism, neutralizing them at their root.

Consequently, what I have chosen to call the *lost classicism of the era of modernity* is not lost in any absolute sense, but rather acts as a vehicle for a kind of cultural anamnesis for which the modern architect is asked to be the agent, if not the demiurge. This observation brings to mind Tafuri's assertion that throughout his career Le Corbusier's essential theoretical position was situated between an infinite past and a will to the future, so that its stance toward the norm involves a sort of *memoire involontaire* inherent in architecture.[10] This hypothesis is reinforced by a fact of which even Le Corbusier himself does not seem to have aware (in spite of his profound grasp of its consequences): that ancient Greek architects, when working on their temples, relied upon the *paradeigma*, an ancient standardization technique consisting of a specimen or model which, placed on that area of the building under construction, regulated the relation of parts to the whole in accordance with a predetermined proportional system.[11] In this sense the technological advances of modernity which Le Corbusier so deeply admired are prefigured in the realized standards of ancient classicism. Le Corbusier seems to acknowledge this when he observes, when commenting on the precision of the entablature of the Parthenon: "All this plastic machinery is realized with all the rigour we have learned to apply to the machine. The impression is of naked polished steel."[12] Nevertheless, his emphasis on the rigor of technical standards should not be taken to mean that the exception has no role to play in the constitution of ancient and modern normative systems. In this regard his celebrated paean to the Parthenon offers eloquent evidence: "There has been nothing like it anywhere at any period… the mouldings of the Parthenon are infallible and implacable. In severity they go far beyond our practice, or man's normal capabilities."[13] Similarly, when Le Corbusier sees the Periclean monument as the apotheosis of the classical code he elevates the norm to a level of perfection usually reserved for the exception:

> In this period of science, of strife and drama in which the individual is violently tossed about at every moment, the Parthenon appears to us as a living work, full of grand harmonies. The sum of its inevitable elements gives the measure of the degree of perfection to which man can attain when he is absorbed in a problem definitely stated.[14]

Thus conceived, the Parthenon not only registers the historicity of Le Corbusier's anti-historicism, but also presupposes a new conception of architecture elaborated on a transhistorical plane.[15] In this respect, the apex of classical Greek architecture (like that of Renaissance

---

10 Tafuri, "'Machine et memoire,'" 214.
11 J. J. Coulton, *Ancient Greek Architects at Work: Problems of Structure and Design* (Ithaca: Cornell University Press, 1977), 55–8, 72–3; on standardization in ancient Greek temples, with particular reference to the orders, John Onians, *Bearers of Meaning: The Classical Orders in Antiquity, the Middle Ages, and the Renaissance* (Princeton: Princeton University Press, 1988), 9–12.
12 Le Corbusier, *Towards a New Architecture*, 201.
13 Le Corbusier, *Towards a New Architecture*, 203–4.
14 Le Corbusier, *Towards a New Architecture*, 134.
15 Manfredo Tafuri, *Theories and History of Architecture* (New York: Harper & Row, 1976), chapter 1.
16 Renato De Fusco, *Segni, storia e progetto dell'architettura* (Bari: Laterza, 1973), 5.
17 Robert Fishman, *Urban Utopias in the Twentieth Century: Ebenezer Howard, Frank Lloyd Wright, Le Corbusier* (Cambridge, Mass.: MIT Press, 1992), 167–8; H. Allen Brooks, "Le Corbusier's Formative Years at La Chaux-de-Fonds," in H. Allen Brooks (ed.), *Le Corbusier*, 27ff.
18 Rowe, "'Character' vs. 'Composition': or Some Vicissitudes of Architectural Vocabulary in the Nineteenth Century," *The Mathematics of the Ideal Villa*, 59–88.
19 H. Allen Brooks, *Le Corbusier's Formative Years: Charles-Edouard Jeanneret at La Chaux-de-Fonds* (Chicago: University of Chicago Press, 1997), 327ff; Passanti, "Architecture: Proportion, Classicism, and Other Issues," 70.

Fig. 2 Le Corbusier, Villa Fallet, La Chaux-de-Fonds, Switzerland, 1906: façade

Le Corbusier, Villa Favre Jacot, La Locle, Switzerland, 1912:
Fig. 3 (above) façade
Fig. 4 (below) plan

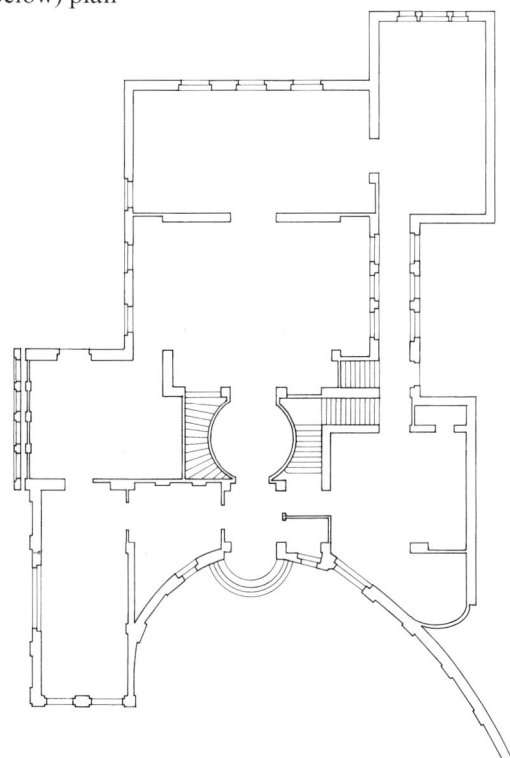

architecture, marked by Palladio) gave Le Corbusier's vision of modern architecture a powerful strategy of legitimation based upon the interdependence of standardized norms and exceptional achievements. It follows that the normative theses specific to architecture, which mobilize regulative principles, theoretical premises, and systematic concepts which Renato de Fusco has identified as so many ways of securing a dynamic orientation toward reality for the discipline, disclose an indispensable, yet often poorly understood, dimension of our history: the implicit relation that links, even as it distinguishes between, the conscious affirmation of modernity achieved by modern architecture and the spontaneous return of the classical in the era of modernism.[16]

Le Corbusier's first realized work, the Villa Fallet of 1906 (Fig. 2), was constructed in his native city of La Chaux-de-Fonds, a hub of Swiss watchmaking which combined venerable craft traditions with exceptional technical precision.[17] Bearer of the artisanal values of the so-called "style sapin" in harmony with the Jura regionalism championed by L'Eplattenier, Le Corbusier's earliest mentor, this house epitomizes a tendency which Rowe himself associated with nineteenth-century codes that emphasized "character" over the Beaux-Arts doctrine of "composition."[18] Insofar as this project is tied to particularist impulses originating in the local architectural culture, it may also be regarded as the earliest instance of an interest in exceptions to academic doctrine, a crucial aspect of Le Corbusier's approach throughout his career.

After working briefly in the atelier of Peter Behrens in 1911, Jeanneret returned to the Suisse Romande, where he executed his first classicizing project, the Villa Favre-Jacot of 1912–13 (Figs. 3, 4). This work, which might initially appear to be the most Palladian of his entire *œuvre*, is in fact quite distant from Palladio, at least in its chief sources of inspiration. And though its idiosyncratic classicism has clear Renaissance precedents—in addition to obvious affiliations with Perret and Behrens—it can be traced back not to the mid-to-late sixteenth-century Veneto, but to early sixteenth-century Rome: instead of a Palladian antecedent for the plan, the clearest model for this feature of this villa is unquestionably Raphael's (and Giulio's) Villa Madama of 1517–21 (Fig. 5).[19] This reading is recommended by Jeanneret's unusual sensitivity to Raphael's characteristic play between symmetry and asymmetry. As such, the Villa Favre Jacot simultaneously registers an impressive control of the classical vocabulary and demonstrates that he took as his point of departure specific contingencies and haphazard elements connected with the unfinished project for Clement VII. When one more carefully considers the implicit network of references informing the new invention, however, one inevitably comes up against a single ancient precedent which is evoked by both Raphael and Le Corbusier: the hemicycle of the Forum of Trajan (Fig. 6).

An equally eloquent example of the use of a classical source linking Le Corbusier's work to Renaissance strategies of invention is provided by the façade of the Villa Schwob of 1916 (Fig. 7). With this project, a specific Palladian model seems to enter Le Corbusier's field of vision for the first time, the Casa Cogollo (Fig. 8). At this juncture the logic of the exception asserts itself most powerfully in the "modern classicism" of *Le Corbusier avant Le Corbusier.* As Rowe has observed, the

20 Rowe, "Mannerism and Modern Architecture," 32.
21 Rowe, "Mannerism and Modern Architecture," 33.
22 For this analysis, I have relied on the insights of my friend Scott Cohen.

Fig. 5 (left) Raphael and Giulio Romano, Villa Madama, Rome, 1515–19: plan
Fig. 6 (right) Forum of Trajan, Hemicycle, Rome, c. 100 AD: plan

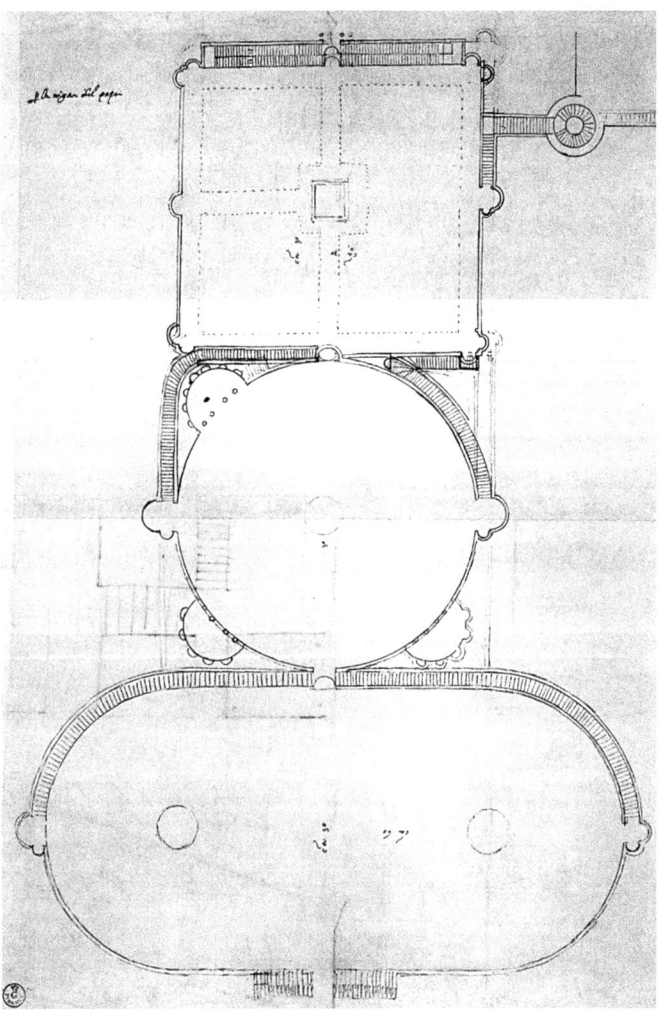
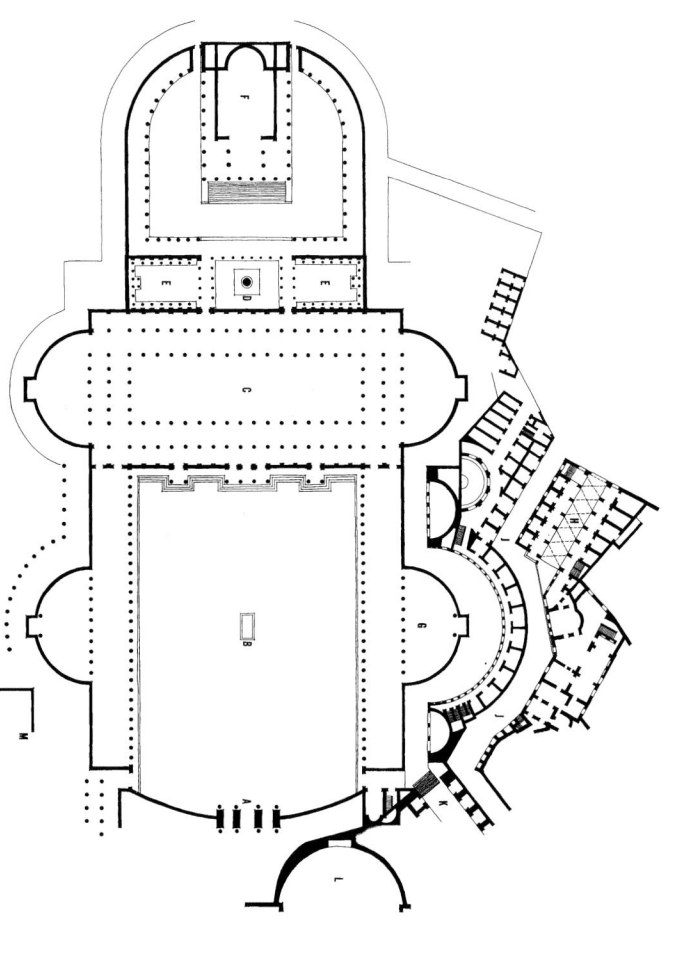

blank second-story panel appears to be a clear response to the voided panel on the Palladian façade, which for its part is generated by the unorthodox combination of a domestic façade and an arcaded loggia.[20] This combination, in concert with the breaking forward of the Ionic entablature of the arch with its anomalous Corinthian superstructure framing the empty space, reads, according to Rowe, as "an inversion of the normal… effected within the framework of the classical system"[21]—the norm in this case being the traditional type of the arch of triumph (Fig. 9).

Since the blank modernist panel of the Villa Schwob reads as the expansion of the upper-level tablet which contains the inscription, just as the base of the façade can be seen as the lateral expansion of the lower divisions of the arch beneath the string course, one can suggest that no Palladian model is necessary, and that both Le Corbusier and Palladio achieved their respective transformations of the classical type independently. In this reading, Le Corbusier's modification reflects a horizontal *and* vertical expansion of the ancient type, while Palladio's registers an exclusively vertical one.[22] (This interpretation is strengthened by the fact that the first documented encounter between Le Corbusier and actual examples of Palladio's architecture occurred six years after the design of the Villa Schwob.) However, it is also possible that the Casa Cogollo did provide a basis for Le Corbusier's complex response to the classical prototype: one that breaks with, even as it cites, the Palladian model. Even if we do not decide in favor of either reading, one thing is certain: when designing the Villa Schwob's façade Le Corbusier played a deft game

Fig. 7 (above left) Le Corbusier, Villa Schwob, La Chaux-de-Fonds, Switzerland, 1916: façade
Fig. 8 (above right) Palladio, Casa Cogollo, Vicenza: façade
Fig. 9 (left) Arch of Trajan, Ancona, c. 100 AD

with the classical language to solve a problem raised by Perret and Behrens—that of finding a classical discourse appropriate to the modern era. In so doing he underscores his own ability to speak the classical language in its highest and most sophisticated form, by inventing a new grammar of the exception, as valid in its own era as the analogous syntax of inversion formulated by Palladio in the sixteenth century.

In light of the foregoing, one might reconsider the normative implications of the emerging modernist code exemplified by Le Corbusier's white villas of the 1920s from the critical perspective formulated by Rowe himself, a perspective whose presuppositions have been elucidated by Paolo Berdini.[23] Emphasizing what is characteristic in Rowe's formalist procedure by underlining the "internal," ahistorical, and more specifically, visual and proportional dimensions of its mode of reading, Berdini maintains that Rowe's formalism does not try to isolate the typological invariants of the villa in its Renaissance and modern incarnations. Instead, it articulates an entire field of differences centering on binary oppositions. These, according to Berdini, and especially the Le Corbusier/Palladio parallel, were formulated to capture the specificity of the modernist achievement by setting it against the Palladian precedent. And yet despite Berdini's assertion that Rowe's analysis, caught up in its comparative task, ends up shedding very little light on Palladio's architecture itself, the attention which the English critic devotes to the inversion of codified languages effected by Casa Cogollo actually does tell us something new and important about Palladio's formal strategy.[24] In this respect Rowe's formalist discourse does not specify what constitutes Le Corbusier's reception of Palladio, but rather helps explain Palladio's and Le Corbusier's architectural languages by means of systematic contrasts emphasizing the "classical" side of the Swiss-French architect and the "modern" aspect of the Palladian legacy.

The images and texts which comprise the *Album La Roche* provide considerable insight into the extent of Le Corbusier's knowledge and study of Palladio (Figs. 10–14). This is not surprising, as the express purpose of the trip that it documents was probably the first-hand study of Palladio's buildings.[25] The album contains seven watercolors of Palladio's Venetian churches (three of S. Giorgio Maggiore, four of the Redentore); five sketches of a Vicentine palace (two of Palazzo Valmarana), a villa (the Rotonda), and a public building (two of the Basilica), all on the same folio, and two sketches of

---

23 Paolo Berdini, "Confronti inaspettati: Osservazioni sulla retorica comparata di Colin Rowe," in Luca Monica (ed.), *La critica operativa e l'architettura* (Milan: Unicopli, 2002), 130ff.
24 Berdini, "Confronti inaspettati," 135.
25 Von Moos, *Album La Roche*, II. 8, 24.
26 Le Corbusier, *Album La Roche*, I. folios 29r, 30r, 31r, 33r, 34v, 36r, 37v (the Venetian images); folio 38r (the Vicentine images).
27 Von Moos, "La Leçon de Venise," 86ff; cf. Kurt Forster, "Le Corbusier, Album La Roche, 1921–22," in Guido Beltramini et al., *Palladio nel Nord Europa: Libri, viaggatori, architetti* (Milan: Skira, 1999), 226. Originally this photograph of the Villa Rotonda was intended for an *Esprit Nouveau* article dedicated to Palladio which never appeared: see von Moos, *Album La Roche*, II. 26.
28 *Carnet 1916–1922*, Fondation Le Corbusier, 5597–8.

another Vicentine palace (Palazzo Porto Barbarano, mistakenly identified as Palazzo Thiene), both on a second folio.[26] To this list one should add two images not found in the *Album La Roche*: a photograph of the Villa Rotonda, obtained from the director of the Museo Civico of Vicenza, Ongaro—included in two publications by Le Corbusier, the first an article appearing in *Esprit Nouveau* 20 (1924), the second a republication of the earlier essay in *Urbanisme* (1925)[27]—and a line drawing of a portion of the façade of S. Giorgio Maggiore.[28]

Let us start with the Venetian images. These watercolors represent the buildings from an oblique angle and at a considerable distance; as such, they accentuate overall contours, rather than specific details. At the same time, they vividly evoke the buildings' volumetric organization (Figs. 10–12). Turning our attention to the drawings of Palladio's buildings in or near Vicenza (Figs. 13, 14), we see that the one of the Palazzo Barbarano clearly shows the building's tetrastyle vestibule and cortile alla romana, while the sketch of the Villa Rotonda emphasizes the arch inserted in the portico corner (an unorthodox motif derived from the Porticus of Octavia in Rome) (Figs. 15, 16). This last drawing, moreover, appears alongside a rendering of the superimposed arches of the Basilica. Regarding the vestibule of Palazzo Barbarano, the solution which Le Corbusier docu-

Le Corbusier's watercolors and sketches in the *Album La Roche*:
Figs. 10 & 11 (top) S. Giorgio Maggiore by Palladio, Venice
Fig. 12 (middle) Redentore by Palladio, Venice
Fig. 13 (bottom left) Palazzo Porto Barbarano Vicenza
Fig. 14 (bottom right) Villa Rotunda by Palladio near Vicenza

Fig. 15 (above) Palladio, Villa Rotonda
Fig. 16 (below) Porticus of Octavia, Rome, c. 30 BC

29 Von Moos, "La Leçon de Venise," 86.
30 Le Corbusier, *Esprit Nouveau* (1920), in von Moos, "La Leçon," 86.
31 *La Nuova Libreria* (Venice, 1555), 155, cited in Licisco Magagnato, "Introduzione" to Andrea Palladio, *Quattro Libri dell'Architettura* (Venice, 1570), in the edition edited by Licisco Magagnato and Paolo Marini (Milan: Edizioni il Polifilo, 1980), xi; cf. Rudolf Wittkower, *Architectural Principles in the Age of Humanism* (New York: St. Martin's Press, 1988), 64, n. 27.

32 Wittkower, *Architectural Principles in the Age of Humanism*, 6off; James S. Ackerman, *Palladio* (London, 1991), 20–1; Mario Carpo, *Architecture in the Age of Printing: Orality, Writing, Typography and Printed Images in the History of Architectural Theory* (Cambridge, Mass.: MIT Press, 2001), 23, 204, n. 16.
33 Jeanneret and Ozenfant, *Apres le Cubisme* (Paris: Altamira, 1999 [Paris, 1918]), 90ff. On the variant/invariant relationship in Le Corbusier's early aesthetic theory see Gabetti and Olmo, *Le Corbusier e l'Esprit Nouveau*, chapter 6, and the brief yet perceptive observations in Frampton, *Le Corbusier*, 27. On the Ozenfant–Jeanneret exchange and its pivotal role in the genesis of Purism, the best general discussion is still Susan Ball, *Ozenfant and Purism: The Evolution of a Style, 1915–30* (Ann Arbor: UMI Research Press, 1981), a reference I owe to the kindness of Mary McLeod; see also Françoise Ducros, "From Art Nouveau to Purism: Le Corbusier and Painting," in *Le Corbusier before Le Corbusier*, 135ff; Beatriz Colomina, "L'Esprit Nouveau: Architecture and Publicité," in K. Michael Hays (ed.), *Architecture Theory since 1968* (Cambridge, Mass.: MIT Press, 2000), 628.
34 Jeanneret and Ozenfant, *Apres le Cubisme*, 93.
35 Ozenfant and Julien Caron, "Une villa de Le Corbusier, 1916," *L'Esprit Nouveau*, 21 (1921), 692.

mented in his drawing corresponds only partially to the actual Palladian project: as von Moos has observed, the problem is complicated by the asymmetrical form of the complex, which can be explained by the fact that an irregular and narrow part of the site was added to the original plot only at a later date.[29] If this modification made it possible to complete the *cortile* on a grand scale, it nonetheless also constrained it to assume an asymmetrical shape. In the *Quattro Libri*, II, iii, Palladio illustrates nothing else besides the original project (Fig. 17), or, alternatively, may have offered a more normative image to the reader, following his usual practice. Moreover, von Moos is right to point out that it was probably the unforeseen spatial sequence, and particularly the unexpected turn to the left, that caught Le Corbusier's eye: Le Corbusier describes comparable sequences when studying examples of the Pompeiian *domus*, a significant typological precedent for Palladio's Palazzo Barbarano: "Si vous dessinez les maisons de Pompeii que vou imaginiez symmetriques selons le traditions de l'Ecole, votre crayon decouvrira des assymetries etonnantes et des symmetries imprevues."[30] Bearing in mind this taste for the asymmetrical, the oblique, and the unexpected, one should also reconsider the unusual emphasis Le Corbusier placed on the motif of the Porticus of Octavia: a detail which, having captured his attention, changed the way he depicted what is arguably Palladio's most classical work, the Villa Rotonda, by bringing its least classical element to the fore. From these examples one can infer that Le Corbusier's reception of Palladio stressed deviations, aberrations, and in fact anything that is inimical to rigid interpretations of the classical code, even in architectural situations which contravene such patently anti-normative readings.

Le Corbusier's emphasis on the Palladian interplay of rule and invention registers his own predilection for a dialectical understanding of classical principles, and of architectural norms more generally. Palladio, as is well-known (and as Le Corbusier certainly knew) presented himself as the self-conscious proponent of a normative architecture. Indeed, his theoretical project was founded on expressly normative premises: according to Anton Francesco Doni (1555), the original title of the *Quattro Libri* was *Norma di Vera Architettura*.[31] Other similarities between the architects may begin to explain, or at least to contextualize, the formal congruences in their work. Giangiorgio Trissino, Palladio's humanist mentor, conferred a new name, and along with this a new social and cultural status, on the stonecutter Andrea di Pietro della Gondola at the beginning of his career. From that

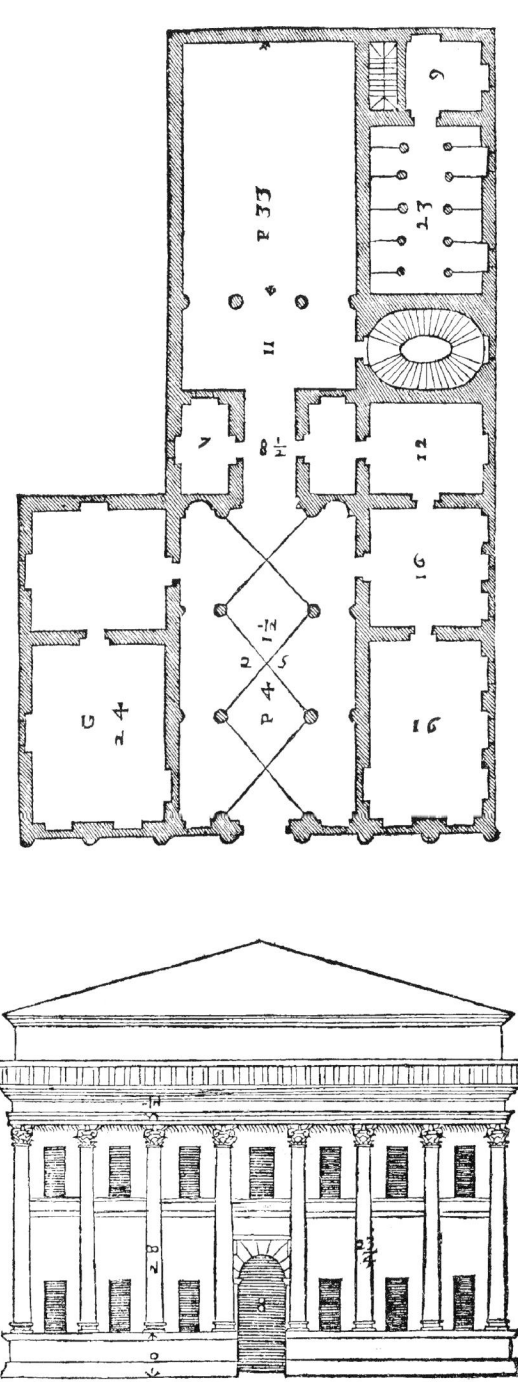

Fig. 17 Palladio, Palazzo Porto Barbarano, 1570: plan and elevation

point forward, Palladio had all he needed to accomplish his transformation from a semi-literate mason into the first architect-theorist of the Renaissance to codify the norms of architectural representation in lucid orthographic images, at least as far as the culture of the printed book is concerned.[32] Like Le Corbusier, Palladio showed a profound awareness of his own intellectual and artistic vocation by assuming a new name; like Le Corbusier, he fashioned a public persona closely associated with a normative idea of architecture based on formal and geometric reduction; and finally, like Le Corbusier, he spread his message by launching a theoretical project and a promotional initiative utilizing the printed word alongside eloquent images of architectural standardization. Because of these specific parallels, Le Corbusier had ample reason to view Palladio not as the exponent of a rigid conception of the classical code (as a superficial but rather widespread view would have it) but as an architect able to exploit the tension inherent in the code itself between typological variation and pure geometry effectively. It becomes plausible to imagine that the modern architect interpreted Palladio's works in terms of his own Purist ideas, a hypothesis that derives further cogency from the central role assumed by the dialectic between variant and invariant motives in the Purist manifesto, *Après le Cubisme*, of 1918.[33] On the one hand, this manifesto argued that modern art and architecture require as their basis geometrical concepts that are primary and rigorous, understood as invariant structures of aesthetic perception; on the other, it maintained that they must be able to accommodate a specific class of deviations which Purist theory "admet... si elle est justifiée par le recherche de l'invariant."[34] However else it may be characterized, this search strives to reveal the intrinsic affinity connecting the fundamental geometric and proportional principles underlying Modern, Roman, and Greek architecture.

In light of what has been said so far, we must ask ourselves if the presentation of the Villa Schwob, which Ozenfant, under the pseudonym Julien Caron, published in *L'Esprit Nouveau* 6 (1921) constitutes indirect evidence for this Purist reading of Palladio.[35] In his essay Caron/Ozenfant presents the interaction between geometrical invariants and perceptual variants as a key to understanding Le Corbusier's design. If the photograph conveys the contingent aspect of perception, the volumetric accent also manifest in this image, when taken together with the critical description furnished by the text, privileges the purity of the overall geometrical configuration:

En plus de ces applications constructives [referring

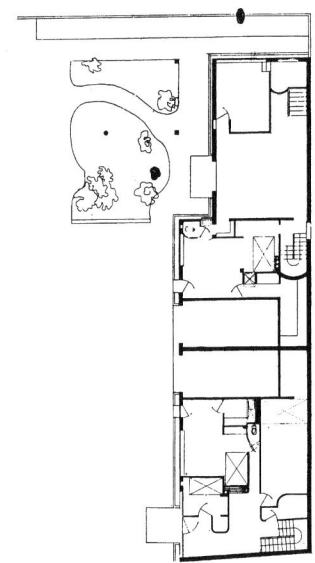

Fig. 18 Le Corbusier, Maisons La Roche-Jeanneret, 1923: plan

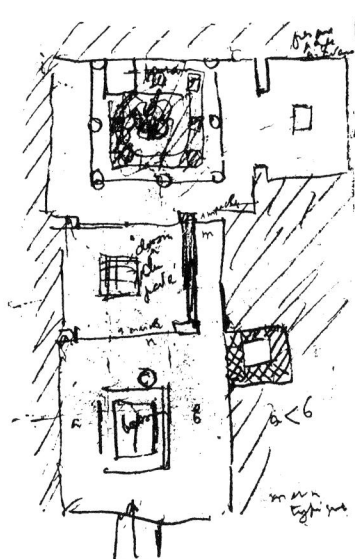

Fig. 19 Le Corbusier, sketch of the plan of the House of the Tragic Poet, Pompeii

to the *beton armé* of the internal structure] Le Corbusier a tente de resoudre un probleme delicat; s'etant donne pur tache de faire une oeuvre de pure architecture, il s'imposa un plan dont les masses ont ete de geometrie primaire; le carre et le cercle. One a rarement tente cette gageure dans les constructions des maisons d'habitation, sauf à la Renaissance.[36]

This passage implies that a specific use of the classical code, stressing its geometrical elementalism, provided an effective normative context for the emergence of Le Corbusier's vision of a modern residential architecture. More precisely, in its reductive focus on the essential, Ozenfant's reference to "a work of pure architecture" identified one of the main problems that Le Corbusier confronted when designing the Maisons La Roche-Jeanneret from 1922 onward: to achieve a synthesis of ancient and modern without reverting to obvious classical allusions. His solution relies on two inherently related typologies: the Roman *domus* and the Palladian atrium house, so that the modern project is endowed with definite, if unobtrusive, classical reminiscences. To be more precise, in Le Corbusier's view the Roman *domus*, in addition to exhibiting a rational distribution of interior spaces, also displays a remarkable volumetric clarity.[37] Both features can be seen in Le Corbusier's plan as he absorbs the lesson of antiquity while rejecting any direct evocation of classical forms.

The most striking thing about this subtle use of the ancient type is that the plan forms a kind of L, recalling —as Kurt Forster argued in a famous essay—the plan of the House of the Tragic Poet which Le Corbusier drew during his visit to Pompeii in 1911 (Figs. 18, 19).[38] Yet, given the fact that Le Corbusier drew a strikingly similar residential plan by Palladio—that of the Palazzo Porto Barbarano (Fig. 17)—on his trip with La Roche, it is more likely that this Palladian model inspired both patron and architect when the two were discussing the Maisons La Roche-Jeanneret. At the very least, the L-shaped plan of Palladio's Vicentine palazzo may have revived memories of the Pompeiian type. In any case, the unusual circulation pattern implicit in both Palladian and Pompeiian precedents must have impressed Le Corbusier when he realized the *promenade architecturale* in the Maisons La Roche-Jeanneret—the first time that this characteristic feature of his architecture appears in his work. After arriving in the garage, the spectator emerges from an enclosed area; following a diagonal axis which leads directly to the threshold of the house, he or she experiences the entire sequence in terms of a barely perceptible contrast between covered and uncovered

---

36 Ozenfant and Caron, "Une villa de Le Corbusier," 692.

37 Kurt Forster, "Antiquity and Modernity in the La Roche-Jeanneret Houses of 1923," *Oppositions Reader* (New York: Princeton Architectural Press, 1998), 20–1.

38 Forster, "Antiquity and Modernity," 20–1.

39 On the *promenade architecturale* in the Maison La Roche, see now Sbriglio, *Les Villas Roche-Jeanneret*, 39ff; Tim Benton, *Les Villas de Le Corbusier*, 1920–34 (Paris, 1975), 64–5. For a more comprehensive reading of the significance of the *promenade architecturale* in Le Corbusier's work as a whole, see now von Moos, "Voyages en Zigzag," in *Le Corbusier before Le Corbusier*, 41–3.

40 On Le Corbusier's and La Roche's shared ideas regarding the gallery's functional parameters and the differentiation of its audience—it was in fact open to the public two afternoons a week, even when La Roche was absent —see Le Corbusier, *Quand les cathédrales étaient blanches: Voyage au pays des timides* (Paris: Plon, 1937), 157.

41 Raoul La Roche, letter of 13 March 1925 cited in Russell Walden, "New Light on Le Corbusier's Early Years in Paris: The La Roche-Jeanneret Houses," in Russell Walden (ed.), *The Open Hand: Essays on Le Corbusier* (Cambridge, Mass.: MIT Press, 1977), 153. My translation.

Le Corbusier, Maisons La Roche, Paris, 1923:
Fig. 20 (top) entrance
Figs. 21 & 22 (middle & bottom) gallery

spaces (Fig. 20). As with the virtual impluvium of the picture gallery (Fig. 21, 22), this highly nuanced game recapitulates a crucial feature of the ancient house: the dialectic between interior and exterior. Charged with antique and Palladian memories while moving decisively beyond them, the *promenade architecturale* prompts an unprecedented articulation of the movement of the body through space. It does this by effecting an oscillation between subject and object, interiority and exteriority, the orthogonality of the volume and the sinuous itinerary joining the different floors.[39]

This mediation between the conventions of ancient typology and the requirements of modern circulation was aimed at accommodating the refined sensibility of a client who fully endorsed the Purist commitments of Le Corbusier and Ozenfant. In the house, La Roche's avant-garde paintings synthesized normative geometries and exceptional episodes so as to express the underlying presuppositions of a Purist concept, translated into a highly articulate architectural language.[40] It is certain that La Roche grasped the implications of this strategy in relation to the aforementioned affinity between antiquity and modernity. This much is clear from a letter he wrote to Le Corbusier after the completion of the project on March 13, 1925, in which he declares:

> The house gives me great joy and I convey to you my gratitude. You have brought to completion an admirable work which, I am convinced, will mark an epoch in the history of architecture. First, the house contains, from different points of view, innovations which have allowed technical progress but which up until now architects have not thought to use… But what especially moves me are certain constant elements found in all the great works of architecture, but which one sees so rarely in modern constructions. Your ability to link our epoch to the preceding ones in this way is particularly remarkable. You have "overrun the problem" and made a work of plastic art.[41]

Inserting itself between architectural codes associated with the residential type and plastic values peculiar to the work of art, the functional dimension of the Maisons La Roche-Jeanneret simultaneously prompts a return to the classical past and a dialectical leap into the future. To be sure, this process precludes obvious Palladian quotations and, for that matter, literal uses of the Pompeiian legacy. Yet in this house one cannot avoid discerning a profound continuity with Palladian and Pompeiian models: a surreptitious classicism whose evocative power derives from the fact that the decisive citations are never explicitly stated.

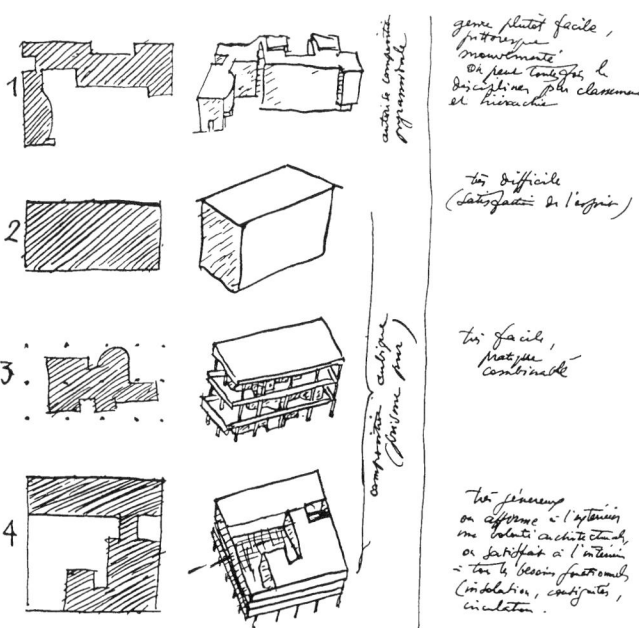

Fig. 23 Le Corbusier, *Les Quatres compositions*, 1929

42 Colquhoun, "Displacement of Concepts in Le Corbusier," 51.
43 Working from a different perspective—and reaching different conclusions from my own—von Moos offers a perceptive analysis of Rowe's comparison of the Villa Stein at Garches and the Villa Foscari at Malcontenta: von Moos, *Album La Roche*, II. 32ff.
44 Berdini, "Introduzione," xvii–xviii.
45 Manfredo Tafuri and Francesco Dal Co, *Modern Architecture* (New York: H. N. Abrams, 1976), 122.
46 Tafuri and Dal Co, *Modern Architecture*, 122.

In the *Quatre compositions* of 1929 (Fig. 23), Le Corbusier's inversion of classical principles finds its most succinct theoretical expression. Presented systematically through a series of new domestic typologies, this inversion acquires the status of a modernist norm. In this context the use of *pilotis* designates the reversal of a classical podium, the *fenêtre en longueur* effects a contradiction of the classical aedicule, and so on.[42] This becomes most apparent in the fourth type, exemplified by the Villa Savoie, whose interior resists the limits set by the absolute geometric integrity of the second type, even as this very same quality seems to be preserved, if only at first glance, on the exterior envelope.

This aspect of the Villa Savoie leads us back to Rowe, and more specifically to the famous analogy he proposed between Villa Savoie and the Rotonda.[43] Yet it is also the case that this specific juxtaposition hinges, as Paolo Berdini has shown, on a more general contrast between a structural system based on a *plan paralysé* and hence on bearing walls and a *plan libre* presupposing a series of *piani nobili* supported on *pilotis*.[44] For Rowe, this structural difference confirms, and yet at the same time contradicts, the effect of formal and geometric similarity that the two houses inevitably share. Yet if we reconsider their relationship in terms of a norm/exception interdependence, something new emerges from the comparison. Turning to the plan, the regularity of the Palladian perimeter remains intact in its Corbusian counterpart. In the modern interior, however, an entire series of spatial singularities and the *promenade* which connects them are clearly privileged. Moreover, when we compare the elevations of Villa Savoie to its planimetric organization (Figs. 24, 25), it is evident that we are not confronted by an abstract exemplification of the norm/exception dialectic, but rather by a concrete manifestation of this interaction, one that strongly marks the plasticity of the surrounding volume. In other words, in Le Corbusier's hands, the typological norm becomes a grid for the eruption of voids and, at the same time, a pretext for the manifestation of exceptions to classical rule.

When followed to its conclusion, the diagonal of the ramp, the primary vehicle of the *promenade architecturale*, shows that the geometrical coherence of the façade, of a pronounced Platonic and Palladian character, is merely a fiction.[45] A paratactic sequence of *objets à reactions poétiques*, exceptions *par excellence*, is secured by the *promenade*, which bears the moving subject along in its spiral journey towards the roof garden (Fig. 26, 27).[46] This itinerary refers the circulatory logic of the Maisons La Roche-Jeanneret to a new spatial model, even as it pits the dynamic lyricism of the singular

Le Corbusier, Villa Savoie, Poissy, 1929:
Fig. 24 (top) façade
Fig. 25 (middle) plans
Figs. 26 & 27 (bottom) ramp to roof garden

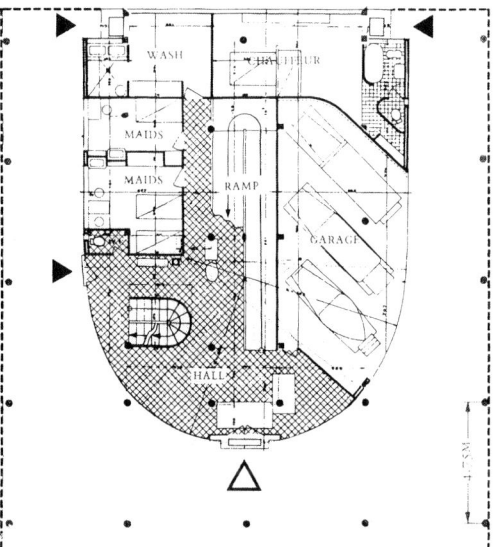
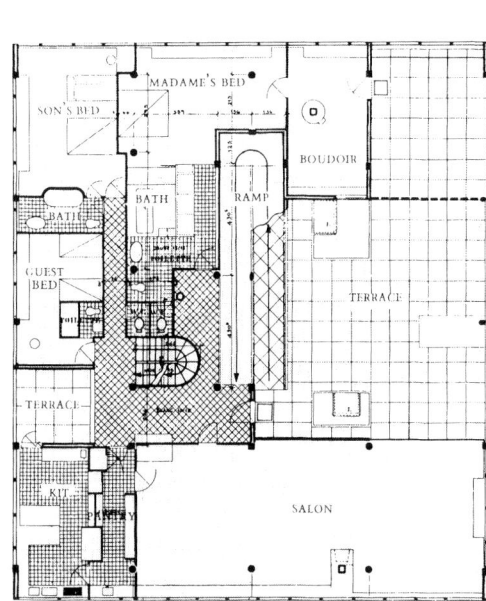
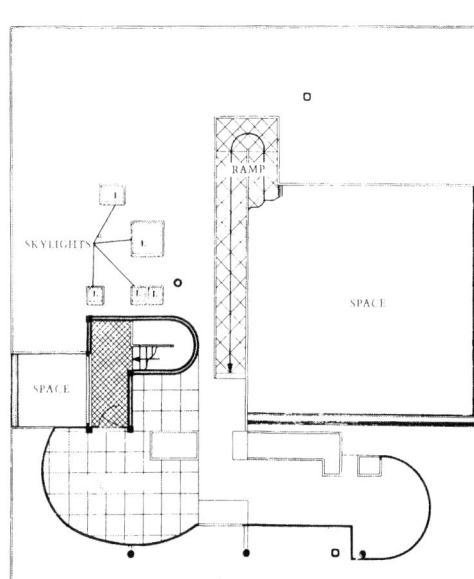

Fig. 28 Le Corbusier, Maison Plainex, Paris, 1927: façade

47 The tetrastyle atrium or vestibule was of special importance to Palladio, who may be said to be chiefly responsible for its subsequent diffusion. Wittkower explains its significance: "The tetrastyle as the leit-motif of the ground-plan is one of the recurrent characteristics of Palladio's palaces.... The ancient atrium had an open roof; since an open atrium could hardly be built by a modern architect, Palladio used the tetrastyle hall for his atrium. But he made the exchange on good authority, for among the five types of atria mentioned by Vitruvius there is one supported by four columns, i.e., a tetrastyle. Palladio's preference for this atrium was based not only upon its structural solidity, but above all upon its square shape which he regarded as a perfect form." Wittkower, *Architectural Principles*, 76.

48 Le Corbusier, *The City of Tomorrow and Its Planning*, trans. Frederick Etchells (New York: Payson and Clarke, 1929 [1925]), 52–3.
49 On Le Corbusier's reading of Nietzsche, with reference to the idea of the eternal return formulated in *Also sprach Zarathustra*, see Tafuri, "Machine et memoire," 214; Frampton, *Le Corbusier*, 201.

episodes against the normative context of the second type of the *Quatre compositions*. In this way, to paraphrase La Roche himself, the architect "outruns the problem," exploiting the tacit equivalence between the *machine à habiter* and the ancient type to stress the distance, as well as the proximity, between classic and modern in a highly sophisticated spatio-temporal game.

It is striking to note that when Le Corbusier stresses the role of the *promenade architecturale* the façade is underplayed: in fact, the Villa Savoie has no privileged façade in the strict sense of the term. But when one turns to the Maison Plainex (1927), an emphasis on façade articulation recurs which has more than one Palladian precedent (Fig. 28). When designing this façade, Le Corbusier confronted problems raised by Palladio's interpretation of the Roman tetrastyle *domus* and reverted to the Casa Cogollo to resolve them. This much is evident from a comparative analysis of the plans of the classical type and the Parisian residence—a comparison authorized by the fact that, during his Vicentine trip, it was precisely the *all'antica* vestibule with four columns of the Palazzo Barbarano that first drew Le Corbusier's attention to the formal possibilities of the type, at least as far as its post-Pompeiian exemplifications are concerned.[47] Here the essential task for the modern architect is to translate a tetrastyle entrance hall characteristic of the ancient (and Palladian) atrium house into formal and visual terms appropriate to the façade of a twentieth-century urban residence. To frame an adequate response to this problem, Le Corbusier generated the most unequivocally Palladian solution in his entire oeuvre: the façade of the Villa Schwob, whose blank panel on the second story cites, as already indicated, a similar anomaly on the *piano nobile* façade of the Casa Cogollo (Fig. 8). In the Maison Plainex, the interior system of columns typical of the ancient tetrastyle vestibule is projected, at least partially, onto the exterior while the void on the second floor is replaced by a solid, blank projecting mass. The latter is reminiscent of the empty, second-story panel of Villa Schwob (Fig. 7)—the chief difference being that, in the Parisian residence, the blank element protrudes, and the *pilotis* recede, while in the villa at La Chaux-de-Fonds, the opposite occurs. Despite this important difference, the façade of the Maison Plainex clearly recalls the Villa Schwob and therefore transforms the model of the Casa Cogollo as well, if only at a second remove. The Maison Plainex, in other words, renews the classical type while addressing the exigencies of the modern urban residence and its implicit Palladian models. In this way, Le Corbusier registers a debt to the Palladian legacy, perhaps the most profound of his entire career, while taking a distinctively modern distance from it at the same time.

A less subtle but equally decisive assimilation of Palladio can be verified in Le Corbusier's theoretical work of the same period. Two years before, in one of the most emblematic pages of *Urbanisme* of 1925, Le Corbusier contrasted Gustave Eiffel's Pont de Garabit and the Villa Rotonda (Figs 29, 30).[48] In addition to offering a striking prefiguration of Rowe's formalist approach by pairing a modern and a classical work, this tension-filled analogy recalls the juxtaposition between the *civilisation machiniste* and the Parthenon advanced in *Vers une architecture* of 1923 (Fig. 1). In the 1925 text, Le Corbusier makes no reference to the Palladian villa, but speaks of the Pont de Garabit, which he regards as the concrete result of a collective will illustrating the "mind of the epoch." Presented as a characteristic product of modern standardization, Eiffel's bridge imposes a limit and establishes a norm: the norm of the engineer, which only Palladio's architecture is able to surpass. On the basis of this contrast Le Corbusier maintains that it is only from rational calculation that one can derive the fundamental value of *pérennité*— a term that denotes something like Nietzsche's "eternal return."[49] Inadequately translated by Frederick Etchells, Le Corbusier's English translator in the 1930s, as "permanence," *pérennité* designates the dynamic recurrence of norms that are infallible and implacable (rather than the static codification of values implied by Etchell's misleading choice of words). Against this notion, Le Corbusier selected a formal achievement that was rationalized and classicizing, yet also imbued with a sense of invention capable of transcending the "culture of calculation." In this sense, the Palladian villa, as an exemplary instance of the art of architecture, is more advanced, at least on the purely aesthetic level, than the most up-to-date productions of the "engineer's aesthetic" such as Eiffel's bridge.

Figs. 29 & 30 Pages from Le Corbusier's *Urbanisme* (1925) showing the photographs of Gustave Eiffel's Pont de Garabit and Palladio's Villa Rotonda

The comparison has a double significance. In the first place, according to accepted conventions of reading, the antithesis which Le Corbusier puts forward here should be read from left to right, from the Pont de Garabit to the Rotonda. However, this procedure seems to be contradicted by the fact that the comparison presupposes a reading which reverses not only the logic of chronology, but even the temporal logic of history itself. According to the terms of the comparison, the Modern is placed before the Classical, so that the Modern corresponds to the *norm* and the Classical corresponds to the *exception*. Due to this paradoxical inversion, it seems as if the Classical derives from the Modern, not the other way around. In the second place, this comparison gives us a crucial theoretical indication which teaches us how to read the history of architecture according to Le Corbusier. It tells us that in this history, *après* and *avant* are not in their usual places, a curious situation which underscores the modernist need to move in a counterdirection opposed to the temporality of all previous histories. Which is to say: the architect is always between buildings, spaces, times and epochs of history, in such a way as to engage a continuous inversion of time and space. In the midst of this, in the promenade between the different epochs, one finds history itself, which discloses its essential contours not by engaging architectural objects, but rather by producing architectural projects, or, to be more precise, by sending the architect on a journey, endless, yet constantly renewed, *Vers une architecture*.

Acknowledgement
I am grateful to Guido Canella and Antonio Monestiroli for their invitation to present a preliminary version of this study as a lecture at the Facolta di Architettura Civile at the Politecnico di Milano on June 5, 2003; to the students in my seminar on "Palladio and Palladianism" at Columbia Graduate School of Architecture, Planning, and Preservation in Spring 2002, for stimulating discussion of my preliminary hypotheses; to Kenneth Frampton and Mary McLeod for their insights on Le Corbusier's relation to the classical tradition; to Scott Cohen, without whose timely intervention this essay would never have been published; and to my friend Andrea Parravicini for his indispensable assistance in editing the Italian lecture, which also proved invaluable in clarifying my ideas in the English version. I am also grateful to the generous support of the New York Foundation for the Arts for a grant that facilitated the completion of this essay. In a broader sense I am indebted to my friend Paolo Berdini for stimulating conversations on Le Corbusier, Palladio, and Colin Rowe, and for the continuing encouragement of Mary Kaplan. The present article is an expanded version of an essay which originally appeared in Italian in *Aion*, 4 (2003), 34–43.

Peter Eisenman

Digital Scrambler

In her two essays "Notes on the Index: Seventies Art in America," first published in *October* 3 and 4 (spring and fall 1977), Rosalind Krauss articulated an idea for defining the diverse genres and styles of art in the 1970s. Rightly or wrongly, she defined this idea as an index. This placed art in a context first used by Charles Sanders Peirce to describe the difference between linguistic signs: between symbol, icon, and index. For Peirce, a symbol was an arbitrary and culturally based referent; an icon had a visual similitude to its object; and an index had a physical and temporal relationship to its referents. Like footprints left in the sand suggesting some prior physical presence, indices are physical marks, traces, imprints, or clues concerning some real event rather than a transcendental truth or signified. In this context the index is the trace of a former presence. The index could also be understood to operate like the clues given in a mystery, or detective, novel, which is the most modern of all literary discourses because it relies on the traces of something prior. The solution to the crime requires a tracing backward to an event and not to some a priori truth; whatever truth may be—that is, who committed the crime—is only revealed in the process of retracing an action or an event that occurred.

Underlying Krauss's invocation of the index was an attempt to explain away one of the major problematics of the poststructuralist era: the metaphysics of presence. That is, many of the formal and pictorial conventions that are sedimented in the arts constitute in most cases their metaphysics. The index then was one way, even if not stated as such, to problematize the metaphysics of presence by moving the art object toward a condition of pure presence.

Minimalism, earth art, and particularly photography

From Index to Codex

were all attempts to empty representation and image of their latent pictorial codes. Presence became the emptier of the metaphysics of presence. For example, when Gordon Matta-Clark sawed a house in half so that it was no longer a functioning house, he not only attacked the metaphysical content of family, the traditions of occupation and function, but, more importantly, he also attacked the form of the house. For Krauss, these cuts are like linguistic "shifters" that empty the house of meaning, because in themselves the cuts have no meaning. The house is no longer a house, but rather an empty presence. No longer did Matta-Clark's house refer to a prior absolute truth or other presence. Rather, it was the site of a simple action, an event which caused such traces to appear.

In a striking difference from the work that preceded it, the art of the 1970s not only emptied out meaning—a relationship to some idea of a transcendental signified, of one object before all other objects—there was also an emptying out of residual pictorial codes, the latent formal manifestations in objects that carry aesthetic information. This emptying out of the pictorial codes is different from what occurred in the abstract expressionism of the 1960s. In this work there was still a pictorial necessity. For example, the picture plane was still active as a datum, as was the edge of the canvas. By the late 1970s, there was a further and important shift in the idea of the index in terms of the photograph. Since the photograph was seen as a record, and therefore a trace, of some event, it became an operative art condition of the index.

Since then, and partly because of the introduction of digital manipulation in photography, the presence of a photograph as a truthful record of an event has been brought into question. Previously, a photograph of a painting with a verified author's signature would certify that the photograph was the representation of the real painting. Today photographs can be doctored in such a way that a signature could either be erased or added without such an action being detected. Thus the photograph no longer stands for an index of presence. The photograph is once again an object being manipulated, and therefore no longer empty of value. It is now open to a more problematic internal manipulation. Just as the photograph is no longer necessarily an index to an objective truth, an uncoded message, the index is no longer a way of assuring a condition of pure presence. When a photograph can be digitally altered, the nature of the alteration returns a code (an internal mathematical logic) to the message. These codes depend on an internal logic that is autonomous from both a context and an event.

In architecture after the 1970s and 1980s other problems with the index surfaced. These concerned the nature of its representational or sign function. Architecture, like photography, is different from painting in that it is already an index. Its signs are traces of its own physicality. But architectural signs are also icons. For example, while a column is the sign of a column, its structuring function depends on it looking like a column for its representational function.

In one sense, architecture has always been about codes, whether literally, in building codes, or metaphorically, in classical codes—the rules of proportion and ordination in building systems. These classical codes often went unexamined because they became iconic and conventional. This was thought to be the natural condition of architectural signs, that is, that architecture as commonly understood will always look like architec-

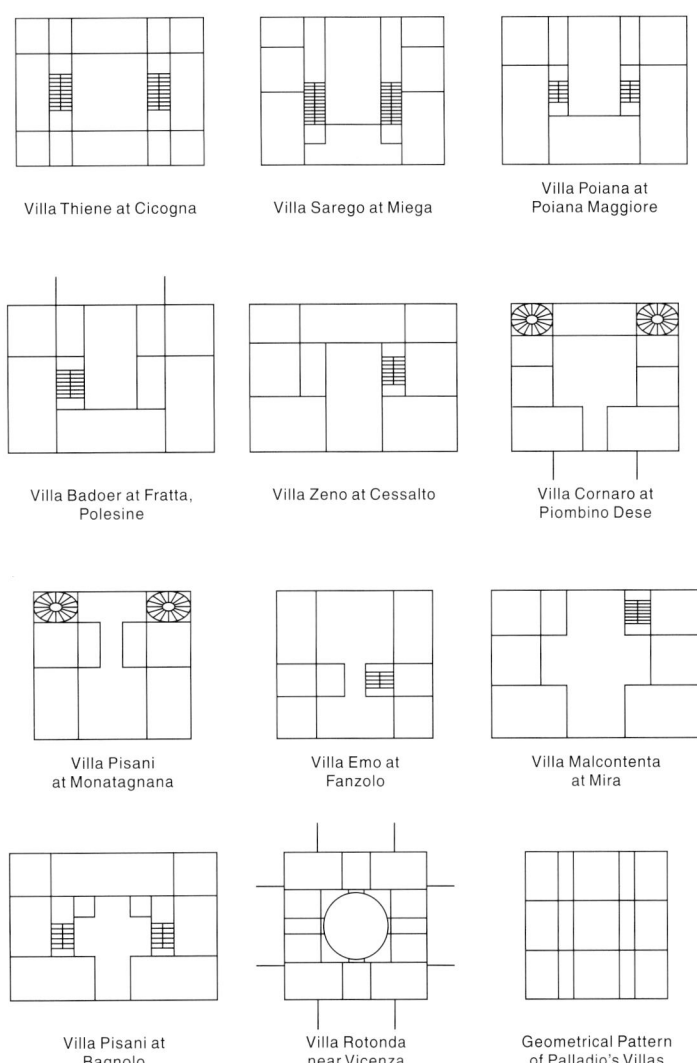

ture—like columns, pediments, bases, etc. In classical ordination, codes were basically a set of rules for the transmission and classification of particular signs, so that these signs could be repeated in different contexts. Proportional conventions were usually measurements of presence and palpable geometries. However, as a series of proportional conventions, classical codes were not generative material; they were proscriptive and still metaphysical.

Many times when an *A–B–A* or *A–B–B–A* relationship was used to denote proportional relationships in plans and sections, these notations did not recognize other relationships, such as those of position. Notation was defined by geometric lines, rather than by spatial position or relationships. The thicknesses of divisions such as the inner and outer edges of walls were rarely considered. For example, Rudolf Wittkower's famous diagrams of Palladian villas (Fig. 1) were line drawings that reduced the thickness of walls and their poché to a constituent geometry. In Wittkower's analysis, space was passive—a residual component. Colin Rowe's later analysis of Le Corbusier's Villa Stein at Garches (Fig. 2) and subsequent urban plans for his book *Collage City* introduced the idea of space, but only as a solid-void, figure-ground, gestalt dialectic, and again not in any way as generative material. Through Rowe, Nolli's map of Rome (Fig. 3) became a mantra for the New Urbanists'

Fig. 1 (above) Diagrams of Palladian villas, Rudolf Wittkower, 1949
Fig. 2 (below) Analysis of Le Corbusier's Villa Stein, Colin Rowe, 1947
Fig. 3 (right) Map of Rome, Giambattista Nolli, 1748

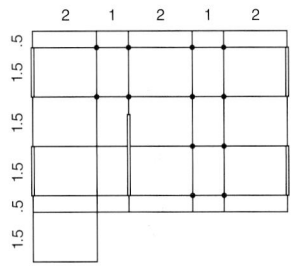

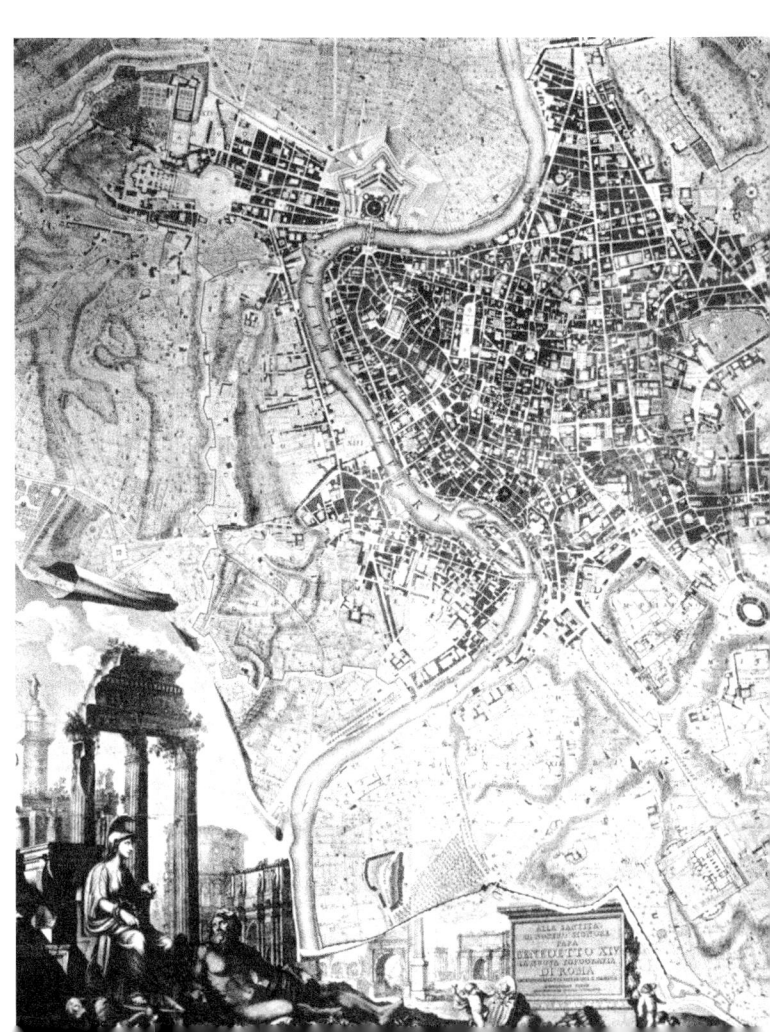

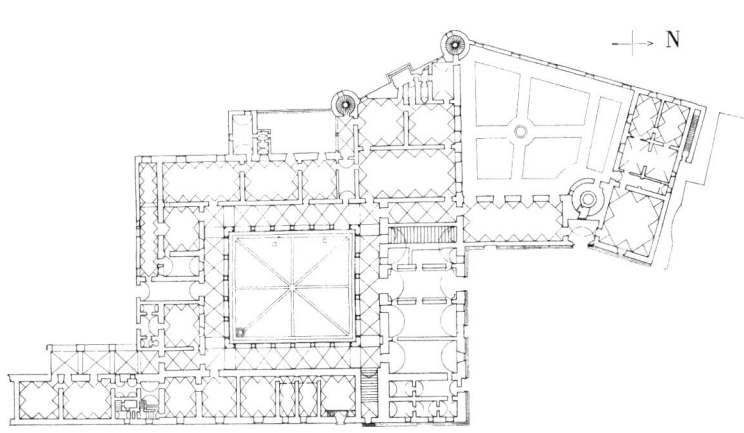

Fig. 4 Plan, Palazzo Ducale, Urbino, Luciano Laurana, 1450

idea of figure-ground as the pictorial frame for a "good plan." However, in the late 1970s, architects questioning the convention of figure-ground began to open up other aspects of the coded conventions in architecture.

Geometry and classical proportions dominated the codes of architecture in the early Renaissance, particularly in the work of Brunelleschi and Alberti. But Alberti began to focus on another problem, one apart from Brunelleschi's attempts to transform a gothic columnar structure into Renaissance perspectival space. Alberti articulated the wall both as a constructional system and as a conceptual entity. Walls, unlike columns, had no agreed-upon conventions, and geometry replaced classical ordination as a guiding principle in wall building. But walls also have thickness, something Cartesian geometry does not necessarily take into account. For example, in Luciano Laurana's Palazzo Ducale in Urbino, the regular geometric grid that defines the courtyard has an extra dimensional layer (Fig. 4). This layer, which is outside of the grid, allows for both the thickness of the column and the spatial interval between columns to remain constant. Each façade ends with a column, which in turn produces a third condition, the intersection of two columns at each corner of the courtyard (Fig. 5). This produces the need for a formal resolution but does not resolve the integration of space and geometry. To consider corners as material being in

Fig. 5 Intersection of two columns at courtyard corner, Palazzo Ducale, Urbino, Luciano Laurana, 1450

Fig. 6 Superposition of Tuscan and Ionic orders in courtyard, Santa Maria della Pace, Rome, Donato Bramante, 1501–4

Fig. 7 Cloister courtyard, Pazzi Chapel, S. Croce, Florence, Filippo Brunelleschi, 1429–61

the fifteenth century also required some form of conceptual or metaphysical resolution.

Recognizing this metaphysical problem, Bramante looked at the corner differently than Laurana did at Urbino. He worked toward a certain organicism of presence, an active unity between geometry and space in which the geometric structural grid and the spatial volume had to be one and the same, without an extra layer to compensate for the thickness of the wall plane. In Bramante's schema, space is not the passive residue of a gridded courtyard geometry but something coactive as presence with it. There is no added layer around the space to take up the thickness of the wall. According to classical ordination the spatial interval between columns needed to be maintained, that is, needed to be a datum of equal integers. At the courtyard of Santa Maria della Pace in Rome, Bramante superposed the existing proportions of two orders—the Tuscan and the Ionic—changing both their iconic condition and their conventionally coded relationships (Fig. 6). This superposition first produced a kind of index from two formerly iconic signs. This was achieved in a modification at the base of the columns at the corner. The resulting corner, however, was neither iconic nor indexical. Rather, in spite of the classical restrictions, the superposition of the Ionic and the Tuscan codes led to something quite startling, something unpredictable, which exceeded both the accidental and the literal corner of the Pazzi Chapel in Florence (Fig. 7) and the formal corner at the Palazzo Ducale.

The corner at Santa Maria della Pace suggests that the volume of the courtyard produces a vectoral force that is outside of any geometric order, compressing the corner into its resultant material being (Fig. 8). In one sense, the result is an index of the space acting on the geometry. But since this was, at the time, a singular and unique event in architecture, there is no semiotic or prior historical condition from which to read the index. Rather, the corner is the uncovering of an internal possibility of architecture, which, because there is no precedent, acts as a different form of index, that is, as something which could be provisionally called a generative or mutational code; a coded index as opposed to a conventional index.

Instead of referring back to the classical orders, or to a specific event, this unexpected outcome referred internally to its own logic. This logic produced a density that exceeded rather than reduced information, and in that excess produced an effect in the object. This effect produced a new autonomous architectural idea about corners, something between a code and a conventional index.

Fig. 8 Courtyard corner, Santa Maria della Pace, Rome, Donato Bramante, 1501–4

All architecture has the possibility to be both a code and an index. Because there is no universal iconic sign system in architecture, and since architecture is always a second language, all architectural representation is coded. This concept of a coded index differs from conventional ideas of a code or index of an event because it could be generative rather than regulatory or secretive. Coding as a form of index reveals upon inspection something that cannot be seen and thus understood at first sight. This seeing is different from that which is recognized by a formal or pictorial reading of a code. For example, the condition at the corner of the Palazzo Ducale courtyard tells us something about what we actually see: two sides of equal value are joined at the corner. This reading can lead to several interpretations. In the first, the plaza is formed in an additive way, with the side arcades tipped up to form the space. In this case the corner is not thematized but is simply the natural result of the intersection. In a second reading, the doubling of the columns at the corner can be read as thematizing the completion of each side, and thus as articulating the corner in a formal sense. When this is compared to the corner of the courtyard at the Pazzi Chapel, the idea of the formal becomes clear. The corner at Urbino suggests something beyond its literal self—a formal proposition—while the corner at the Pazzi Chapel is simply a literal intersection, nothing more. That the intersection at Santa Maria della Pace seems to suggest the collision or disappearance of matter through some sort of force is only a further instance of the manner in which this corner problematizes conceptions of the formal. In many respects, Urbino and Santa Maria della Pace are similar, but there is an important difference. What is at work at Santa Maria della Pace is neither a conventional code nor a literal or formal presence. Where previous architectural codes only dealt with positive integers—columns, capitals, pediments, etc.—here coding also incorporates space as an active force, the presence, as it were, of an absence. Both the materiality of the arcaded wall and the spatial volume of the courtyard are engaged. The code is read not because of some previous external example but because of an internal superposition of the two orders, which creates a new effect.

The possibility of reading such indices and codes today was preceded by the transition from a purely formal reading to a semiotic one that occurred from the 1960s to the 1980s. Relationships of rectangles and squares were no longer sufficient to explain the complexities that architecture faced. The epistemology that related some stable condition of form to some progressive condition of an ideal universe, seen as some absolute condition, was questioned. Again, in order to overcome its metaphysical connotations, architecture began to be examined as a semiotic system, one without any pictorial or formal conventions. However, any reading of a Bramante or a Palladio that no longer searched for an ideal still had to contend with the aesthetic residue implied in any iconic or semiotic system, which were assumed to be fundamental to any architectural condition. Some historians even argued that the new semiotic systems did not take into account the affects that geometrical relationships and spatial being, i.e., height, material, surface, etc., of buildings produce. Similarly, in the limitation of formal analysis, whether proportional or aesthetic, was a latent and perhaps unconscious desire to reduce conditions of complexity to simple geometries, like reducing architectural thickness to simple lines. Through the introduction of different geometries—topological, fractal, etc.—nature is no longer understood as a series of complex forms that can be reduced to simple forms. Rather, all forms can be seen as suspensions of more complex systems—as exemplified by earthquakes, landslides, and tsunamis—whose geometries, like fractals, are not even based on whole numbers. Neither static nor necessarily linear, and seemingly dislocated, they demand other interpretations. How these disturbances of form implicate space might propose what could be called a less activated object. How such a space becomes coded to produce a less motivated

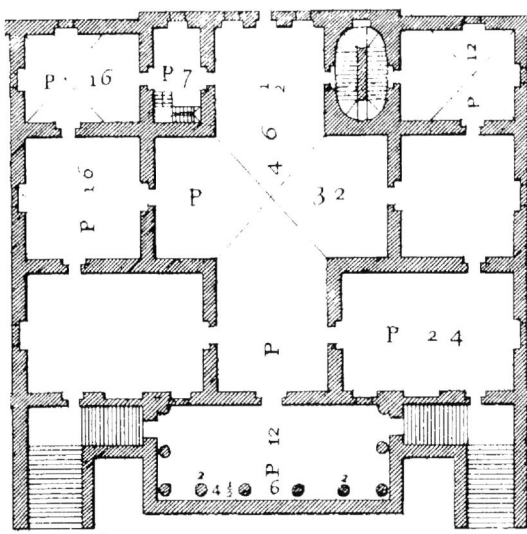

Fig. 9 Analysis of Palladian villa by proportional size of rooms, Andrea Palladio, 1570

Fig. 10 Diagram of *A–B–C–B–A* analysis of Palladian "virtual villa," denoting positional and functional relationships both front to back and back to front, Peter Eisenman

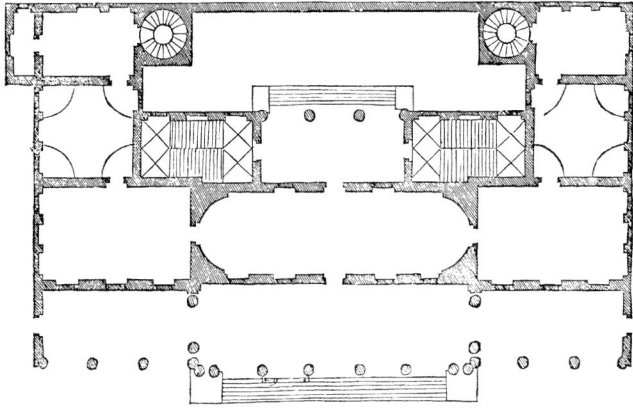

Fig. 11 Plan, Palazzo Chiericati, Vicenza, Andrea Palladio, 1550

object of space and geometry is a key issue, for it requires different ways of thinking and reading architecture.

As reading architecture moved from a formal system to a semiotic one, there was a concurrent movement in the general condition of culture from a technological and mechanical explanation of the world to one that is more biological, in which different conditions of the physical objective world as explanatory models are proposed. This also made it possible to suggest models of explanation other than mathematical, that is, geometric— Platonic and Cartesian or Euclidean—and other than general relativity theory, quantum mechanics, and so forth. For example, difference could be seen as dynamic, as in biological models with organizing principles that no longer required stable, static whole integers.

To open up ways of reading and making architecture is to propose another strategy of reading and another kind of "writing," other than indexical, that is no longer defined only by geometric ordering. It requires that semiotic and geometric systems become secondary to ways of producing objects that have more to do with spatial position, superposition, and misreading than with the geometry of the shape. This can also lead to a reevaluation of the work of an architect like Palladio and produce through other readings the revelation of a different writing of space and position.

Historically, Palladian villas have been read in several ways. One, proposed by Palladio himself, is a proportional analysis of the size of a room (Fig. 9). Other readings look at the villas as variations from an ideal cube. These variations always work from an ideal square in plan. Usually they are read from in front of the steps of a portico to some exterior line in the back, but always within the limits of a square form in plan. Similarly, other readings of the same ideal square can begin at the back and extend to the front. But there are still other ways of reading Palladio that have no relation to the proportions of rooms or the ideal geometry of a square. One such reading proposes a virtual and fluctuating condition of the volumes of space, as opposed to a literal reading of the lines of a static geometry. A virtual condition in Palladio begins from a symmetrical sequence of spaces, which, reading from front to back, can be coded *A–B–C–B–A* (Fig. 10), denoting both positional and functional relationships but not ideal geometric relationships; these integers have no specific shape or proportion. While the volumes of such a virtual villa can be defined by conventional functional terms such as *portico*, *circulation*, and *main space*, or proportional or letter distinctions, in an attempt to displace the established means of reading a different notational

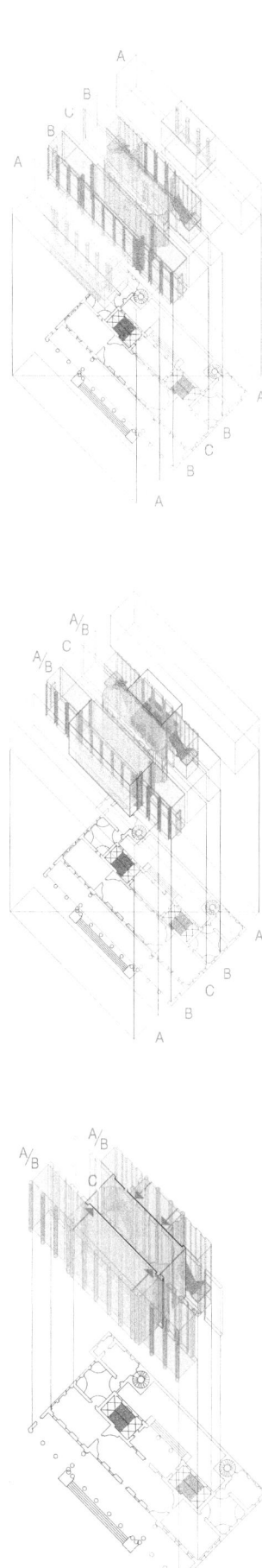

Figs. 12, 13, 14 Diagrams of Palladio's Palazzo Chiericati, Peter Eisenman

system, or coding, can be proposed. The idea of such a coding opens up the Palladian tropes to a notational reading strategy. In this sense, it is possible to look at a building such as the Palazzo Chiericati differently from previous analyses (Fig. 11).

The Palazzo has two distinguishing characteristics. First, the loggia runs across the full façade and simultaneously acts as a portico. Second, unlike any other Palladian villa, it consists of a series of horizontal layers in plan, parallel to the picture plane. The key to understanding the mutations that occur, like the odd corner condition at Santa Maria della Pace, is the pairs of doubled columns that are compressed together at the center of the front loggia. These suggest a reading of a portico that also is compressed into the loggia, or body, of the building. This can be read as a coded as opposed to a formal relationship of position A of the portico and position B of the circulation space in a conceptual idea of a villa (Fig. 12). At Chiericati, the missing portico A has been compressed into the transverse circulation space B (Fig. 13). This space is usually between the portico A and the dominant major space C. The C, or main, space is compressed from an ideal centralized form, as if it had been placed in a vise and a pressure applied to it. In Palladio's vocabulary the major space C is articulated by a figural poché (Fig. 14). The next layer is a rear circulation space B, and then an actual portico A. One way to understand Chiericati is to compare it to a mental idea of a villa consisting of a portico, circulation space, main central space, circulation, and rear portico. In a first reading of Chiericati one sees the absence of an actual portico, a loggia for a circulation space, and an implied portico in the rear. Thus any A–B–C–B–A comparison to a conceptual condition includes a virtual A at the front and rear. This reading of a hypothetical villa only approximates the real building. Another reading reveals two other virtual A conditions: a compression from front to back, and then from back to front. In the first, A is compressed over B, with the portico and its stairs and columns pressed into the loggia. In the second reading, the portico is pressed into the B circulation bay from the rear, leaving a void in the rear yard. This A over B condition, this compression, creates a conceptual spatial density, which is keyed by the pair of columns in the portico pressed into the second pair of columns. This compression of A into B results from a spatial force that produces a conceptual density in the condition of space B.

This particular coding contains three major characteristics. The first is the relation of the actual components to a conceptual or hypothetical villa. The second is the conceptual density that is then created by the mental superposition of the coded two components, that is, the portico space pressed into the loggia. The third reading is the compression of a hypothetical ideal villa type into a series of linear elements. No one reading is better than or to be preferred over another. Each merely contains different information. These readings fluctuate. If one is taken as a stable or dominant base, the other reading can no longer be sustained. If the second reading is taken as a base condition, the first is no longer possible. The only way to have both is to deny a base condition which problematizes any hierarchical or dialectical reading.

From Palladio's Palazzo Chiericati, it is possible to look at Schinkel's Altes Museum in Berlin, which resembles Chiericati in its overall massing and layering. Here another set of codes is operating, which breaks from the formal conventions of the neoclassical. Here a displacement of position creates a different kind of conceptual spatial density. This is initially caused by the unstable location of the dominant spaces, particularly the central rotunda in relation to the exterior enclosure.

While both Chiericati and the Altes Museum have porticos and central ceremonial spaces, and both are

Fig. 15 Altes Museum, Berlin, Karl Friedrich Schinkel, 1823–30

layered from the front to the back, each is a misreading of different codes. Chiericati is a frontal, layered Renaissance building. The viewing subject is meant to be centered at the front. Schinkel's building is neoclassical; it is to be seen in a receding perspective from an oblique corner (Fig. 15). Palladio's work is often seen as the deformation of a nine-square geometric grid; Schinkel's is not. However, by putting them in a similar textual context, it is possible to assign a similar *A–B–C–B–A* conceptual notation (positional as opposed to geometric, proportional, or dimensional) to both.

On first appearance, the Altes Museum is a cross between Palladio's Villa Rotunda and Chiericati, because Schinkel inserts a central drum into the parallel layers. The drum is bilaterally symmetrical from side to side, but not from front to back. This is the key to a series of internal displacements (Fig. 16).

The strategies of reading and interpreting provoked by Schinkel's plans are similar to those of reading Palladio. When one condition is assumed to be stable, as in the exterior side façades, which are symmetrical front to back, the asymmetrical location of the major elements of the plan appears to have shifted inside the symmetrical shell. In the plan of the building, the three internal figural volumes—the central drum and two flanking courtyards—are seen as shifted off center from front to back. Alternatively, if these three volumes are seen as stable and centrally located, then the front stoa is seen as something added, as a frontispiece to the building volume. This latter reading confounds the initial reading of the side façades. In a final reading, the drum and the two horizontal bars are themselves seen as shifted to the rear with the addition of the layer of small rooms in the rear of the two courtyards. Notably, the conventions of the symmetry of the traditional neoclassical palazzo are disrupted in these new readings, which again introduce a new idea of coded relationships.

The idea of coding as a notation of spatial force and position allows a rereading of the formal in terms of what can be called different textual conditions in Bramante, Palladio, and Schinkel. This kind of reading uncouples the traditional formal relationship of proportional ratio to functional use (both "form follows function" and "form defines function"). It is also possible to take the same idea as a reading and produce a project from it, a project that provokes a writing, that is, provokes the potential generative nature of a coded notation. This idea animated our project for the City of Culture of Galicia in Santiago de Compostela, Spain.

The idea of a *codex* is an important one to locate the theoretical strategy of our project in Santiago, because the word combines ideas of index and code. Originally a *codex* was a Christian manuscript written on leaves of parchment. The word stems from the Latin *caudex*, or wooden stump. Christian manuscripts were written on parchment because both sides of the page could be used, while a papyrus scroll, the traditional form of Hebrew Scriptures, could only be inscribed on a single side. By the second century, Christian iconography depicted Evangelists holding codices, while Hebrew prophets were shown with scrolls. The introduction of a *codex* or manual in the secular arts and sciences occurred in the fifteenth century. Among the most well known are the codices of Leonardo da Vinci. Many of Leonardo's codices are written backwards, from right to left, so they can only be read through a mirror that reverses the text. Acting as a signal that one must read differently, this reversal displaces the established means of reading. This is precisely what a coded index requires: a way of reading differently. Coded indices disperse meaning in such a way that the display of language for itself is questioned.

While traditional codes can be seen as the basis of the pictorial conventions—frontality, edge stress, etc.—that

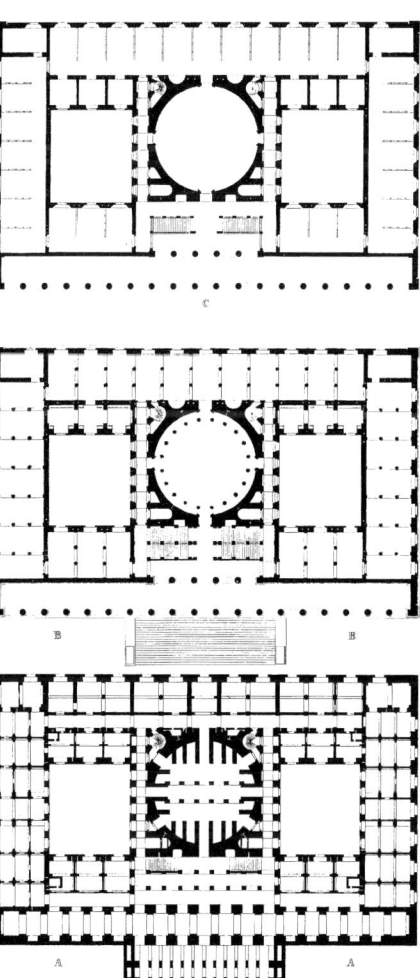

Fig. 16 Plan, Altes Museum, Berlin, Karl Friedrich Schinkel, 1823–30

Fig. 17 Sketch by Peter Eisenman showing superposition of historic Berlin maps, IBA Social Housing, Eisenman Robertson Architects, 1981–5

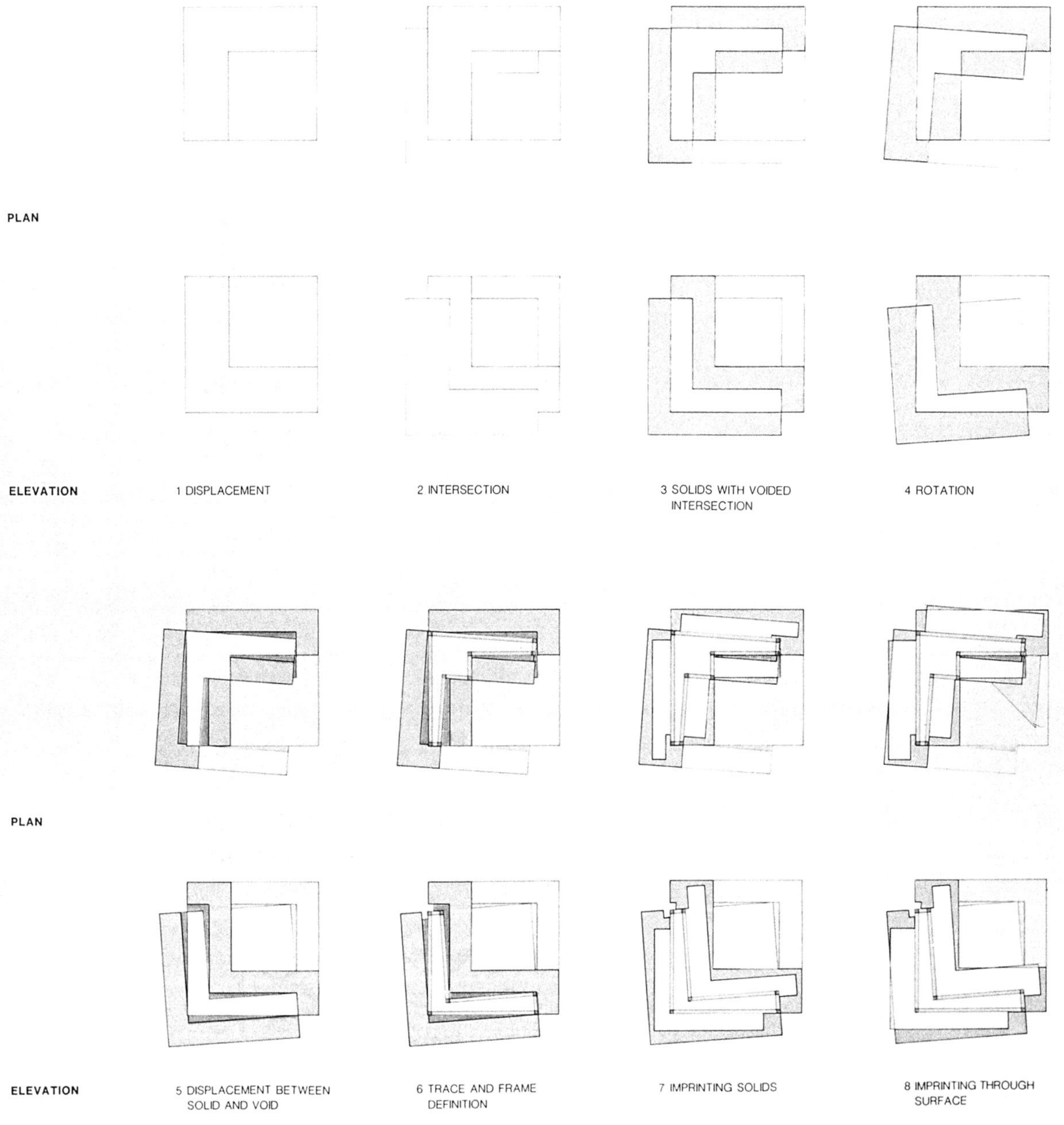

Fig. 18 Diagram of traces, Guardiola House, Eisenman Architects, 1988

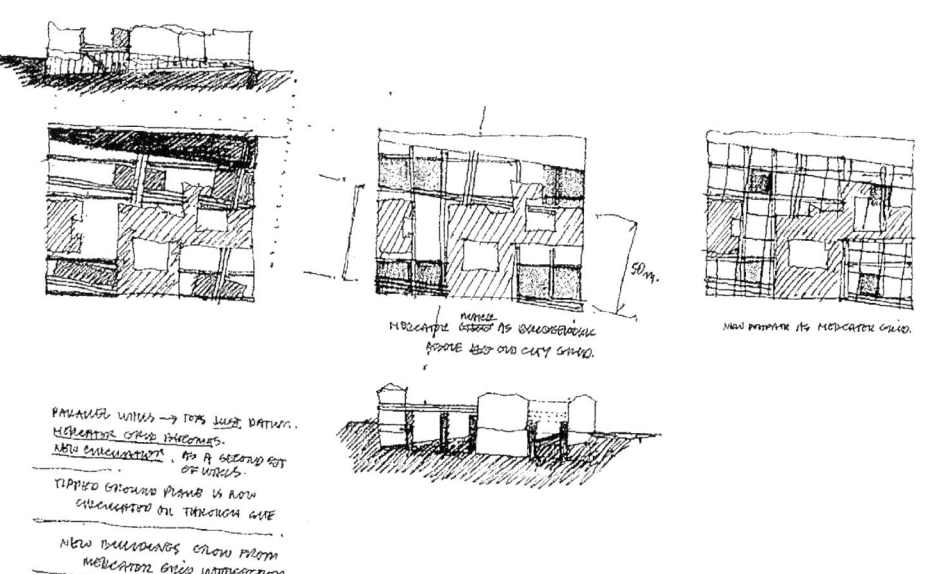

operate in painting, these conventions are almost unknown to most ordinary viewers but not to serious painters. When codes become conventions they only act on memory, on what has been known in the past history of any discipline. Once these codes have become conventions they lose their strangeness. It is this strangeness that differentiates imagination, that is, the possibility of new effects, from memory. In this sense, codes operate differently than ordinary language usage (excluding poetic and literary forms) because they have a different interiority, a different relationship of sign to signified. In common language, the sign-signified relationship is supposed to be transparent; in a code like poetry and literature this relationship is more opaque, creating a strangeness in the object, and thus questioning familiar conditions of reading.

The use of the word *codex* in the context of architecture and in the particular project at Santiago signals an important shift in our work, from traditional coded conventions to a form of coded index. Much of my own work in the 1970s and early 1980s was an attempt to reduce the classical pictorial conventions of a so-called "good" plan by also introducing the idea of the index. This work was characterized by ideas of trace, imprint, and superposition (see *Cities of Artificial Excavation*, 1994). Most of these projects dealt with two-dimensional traces in plan, which, in order to achieve a third dimension, were extruded vertically (Fig. 17). Only in the case of the Guardiola House (1988) were both imprints and traces attempted in section (Fig. 18). But in every case this work was marked by the absence of a former presence, through some kind of imprinted geometry; like two halves of a plastic mould, these traces were never spatial in a volumetric sense.

While the project at Santiago begins as a series of plans overlaid as a palimpsest, an archetypal form of an index, these overlays are then extrapolated into a three-dimensional matrix. Whether as a palimpsest, a photograph, or a cut in a building, indices are precise records of former presences (Fig. 19). At Santiago, the indices become scrambled by a series of deformation and flow lines extrapolated from the original tartan grid.

These represent the activity of a new digital—as opposed to analogic—code: a code that scrambles the prior notations. Neither geometric nor planimetric, they are analogous to the strands of the nucleotides of a molecule. As they change spatial position, they change notation. Here they are no longer indices of meaning but schemata of a three-dimensional matrix (Fig. 20). The generator of the forms is now a torqued digital vector, a scrambler of the superposed grids which registers

Fig. 19 Site diagram showing layers of historical and topographical information used to generate three-dimensional forms, City of Culture of Galicia, Santiago de Compostela, Spain, Eisenman Architects, 1999–in progress

something other than an extrusion from the horizontal plane. The resultant matrix is no longer an index of this activity. Because of the scrambler it cannot be traced back to some origin. There is no longer a linear narrative or legibility in presence.

What is created by the force lines in the vertical (third) dimension was something other than a projection or morphing of geometry (Fig. 21). Any mechanical warping, such as a vertical rotation of the lines, would be no different than a vertical extrusion. These actions, similar to the spatial vectoring of the cortile of Santa Maria della Pace, produced a result which no longer was the outcome of a mechanical process.

It must be understood that grids, endowed with a rationality since the Renaissance, and regulating lines, which have a more metaphysical dimension, are not the same thing. In the City of Culture, both are combined to produce something that is no longer a geometric grid but is more akin to the organicism proposed by Bramante, in which a geometry of surfaces and spatial flows no longer distinguishes between points, lines, and planes.

In contrast to the proscriptive codes of classical architecture and the Cartesian geometry of modernism, the generative use of geometries today can be understood in the context of developments in our understanding of nature and biological systems. D'Arcy Thompson's *On the Growth of Forms in Nature* was a compendium of organic formal organizations that influenced an entire generation of architects, beginning with Le Corbusier in the 1920s, who saw in these known organizations a natural condition that could be mirrored in man-made forms. Our understanding of nature today no longer conforms to these easily recognizable patterns. Natural organizations such as avalanches and tectonic plates, clouds, and coastlines are seen to have dynamic organizations that involve forms in a space-time continuum. These "new natures"—new coded systems that can now be modeled on a computer—form the basic energy behind our project at Santiago. They act both as a substrate for organizing the required elements of the building and, simultaneously, as a *codex* that requires a reverse reading to a nonexistent origin.

Fig. 20 (left) Deformation diagrams showing how vector lines of force create new interior volumes within exterior forms, City of Culture of Galicia, Santiago de Compostela, Spain, Eisenman Architects, 1999 – in progress

Fig. 21 (below) Competition model, City of Culture of Galicia, Santiago de Compostela, Spain, Eisenman Architects, 1999 – in progress

Winy Maas: Interview

A practicing architect from Rotterdam, Winy Maas held the Eero Saarinen Visiting Professorship of Architectural Design at the Yale School of Architecture in the spring of 2003. After exchanging questions, notes, and ideas for a potential text to appear in Perspecta 35, *an interview was finally scheduled during the week of end-of-term juries. On May first, Maas joined* Perspecta 35 *in a third floor office of Paul Rudolph's Art and Architecture building to discuss the role of codes in the work of MVRDV, the office he co-founded in 1991 with Jacob van Rijs and Nathalie de Vries. After taking a moment to recover from the full day of reviews, he offered his thoughts on the impact that systematized forces originating outside of architecture impose on the built environment.*

Perspecta 35: In the talk you gave at the Architekturzentrum in Vienna (19 January, 02), "Next Steps, the Chronological Sinusoid of Research," you note that in developing *FARMAX*, and *Datascapes* specifically, "there were certain limits, pressures, resistances, and actually the unrevealed, hidden boundaries of our society that we experienced in coincidence at that very moment as an unexpected side-effect of that research… if you want to go beyond the existing urban conditions, if you want to make a higher density or another typology, then these boundaries—described by laws—should be criticized and elevated." What was the motivation for that research, and what role do the conclusions you've drawn from it play in your work now?

Winy Maas: There were two motivations. First, these observations originated at a moment when the whole architectural world was dealing with complexity, with the idea of endlessness. There were architects on the American East Coast, drawing on the work of French philosophers, who wanted to address architecture in a more "philosophical" way by literally mirroring chaos in their buildings. There were deconstructivists who would simply put bits of rubbish on top of each other and say, "that's complexity." And there were also intital steps taken at places like OMA, where people were suggesting that there could be a way to understand complexity through research. It was in the context of these two positions that *Datascapes* emerged as an attempt to develop research through the explorations of spatial "limitations," showing what happens when you push things to an edge, showing that indeed this reveals some clarity in that moment of complexity. But, on the other hand, we wanted to push the idea of research, because we felt that research was still being carried out in a more or less observational way. We wanted to instrumentalize research to lead to the production of something new. The idea was to first show the limits, and then to go beyond them.

And what emerged from that?

You want to work on finding new ways of dealing with these limits. This can involve very small details, as was the case with the Hageneiland project, where we were initially not allowed to make houses without gutters. It was an issue with the health and safety laws. When we did the project, there was concern that the water would glide down along the walls and that mold or algae would grow, which could pose health risks for the inhabitants. But rather than giving in and simply adding gutters, we found materials that would produce a kind of algae that posed no health risks.

A larger example is the Flight Forum proposal, where we wanted to make a non-hierarchical traffic system without traffic lights or discrete intersections. This required space for acceleration and deceleration, but at only 60 hectares the site was too small. The scale of the site suggested oblique connections that would decrease the speed enormously, which we had wanted to avoid, so instead we suggested a zone of 150 meters, which would merge traffic to provide 70 kph access everywhere. This system was adopted by Dutch law as a viable alternative for the current "safe traffic" rules. One is no longer obligated to use solely oblique connections.

These projects represent one aspect of what has developed from our research. Currently we also look particularly at larger scales, as a ground for innovations, as a scale to address architectural agendas—an Oldenburg approach. You can see things in a larger perspective; sometimes innovations will appear as a result of the scale shift. We like to work with small scale solutions whose effects are felt at a very large scale. This interest in larger scale phenomena goes beyond the research for *Datascapes*; it presents different issues for architecture.

The two projects you mentioned both challenged and subsequently changed existing laws that had originally been established with the intention of protecting health and safety, though at vastly different scales. Given that one could say the points of focus for these projects were aesthetics and efficiency, respectively, what do you see as the exigencies that justify a reevaluation of existing codes, or systems of regulation?

Capacity, quality, efficiency, ecology. We are currently working with optimization software, with optimization being very closely related to efficiency. We are interested in optimization in terms of the densification of the globe, so capacity. And yes, there are also aesthetic and other motivations. For example, with the Hageneiland houses, both aesthetic and ecological concerns informed the design. By not using gutters, we avoided dumping water directly into the sewer system, instead dispersing it over a wider area, allowing it to be used for hydrating the surrounding soil. However, the decision to not use gutters also came out of the desire to reduce the image of the house to an abstraction. We wanted to make the houses so sculpturally strong that whatever the individual occupants might do to customize their property—whatever fences, shrubs, or lawn ornaments they might add—would exist against the iconicity of the house. So the decision to not use gutters was made in an attempt to produce the most abstract house possible, one that would resemble the house a child might draw with a crayon. It has something of an ironic agenda in this sense.

Ironic because it assumes the default outline of a house?

Yes. Although I should note that this is the default outline for economic reasons. So in this sense there is an economic motivation for eliminating the gutters embedded within the aesthetic one, on which we decided to capitalize as a way of spending more money on the urbanistic aspects of the project. In an effort to create a type of urbanism

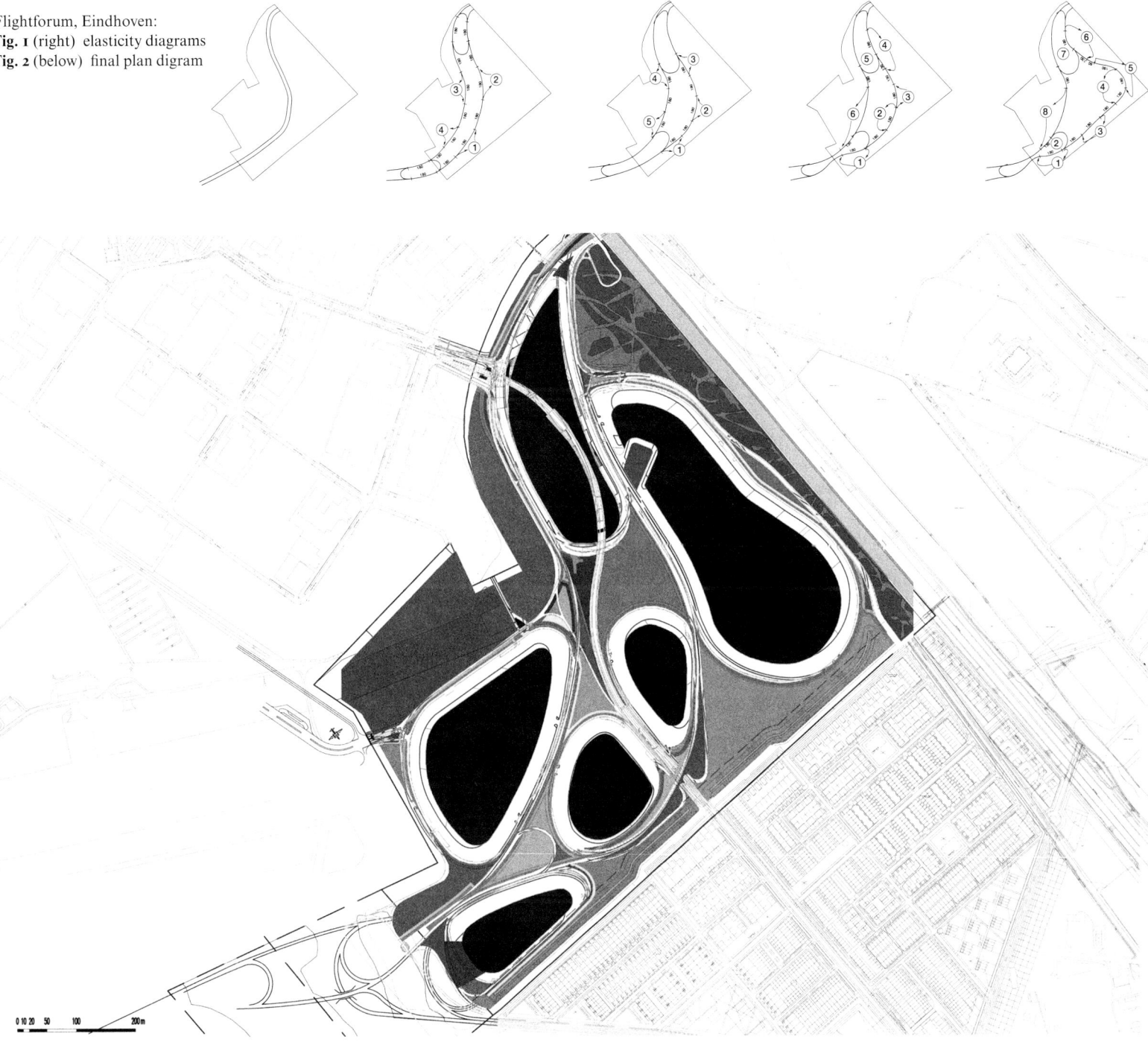

Flightforum, Eindhoven:
Fig. 1 (right) elasticity diagrams
Fig. 2 (below) final plan digram

Haageneiland Housing, Ypenburg:
Fig. 3 (left) sections
Fig. 4 (above) elevations
Fig. 5 (right) exterior view

that was not solely focused on the street front, we shifted the houses on the plots so that you could see the backside of a house through the view corridor created by two houses on front of the street. However, the fact that we were exposing an additional façade, along with the choice to use detached houses as opposed to row houses, meant that we had to find new ways to minimize costs. One strategy was to more or less eliminate site traffic, making a circular road around the entire project. Another strategy employed was to minimize the amount of detail in the houses. We realized that the transitions between materials cost more than the materials themselves, so we decided to just use one material for the entire house. So these three concerns—aesthetics, ecology, and economics—were the motivations for this project.

That's interesting because it seems such a contrast to architectural practice here in the States. It seems that architects here tend to be so passive towards these sorts of constraints. Basically, you are saying that as an architectural office, it is possible to use a project to question, even challenge, existing regulations, and that in doing so, architecture could have a role in shaping the regulations involved in its production.

Why do the architects not do that here? Is it because they are lazy, or too comfortable? Is it fear?

I don't know. It's hard to say whether it is a control issue, because municipalities find such an approach hard to accept, or are slow to change, or whether it is because there is a dogmatic belief in the health and safety letter of the law, and that is seen as paramount. Unless you are proposing something empirically proven to be healthier and safer, no one wants to hear it.

And perhaps there are also fears that it would delay the process, that clients wouldn't want to invest in it.

The triumph of a different sort of efficiency.

Yes, that's true.

Next, let's return to your comments earlier about working at large scales. What, in your opinion, should be the parameters for the regulations governing the increasingly expansive scale of urbanism? For example, with the Functionmixer, you propose that the city can be described as an immense collection of data. What is the logic that you use, or that should be used, to establish the rules by which the information is organized and put together?

This larger scale of urbanism is something that we have been investigating at both the Berlage and in the office. At the most basic level, it is probably fair to say that what characterizes the forces driving urbanism is that they are politicized. There are a number of concerns that are extremely influential: ecological concerns, issues of mobility and migration, issues relating to food and industry, and even climactic issues. This may seem obvious, but climactic change is much more drastic than I had thought, and has significantly informed our work, especially in relation to agriculture and its relationship to urban patterns in the way it influences water and temperature systems.

As to how we address these issues in architectural production, we use several strategies. One method is to simply extrapolate the data in an attempt to magnify the issue, bringing it to the public's attention such that we will have support to work on it. With *Metacity/Datatown*, we started by researching how much waste we produce, and then attached it to a specific city such that one can understand the amount of waste that will be produced in that city in the coming future. In the end, people are shocked by the results. We've used the same strategy of extrapolation with water and climactic issues. The large scale involved has led to apocalyptic proposals; that accelerates the need for deeper solutions.

Another strategy is to create opportunities to combine the individual with the generic. We had observed that a lot of policy is structured to be top-down in terms of its official implementation, yet needs an enormous amount of bottom-up attention in order to be successful. The Kyoto Treaty is an example. To engage the individual in the implementation of these policies targeted at the collective, we place a lot of hope in new media, the Internet, and software. We hope to use these technologies to produce a series of instruments that can reconcile the individual and large scale phenomena, and demonstrate what type of

cities and neighborhoods will be produced as a result. These "machines" would evaluate and visualize existing data across a designated scale—a neighborhood, or a region, or an even larger scale. The GIS and other types of data already exist. So now the task is really to investigate how it can be combined and applied to create possible solutions and new ideologies. In a sense it comes back to optimization. Also, I think that at the moment, people understand data very well, and we try to exploit that.

You concluded your talk in Vienna with the Regionmaker, which proposes that, in effect, it is not only the nature of the existing codes, but also the geographic limits of what they seek to regulate that must be questioned and revised. It seems that one could find something of a political agenda in this passage. Do you consider your work to be political, or perhaps more accurately, to be politicized?

I hope that our work is not political, but that it is an instrument for innovations, changes. The Regionmaker plays with politics. It mirrors politics. It can reflect developments and trends like an election poll that indicates the political direction at the time.

But while maintaining some semblance of neutrality, or is there something of an agenda there?

Both. There can be agendas. An entire range of possible agendas can be set up by the individual within it. So it can be more or less neutral, but it also has the capacity to produce agendas, and to parametrize agendas within it. You can use it to follow a Krierian method to produce that kind of city or region. That is the norm, or the default. This is one of its possibilites, but I am more interested in its ability to function as a polling device—to visualize data as fast as it can be collected, such that we can understand the political conciousness of the times and the direction in which it is headed. This differs from Pig City, which was an apocalyptic extrapolation, rather than a device to reframe the current political situation through the gathering, analysis, and visualization of data. The goal is to be able to show the status quo, and then question or reframe it.

So this, for you, is one of the ways you see your research getting beyond observation.

Yes.

Would you consider your position concerning density, the manipulation of data, and the need to regulate what is built on a much more holistic scale, specific to a contemporary condition? If so, what distinguishes this point in time and how has it necessitated this position?

One can describe this momentum as an acceleration of information knowledge, scale, mobility, globalization; these issues evolve from that process. I definitely want to say something about this, because some people say that these issues—like density— are issues of the sixties. They might claim that it is no longer relevant, or that we are merely addressing that which was already addressed in the sixties. I would like to stress that densification is a contemporary trend not only in terms of urbanism, but also in respect to many other domains as well. Technologies allow us to densify our use of the earth. Knowledge systems operate by building up data, becoming denser and denser. Our global status is, in a way, about densification as well. We travel more, we create new situations, we want to do more, and all these desires lead to an enormous densification beyond just the physical growth of the population. I don't think that densification has stopped yet, and I doubt that it ever will, aside from some major disaster. But instead of looking at this process in a negative light, we try to understand it and use it as a tool. We try to find the possible adventures, discoveries, and unexpected occurrences that are a result of densification, and understand them optimistically.

But what is it it is that distinguishes the contemporary situation from the sixties? Is it simply that the world, understood to comprise the physical world, as well as information systems, etc… has become even denser and therefore it is a more pressing issue?

Yes, as simple as that. Isn't that enough? Our knowledge of the issue of densification was much more primitive in the sixties, and accordingly, so were the architectural proposals. Take Peter Cook's work for instance—it is beautiful, but incredibly naïve, and not founded on thorough investigation of the issues. It would be difficult to say that Kissing Towers are a direct translation of something like Cook's work. The differences between the sixties and today are enormous, particularly in terms of the

 Diversity: everybody has a different neighbor…
 with Costs: the building height is reduced…
 with Daylight: housing and park are lifted to roof level…
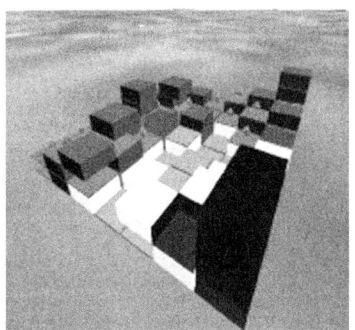 and with Noise: noise is concentrated on one side of the area

Fig. 6 Functionmixer: combination of parameters

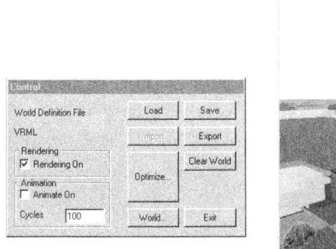
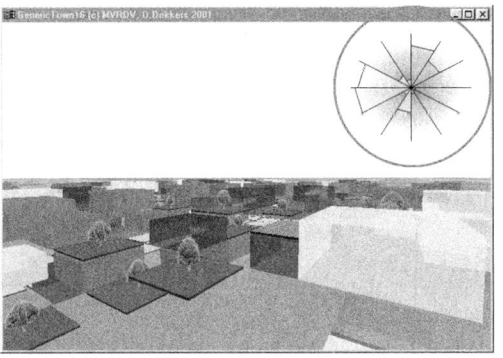
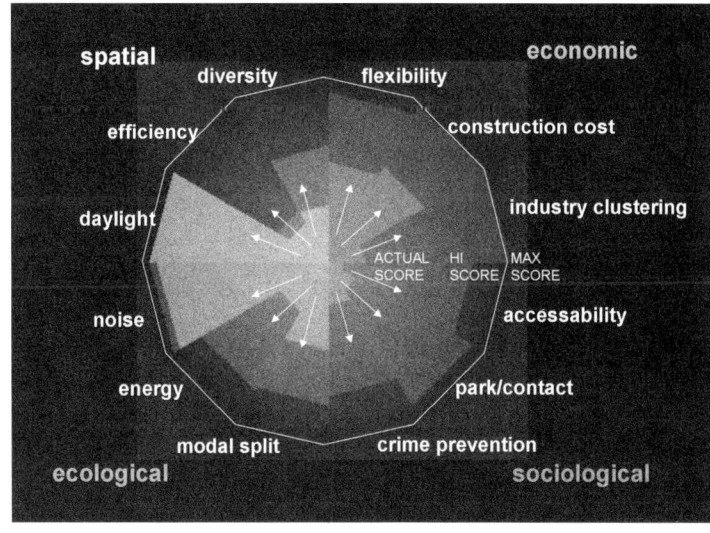

Fig. 7 Functionmixer: program interface

capacity of technology and its effects on information and mobility. The constraints of ecology have led to a kind of pessimism when thinking at the very largest scales, yet individualism has been encouraged. One of our concerns is how these contradictory forces can be reconciled and integrated into our work addressing densification. As we learned with *Datascapes*, there is enormous resistance to this. The resistance is elaborate and difficult to trace, and unbelievably fluid. The Regionmaker and Functionmixer are attempts to overcome this resistance. We're trying to find a way to deal with density given the parameters that have developed since the sixties.

Given the importance of external forces affecting architecture in your work, I'd like to know more about your thoughts on the issue of design. For example, in discussing your proposal for Almere—a design made through the Functionmixer (also at the Architekturzentrum)—you have described it as "The city: an environment without architecture—quite a dream!" What is the expertise of the architect under these conditions, or is it even helpful to think of architecture as a discipline that is different from, say, planning or management consulting? Is "design" still something that architects do?

We translate design as the visualization of spatial effects and constraints. This translation questions the intuitive, form-driven approach of colleagues. That is what the project at Almere does—it finds a spatial solution that best mediates the issues of the politicians and investors. In a sense, the architecture is simply a product of the negotiation process between interested parties. It is a product of optimizing their concerns. Any taste or style, any architecture, in a classical sense, that could have been attached, would only have been a distraction from the discussion. We wanted to concentrate on the more communicative aspect of the buildings.

You would say there is a conscious avoidance of style, or form, to allow for the focus to fall on other more universally tangible issues?

Well, it creates more possibilities, more possible "encounters." Perhaps it would be interesting, given the nature of this sort of project, to see what different architects would produce. If such a project were split into three pieces, say one for us, one for Leon Krier, and one for Peter Eisenman, I doubt the outcomes would be as different as people might imagine given the constraints. Aside from the designated parameters that everyone would have to negotiate, it would really be a stylistic exercise.

So, what are the parameters that you choose to resist? How do you go about choosing what parameters to accept, and which to challenge?

Opportunism calls; the ones you meet in both practice and in theory. But for Almere specifically, what we sought to resist was the issue of style. I think it was important to show that the more you dress up architecture, the more the actual goals of the project, which in this case were to mix, or to heterogenize, become compromised. For this project we tried to make the architec-

Fig. 8 Kissing Towers – Donau City, Vienna (competition entry)

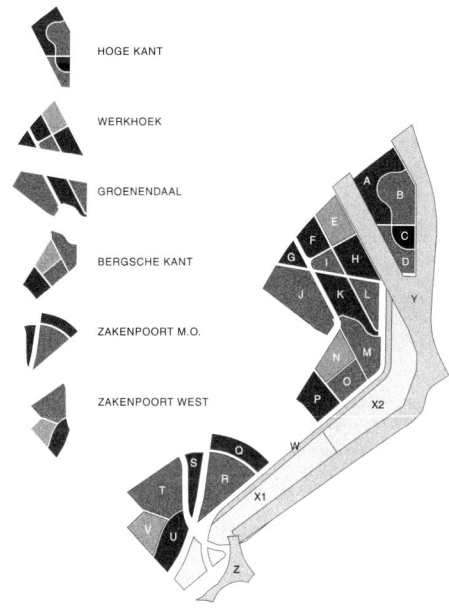

Fig. 9 Almere Poort: programming diagrams

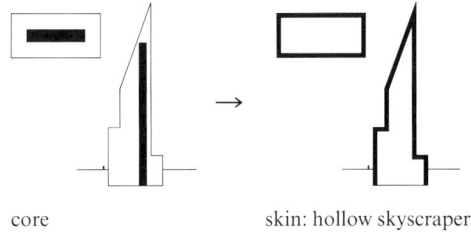

core   skin: hollow skyscraper

Media Galaxy – Eyebeam Institute, New York (competition entry):
Fig. 10 (above) "hollow skyscraper" diagram
Fig. 11 (below) section

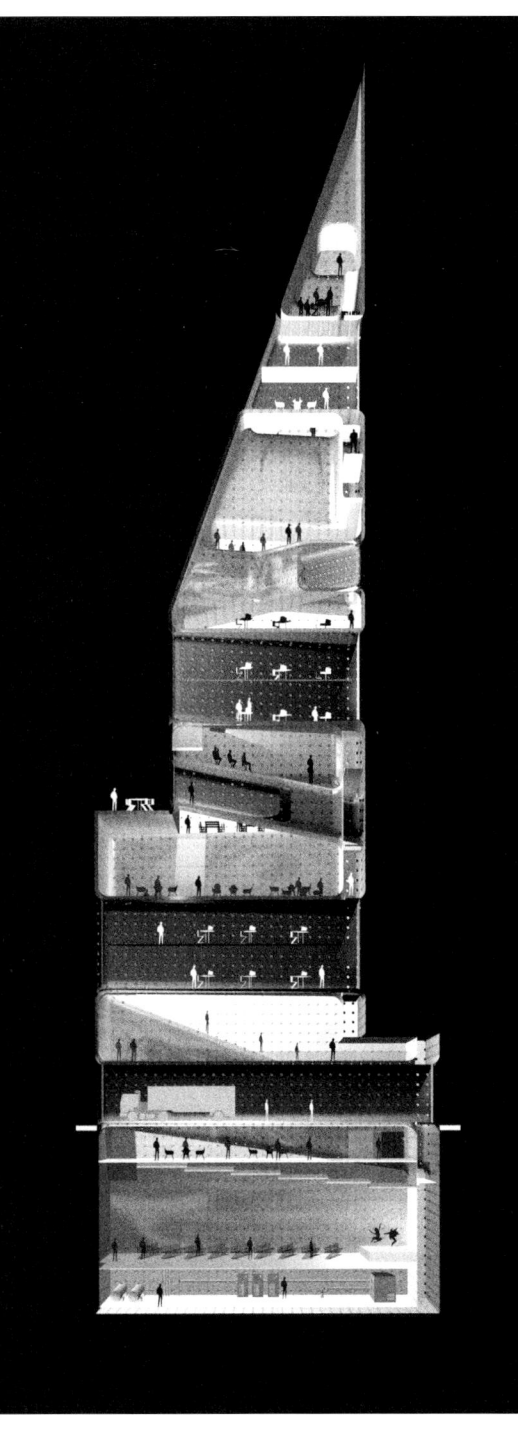

ture as much a part of the background as possible. An unadorned and simple façade made it easier to check as to whether the environment was becoming too mono-functional, whereas a dressed-up building could pull our attention away from issues of use to issues of style.

There is in that this latent modernist argument about the honesty…

Of transparency.

So you are saying that, in this instance, you chose to work within the constraints the developer set out, treating the architecture as the neutral backdrop?

But the interesting thing you are saying is that maybe we need the clarity of modernism at the moment when we want to discuss, through architecture, the limitations placed on architecture. It seems that with a clarity borrowed from modernism, these external exigencies become visible. With modernism, in this sense, architecture becomes communicative, and can relay the discussion of the agenda to people who are outside our expertise— to laymen. So here we can say that a clear and obvious architectural language can actually help you to communicate.

That's interesting, because so much of the post-modern critique of modernism framed modernism as a dead-end; that formally it had run its course. You can only take so much away before you're left with, well, nothing. You're saying that by focusing on other parameters, formal vocabulary becomes less important. It simply allows for the possibilities to be played out in a way that the focus on form has neglected, at least in this country, for the past 20 or 30 years.

Absolutely. I personally hate this hermetic focus on formal vocabularies. It is what I would call an architecture of fear, because it does not want to talk about the very things that actually need discussion today. Perhaps at that moment it pleases a lot of people, which cannot be ignored, but it can distract enormously from the number of possible important issues that surround the production of architecture. In our project for Eyebeam, we suggested an inversion of the traditional hollow Manhattan tower. Rather than placing work space around the periphery, we used the periphery for services so that the core became a dark

work environment that could accommodate new media work. This could lead to a new type of building, a semi-public interior, but not through a language. Of course, you could say it uses a modernist vocabulary, but this building would never have been produced in those times because its design addresses issues raised by new technologies and conceptions of art and the museum. Perhaps you could say that its rhetorical obviousness is borrowed from the sixties.

While the regulatory laws and by-laws you mention in *Datascapes* are usually highly politicized, involving issues of government control over private land use, community identity, health, and safety, architecture is usually not perceived to be a political act. In your interview with Nina Rapaport for the *3-D Cities* exhibit that was in the gallery here, you note: "Political architecture doesn't exist in the end. Forms are not as dangerous. Beauty solves everything, no?" How would you describe the apparent paradox of an apolitical architecture which is nevertheless subject to the political intentions of regulatory laws?

Your question is not so clear. Apolitical architecture is almost always used or commissioned for political reasons. One could say the Guggenheim in Bilbao is built to bring more attention to the city, and there it works.

To reframe it, is architecture necessarily apolitical? Is it that the motivations involved in architecture, or the parameters involved in the creation of architecture, may be politically motivated, but the object itself remains decidedly apolitical? Or is there something in architecture besides for beauty? Is there an embodiment of these external factors?

I think that within the framework that has been set for any project—say, that a city wants a new museum, which can be a highly political project, there is always room to maneuver. There are always the obvious choices to be made: is it transparent or not; focused on the environment or not; should it question the institutionalized spaces of the museum or not? But there are opportunities to be critical of that framework as well. With every commission one must discover on what one can comment, and at what level one can comment. I think that is always the most interesting component of a competition or a preliminary design phase. What are the issues you would like to

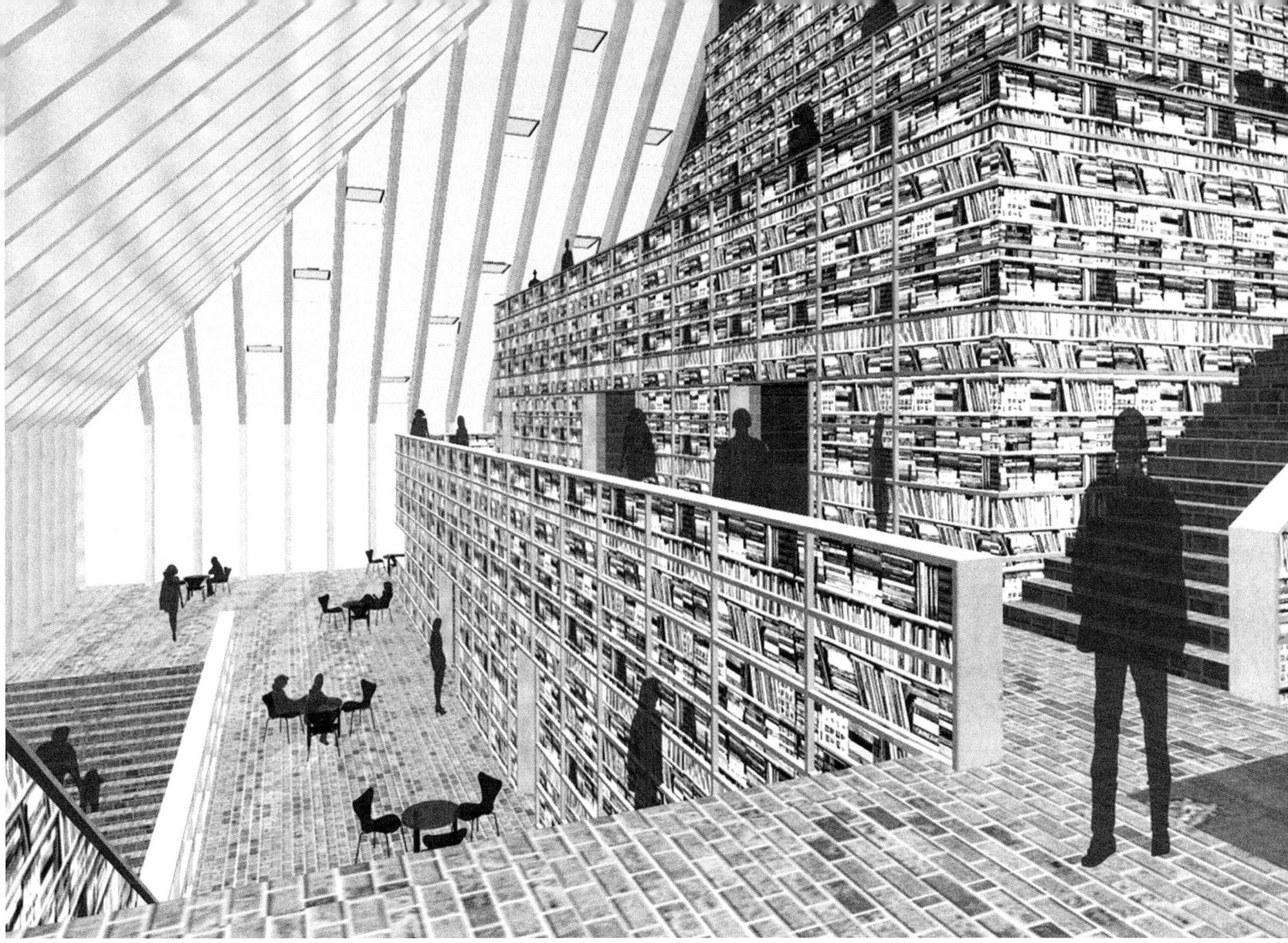

Fig. 12 Public Library, Spijkenisse (competition entry): interior view with glass "cupola"

manifest, and how would you show that in juxtaposition with what is given? For example, with the VPRO building, which was to occupy the maximum envelope allowed, we chose to not make a show of the façade, stressing that the main identity of the VPRO is their broadcasting products. Instead we stressed the importance of the interior, which is visualized in the façade. We cut the building like a piece of lasagna; a cut of an endless interior. And that was in criticism of the envelope, and the urbanists who set and enforced it. We argued that it should be able to continue, and that it is ridiculous to have stopped it with the maximum buildout envelope we were required to maintain. That is a modest way of criticizing while working within reality.

We are currently working on a library, a competition we won two weeks ago, where the envelope that was given was so ridiculous that we simply made it into a kind of giant cupola. Beneath it we made an enormous display of the message we would like to show to the city about how a library should be organized, and what kind of instrument it can be. It became an advertisement for the book, placed underneath this absurd envelope, which was made even more ridiculous by proposing to physically build it entirely of glass, say, almost invisible.

You would argue that flaunting the arbitrary envelope that the planners had given you—an envelope based on god knows what—is a critical gesture?

It is critical because you don't want to deal with it formally. You simply accept it for the moment, and focus efforts on the other issues.

So, in a heavy-handed way, you simply define the boundary based on the parameters, and then develop other aspects of the problem?

Well, that envelope was given to us by planners, so we simply made it manifest. It was what the city was giving us, and we wanted to show that it was not the best envelope to work with given the program. This was the case for Eyebeam as well. We could have made a much better building without the zoning, but at the moment, these are things that I cannot change, so I will show it clearly, and put it on hold so that we, or the generation after us, can do more about it in the future. If these given constraints are at least shown clearly, the following generation of architects can then at least act in response to them, creating new types of buildings. In this sense architecture is a machine of that transition from one epoch to the next. There are a lot of things in the VPRO building that we wouldn't do again, and that we wouldn't have to do again. Yet because of the building, strategies for urban planning have changed, which could yield a new building type of building in the future.

Your buildings build on one another? Their logics build on one another?

They are indeed not autonomous. Architecture is never autonomous.

Edward Eigen

The Housing of Entropy

In the world of physics we watch a shadowgraph performance of familiar life. The shadow of my elbow rests on the shadow table as the shadow ink flows over the shadow paper.... The frank realization that physical science is concerned with a world of shadows is one of the most significant of recent advances.
A. S. Eddington, *The Nature of the Physical World* (1928)

What is Life? This is the question addressed by Erwin Schrödinger in the series of lectures he delivered in February 1943 from the security of his self-imposed "exile" in Dublin.[1] The very ambition evinced in the title might have seemed preposterous, had the Nobel laureate physicist not used the occasion to outline the quantum mechanical design of life's genetic "code-script." Code-script was DNA *avant la lettre*. For Schrödinger, explaining the endurable nature of its molecular structure (the so-called aperiodic crystal) went halfway toward deciphering life's enigma, namely its "gift" for withstanding for long periods of time the disturbing influence of entropy. Contrary to the irreversible course of events in nature, living organisms presented singular evidence of the (re)production of "order from order." Code-script was the key to life's genetic immortality. Yet life's seeming exemption from the second law of thermodynamics was not the product of some nonphysical or supernatural force. Its ability to "keep going" stemmed rather from its "concentrating a stream of order on itself:" the organism restores itself by continually "feeding on 'negative entropy.'"[2] Or, as Schrödinger expressed it in still more vivid terms, the organism goes on by "sucking orderliness from its environment."
The organism is not a closed system fated by the second law to "death by confinement," in the physicist Léon Brillouin's phrase. For Brillouin, who interpreted Schrödinger's notion of negative entropy in terms of the new language of cybernetics, "confinement implies the existence of perfect walls, which are necessary in order to build an ideal enclosure.... Do we really know any way to build a wall that could not let any radiation in or out?"[3] In thus questioning the physical nature of confinement Brillouin might unwittingly have pointed to

1 Based on lectures delivered under the auspices of the Dublin Institute for Advanced Studies at Trinity College, Dublin, in February 1943, *What is Life? The Physical Basis of the Living Cell* was originally published in 1944. All references in this essay are to the Canto edition: Erwin Schrödinger, *What is Life? with Mind and Matter and Autobiographical Sketches* (Cambridge: Cambridge University Press, 1992). Schrödinger's arrival in Dublin marked the beginning of the period that, in his "Autobiographical Sketches," he referred to "My Long Exile (1939–56)."
2 This characterization of *What is Life?* derives from Evelyn Fox Keller, *Refiguring Life: Metaphors of Twentieth-Century Biology* (New York: Columbia University Press, 1995), 69.
3 Léon Brillouin, "Life, Thermodynamics and Cybernetics," in Harvey Leff and Andrew Rex (eds.), *Maxwell's Demon: Entropy, Information, Computing* (Princeton: Princeton University Press, 1990), 93.
4 Sigmund Freud, "The Uncanny," [1919] in *The Standard Edition of the Complete Psychological Works of Sigmund Freud*, 24 vols., trans. James Strachey (London: Hogarth Press, 1953–74), XVII. 220.

Fig. 1 Brownian movement of a sinking droplet, from Erwin Schrödinger's *What is Life?*

On Schrödinger's Code-Script

the disjointed framework of Schrödinger's writing on life, including his own—punctuated as it was by periods of exile, wandering, and homelessness.

Schrödinger's approach in *What is Life?* was to ask, "How can the events *in time and space* which take place within the spatial boundary of a living organism be accounted for by physics and chemistry?" By "spatial boundary of a living organism" he was referring first and foremost to the cell, what he called the "tiny central office" in and from which code-script carried out the work of ordering life. This mention of the cell marks the migration of architectural figures of thought into the discourse of life. Articulated by analogy to a honeycomb, which was said to resemble a building made up of small rooms (or cells), particularly those of a dwelling, the cell shelters the hereditary substance, itself an "unusually large molecule of highly differentiated order." That said, it is not the primary intention of this essay to examine the physical and chemical account of events *in time and space*. What are these events, anyway? They are, to use Schrödinger's term, the "devices" of life itself, preventing it from "fad[ing] away into a dead, inert lump of matter," or what physicists call "maximum entropy" (69). Rather, in drawing attention to the question of spatial boundary, to what Brillouin calls "perfect walls"—including those separating life and death, as well as the living and the dead—this essay examines the role that conceptual and real architectures play in Schrödinger's conception of life's governing plan, or code-script. Correctly anticipating the difficulty of explicating code-script in terms of physics and chemistry, Schrödinger ably resorted to figurative language. To wit, the chromosome is both "law-code and executive power—or, to use another simile, it is architect's plan and builder's craft—in one"

(22). To be sure, the simile fits within the present attempt to examine the role played by real and conceptual architectures in Schrödinger's writing on life. Yet the discussion does not rest with the life of the cell but examines how confinement and its opposite are dramatized in Schrödinger's elliptical "Autobiographical Sketches" (1960). Translated and published for the first time as a supplement to the Canto edition of *What is Life?*, the "Sketches" offers another level of (self) reflection on the events in time and space that shape a life (story).

Schrödinger would seem to have appreciated the incentive for juxtaposing the two texts, offering as he did the deceptively bland opinion that "it takes both a code of chromosomes and civilized human surroundings to produce people of our kind" (174). And indeed, while *What is Life?* examines the molecular structures of inheritance, the "Sketches" painfully reveals how one can be kin but not kind. The autobiographical subject of the "Sketches" neglects his familial bonds and betrays his hereditary obligations; worse yet, to his own thinking, he unwisely and unkindly closes out his parents' home following the death of his father. The reversal of his family's fortune—in which, as an errant son, he felt himself to play a part—becomes the text of his dream life. As recorded in the "Sketches," the dream sequence is symptomatic of what Freud, in his 1919 essay on the "Uncanny," described as the realization that the familiar already contains the unfamiliar—or life already contains death—making the very idea of the homely *unhomely*.[4] It is from the nature of these reversals, which bear a relationship to the entropic tendency of all things, that clues to the meaning of life's code-script must also be coaxed.

What, for Schrödinger, constituted the outlines of familiar (and familial) life? To judge from this essay's

Fig. 2 Ludwig Boltzmann's Tombstone, Vienna Central Cemetery

epigraph, quoted by Schrödinger in his essay "Mind and Matter," the physicist is at home in a shadowy reality. He works with models, pictures, and constructs which stand in for "the world itself." But which world? How does the physicist's watching "a shadowgraph performance of familiar life" square with the autobiographer's sorting through memory? It is not simply the case that the "Sketches" offers something apparent and sensible that is missing from *What is Life?* Almost the opposite is true. On at least two occasions, Schrödinger emphasizes that entropy is not a "hazy concept or idea" but rather a measurable physical quantity expressed by the equation: $S = k \log D$. Ludwig Boltzmann's "famous equation," as Schrödinger referred to it, may appear offputting to the nonspecialized reader (this author included). How is one to translate its meaning?[5] S is the organon of disorder; it predicts the dislimning of life's familiar outlines. It disrupts communication between generations. Curiously, the equation was inscribed on Boltzmann's monument in Vienna's Central Cemetery, in which setting it serves as a particularly cryptic memento mori. Biography, literally a form of life writing, would seem to restore if not establish life's familiar outlines. Yet the act of writing itself is seemingly implicated in Boltzmann's equation. As Schrödinger explained, the tendency of things to approach a chaotic state is the same tendency that the books in a library or the piles of paper on a writing desk display unless disorder is obviated. "The analogue of irregular heat motion, in this case, is our handling those objects now and again without troubling to put them back in their proper place" (73).

Putting things in their proper place is essentially the discipline of architecture. Architectural theory was concerned through much of its history with the nature of order as such; the specific origin of the genera (orders) of columns in divine and/or natural models was the matter of frequent and occasionally illuminating debate. Equally as important to the codification of architectural theory is the rhetorical insistence on the part of the Roman author Vitruvius, the so-called father of architectural theory, on the genetic immortality of exemplary ideas and practices:

> Our ancestors, not only wisely but also usefully, established the practice of transmitting their ideas to posterity through the reports of treatises, so that their ideas would not perish, but instead, as they grew with each passing age and were published in books, they would arrive, step by step, at the utmost refinement of learning.[6]

When Vitruvius's work was "rediscovered" in the fifteenth century, the architect and scholar Leon Battista Alberti had legitimate cause to grieve that "so many

---

5 For Schrödinger, Boltzmann's demonstration of the "directedness" of things in nature, the life-history of the organism from birth to death, the "arrow of time," as Eddington called it, was simply the most important intellectual accomplishment between Kant's idealization of space and time and Einstein's theory of relativity.

6 Vitruvius, *Ten Books on Architecture*, trans. Ingrid Rowland (New York: Cambridge University Press, 1999), 85.

7 Leon Battista Alberti, *On the Art of Building*, trans. Joseph Rykwert, Neil Leach, and Robert Tavernor (Cambridge, Mass.: MIT Press, 1988), 154.

8 Alberti, *On the Art of Building*, 3.

9 Erwin Schrödinger, "Science, Theory, and Man," [New York, 1957] cited in Nicholas Georgescu-Roegen, *The Entropy Law and the Economic Process* (Cambridge, Mass.: Harvard University Press, 1971), 75.

10 A. S. Eddington, *The Nature of the Physical World*, cited in Gillian Beer, *Open Fields: Science in Cultural Encounter* (Oxford: Clarendon Press, 1996), 171.

11 Notably, Schrödinger makes no mention of George Beadle and Edward Tatum's important "one gene – one enzyme" theory of 1941.

12 On the "coding problem" see F. H. C. Crick, J. S. Griffith, and L. E. Orgel, "Codes Without Commas," *Proceedings of the National Academy of Sciences of the United States of America*, 43:5 (May 15, 1957), 416–21.

works of such brilliant writers had been destroyed by the hostility of time and man."[7] For Alberti, these chaotic forces were counteracted by a life-giving flame. "How many respected families," he wrote, "would have totally disappeared, brought down by some temporary adversity, had not their family hearth harbored them, welcoming them, as it were, into the very bosom of their ancestors?"[8]

Considering this legacy, is it not curious that the space upon which the trauma of the "Sketches" settles is Schrödinger's father's library? In selling off its contents Schrödinger mortgaged the intellectual basis of the "civilized human surroundings" in which he himself had been raised. If kept in good order, the house is a principle source of low entropy; to paraphrase a well-known refrain, it is a device for living (in). Revealingly, Schrödinger found no better analogy for the meaning of entropy than the chaos wrought upon a library by the sudden entry of an unruly mob, that definitive human agent of disorder.[9] As it happens, the library in question was the focus of the so-called gas calamity of 1918, which forced his father to work under the light of noxious carbon lamps, the physiological repercussions of which proved fatal.

The "coding problem"

The structure of the vital parts of living organisms, Schrödinger explains, differs entirely from any piece of matter "ever handled physically in our laboratories or mentally at our writing desks" (4). This first section examines how Schrödinger's metaphoric design of the writing desk (and by extension the library, and ultimately space and time) fits within the same model of figurative usage as the simile of the "architect's plan and builder's craft." First about the desk: in his essay "Mind and Matter," Schrödinger discusses the gifted scientific expositor Arthur Eddington's picture of physical reality. As if to eulogize the passing of familiar notions of time and space, Eddington wrote: "I am standing on the threshold about to enter a room; it is a complicated business."[10] Eddington thence offered a parable of the two writing desks to illustrate the business at hand, giving sense to a flux of interpenetrated elements ungraspable by the intellect. In Schrödinger's words:

> Some readers may remember A. S. Eddington's "two writing desks;" one is the familiar old piece of furniture at which he is seated, resting his arms on it, the other is the scientific physical body which not only lacks all and every sensual qualities but in addition is riddled with holes; by far the greatest part of it is empty space, just nothingness, interspersed with innumerable tiny specks of something, the electrons and the nuclei whirling around, but always separated by distances at least 100,000 times their own size. (120)

The genius of *What is Life?* is to treat the genetic code as if it were this "old piece of furniture," something that was fabricated, that was inherited from the previous generation and destined to be passed along to the next.

Schrödinger began investing the genetic code with familiar physicality by "inventing the molecule," the aperiodic crystal, in which the contents of code-script were borne. He suggested that if the regular, lattice-like geometry of solid matter were like ordinary wallpaper in which the same pattern is repeated again and again, the aperiodic crystalline structure of the genetic fiber was a "masterpiece of embroidery, say a Raphael." In it there is no dull repetition but rather an "elaborate, coherent, meaningful design traced by the great master" (5). Every atom, every group of atoms, plays an individual role, not entirely equivalent to that of any other. Only such a well-ordered association of atoms possessed a variety of possible arrangements sufficiently large to embody a system of organic "determinations" (61). Thus Schrödinger writes of a possible "correspondence" between this "miniature code" and a highly complicated and specified plan of organic development.[11] According to Schrödinger the great "revelation" of quantum theory was that "features of discreteness were discovered in the Book of Nature." That is to say, so-called solidifying forces and threshold energies "vouchsafed" the permanence and stability of the molecule. On this basis it was possible to imagine a "correspondence" between this code-script and a highly complicated and specified plan of organic development. Yet code-script was not a set of fixed and unmoving symbols. The genetic fiber was at once reader, writer, translator, and, according to some accounts, editor of life's enigmatic text.

These editorial functions presupposed, of course, that code-script was in some way like a text. As with the Book of Books, with its narrative of Genesis and litany of begetting, the Book of Nature, seemingly compressed into code-script, contained exoteric and esoteric meanings. No ordinary interpretation (or interpreter) would do. The first generation of molecular biologists, many of whom were inspired by *What is Life?*, would make a disciplinary issue of the so-called coding problem, seeing in it a formal question of how genes themselves sifted "sense" from "nonsense" within the potential determinations of the chromosome.[12] For while it is composed of discrete signs (codons), code-script has no extrinsic meaning; it simply constitutes a differentiating (and internally differentiated) structure. If there are signs in nature, then these signs must be read, after a fashion. What Schrödinger was after, by contrast, was nothing less than the philosophically intoxicating issue of being and becoming. Indulging in language that by his own account was "perhaps less becoming a scientist than a poet," he made attempts at approximating the relationship between the structure of the genetic fiber (plan) and its role in development (craft). The inspiration for Schrödinger's poetic agony is evident. *What is Life?* is punctuated by epigraphs from the writings of Johann Wolfgang von Goethe, the master poet of metamorphosis, for whom the essence of poetic language was its inability to be paraphrased adequately. By contrast, science, Schrödinger unadventurously claimed, "aims at nothing but making true and adequate statements about its object" (117).

To this end, Schrödinger evoked as the ideal reader of code-script an imaginary being of physic's own parturition: the "all-penetrating mind" conceived by the eighteenth-century physicist Pierre-Simon de Laplace. Laplace's "Intelligence" was an entity to whose eyes "the future, like the past, would be present" (21). Its combined capacity for unerring prevision and retrospection allowed it to comprehend the epigenetic pattern inscribed in code-script. Thus it "could tell from [the chromosome fibers'] structure whether the egg would develop, under suitable conditions, into a black cock or into a speckled hen, into a fly or a maize plant, a rhododendron, a beetle, a mouse or a woman" (21). The Intelligence read from the code-script not only the adult form of an organism but also the "four-dimensional pattern" of its development. The Intelligence was the product of a mechanical world of reversible events and predictable turns. By contrast, most discussions of life and the second law, Brillouin's included, evoke another imaginary entity: James Clerk Maxwell's Demon. Maxwell's "intelligent demon," as he was christened by William Thomson (Lord Kelvin), himself the author of the second law, was born of a thought experiment meant to show that the second law was only statistically true. This "very observant and neat-fingered being" was capable of sorting individual molecules by operating a frictionless sliding door separating two chambers of gas, thereby reversing the direction of heat flow.[13]

Schrödinger never mentions Maxwell's Demon, the "doorkeeper" at the aperture between two chambers, which would otherwise mutually tend to maximum equilibrium. However, as Evelyn Fox Keller has observed, Schrödinger does not manage to solve the problem of life and second law without recourse to

---

13 E. E. Daub, "Maxwell's Demon," in *Maxwell's Demon*, 37.
14 Fox Keller, *Refiguring Life*, 72.
15 Gaston Bachelard, *Lautréamont* (Paris: Librairie José Corti, 1956), 54–5.
16 T. E. Hulme, "Romanticism and Classicism," in *Speculations: Essays on Humanism and the Philosophy of Art* (New York: Harcourt Brace, 1924), 132.
17 Letter dated December 22, 1818, John Keats to George and Tom Keats, in Hyder Edward Rollins (ed.), *The Letters of John Keats*, 2 vols. (Cambridge, Mass.: Harvard University Press, 1958), I. 191.
18 Erwin Schrödinger, *Nature and the Greeks*, (Cambridge: Cambridge University Press, 1996 [1954]), 18.
19 Schrödinger, *Nature and the Greeks*, 56.
20 Robert Hahn, *Anaximander and the Architects: The Contribution of Egyptian and Greek Architectural Technologies to the Origin of Greek Philosophy* (Albany: State University of New York Press, 2001), 181.
21 Hahn, *Anaximander and the Architects*, 3.
22 Max Delbrück, Nicolai W. Timoféeff-Ressovsky, and K. C. Zimmer, "Über die Natur der Genmutation und der Genstruktur" [On the Nature of Genetic Mutation and Gene Structure], *Nachrichten von der Gesellschaft der Wissenschaften zu Göttingen* (1935), 189–245.

something very like the Demon. The deux ex machina in his solution returns hidden in the structure of the most essential part of a living cell: the chromosome.[14] Evidently the discussion turns again to the question of thresholds and cells. Yet before sorting the evidence, largely derived from the "Sketches," suggesting just how imperfect are the walls that shelter life, it seems necessary to examine the interpretive consequences of Schrödinger's conception of the chromosome as "architect's plan and builder's craft—in one." The Demon, for its part, occupied the architecture of a thought experiment devised to "pick a hole" in the second law of thermodynamics. Acting in the place of the Demon, code-script keeps disorder at bay by perpetuating order. Arguably, Schrödinger's simile betrays his desire to penetrate the architecture of thought itself. That is, it makes sensible the events—coding, sorting, determining, sheltering—that take place within the boundary of the living organism.

"All images of inner fire," Gaston Bachelard writes, "hidden fire, fire smoldering beneath the cinders, in short, of fire that is unseen and hence demands metaphors, are 'images of life.'"[15] Schrödinger's simile transports his reader to the Demon's station at the door between order and disorder, between life and heat death. This suggestion is borne out by attending to the *what* of metaphoric usage as well as to the *how*. Schrödinger deployed the set of instruments that the literary critic T. E. Hulme metaphorically called the "architect's curves." These are the templates the architect uses to draw nonorthogonal lines, when the "normal" means of the T-square is of no use. By a suitable selection from these he could produce nearly any curve he liked.[16] Figural language (as represented by so many literal curves or figurative tropes) can never and ought not precisely fit its object. Rather, it nurtures the quality that the poet John Keats once called Negative Capability, that is, "when a man is capable of being in uncertainties, mysteries, doubts, without any irritable reaching after fact and reason."[17] In fact, Schrödinger addressed what he called the "competition of reason *v.* senses" in a discussion of the original importation of architectural techniques into cosmological thought, a genre of writing from which *What is Life?* clearly descends.

As if to test the mechanisms of intellectual inheritance, in his 1948 series of lectures *Nature and the Greeks* Schrödinger examined which elements of Greek thought had been "taken over by the fathers of modern science." He argued that the legacy of antiquity was not a body of immutable truth but rather accidental and contingent habits of thought.[18] In other words, it reflected so many styles of making sense of the world. On the side of reason he placed the Pythagoreans, who were bent on "reducing the edifice of nature" to number. Even so, Pythagoras's discovery of the rational subdivisions of a string—that is, musical intervals—led to the composition of songs, the harmony of which "may move us to tears." On the side of sense, he placed the Milesian *phusiologoi* (nature describers) who applied themselves to abstract problems about the physical constitution of the world based on the evidence of *techne*. Their way of thinking shows "traces of the practical origin from which it started."[19] The most notable example is Anaximander's cosmogony, which was rendered in terms of a *syngraphe*, or the set of technical specifications commonly produced by an architect. Just as often, these specifications were accompanied by a *paradeigma*, or a physical model.[20]

Anaximander *imagined* the shape of the cosmos: as the philosopher Robert Hahn has written, his explanatory models for its law-like patterns were derived from the world of making and above all the architect's undertaking of monumental temple construction.[21] What does Schrödinger's self-styled return to antiquity reveal about the role played by plans, models, and more generally architecture in the project of world-making? The modern physicist, he explains, "plans" pictures and models for the purpose of seeing whether they confirm expectations based on experimental results, and thus whether the pictures or models are themselves adequate. Indeed, Schrödinger offers his "General Picture of the Hereditary Substance" in the chapter of *What is Life?* entitled "Delbrück's Model Discussed and Tested." The physicist Max Delbrück and his co-authors demonstrated in their famous so-called three-man paper of 1935 that genetic mutation consisted of a "single event" that takes place at a specific locus in the hereditary substance.[22] Here is the essential event in space and time upon which the explanatory force of quantum theory was to be focused. Thus Schrödinger addresses "The Uniqueness of the Picture," referring to singular features of Delbrück's molecular model from the quantum mechanical point of view. Yet in the following chapter, "Order, Disorder and Entropy," he suggests that while the model is coherent it offers no understanding of how the gene is put into operation. "How," he asks, "are we going to turn 'conceivability' into true understanding?" (67).

The philosophical legacy of Anaximander rebalances the equation of mind and body; it brings the *use* of models (as opposed to their shadowy essence) in line with origin in the world of making. Sense and reason both have a part in furnishing Schrödinger's "construction" of reality. But for Schrödinger the chief question is how that world endures. What could have served for Schrödinger in place of Anaximinder's temple? The writing of *What is Life?* in fact coincides with the call by architects for a "new monumentality" following the all-consuming inferno of the Second World War. As articulated by Siegfried Giedion, the need was to develop non-monumental (i.e., nonmassive) means for creating symbolic forms that will "constitute a heritage for future generations."[23] What is striking in this statement is the concern for what Giedion referred to in his *Space, Time, and Architecture: The Growth of a New Tradition* of 1941 as the question of "architectural inheritance." There he wrote that "history can reveal to our period the forgotten elements of its being, just as our parents can recover for us those childhood and ancestral particularities which continue to determine our natures though they are not found in our memories."[24] Consider Schrödinger's dedication of *What is Life?*: "To the Memory of My Parents." While the work pays respect to the departed prophets of its own being, its author considered himself to be "the bodily heritage of his ancestors." He possessed their "chromosome treasure." He was their living memory.

The gas calamity

It is not necessary to turn to the "Sketches" to gather glimpses of Schrödinger's life. In the initial discussion of the hereditary mechanism in *What is Life?*, for instance, he improbably notes the events that took place within his father's body in November 1886 (meiosis) that led to his own conception. More revealingly, a long parenthetical aside in a discussion of "Different 'States' of Matter" draws on Schrödinger's memory of the asphalt-like substance that substituted for coffee in Vienna during the First World War. The ersatz coffee was initially rock-solid but over time behaved as a liquid, closely packing the vessel in which it was kept; it was an example of the "amorphous" substance, which was the opposite of the crystalline stuff of which the gene was built.[25] That such a recollection seeped into his account of the events in space and time that take place within the spatial boundary of a living organism is not in itself remarkable. Yet to the extent that the "Sketches" localizes the events of a lifetime, it potentially redefines these boundaries. That is to say, it points beyond the cell to the identity of the household— the very word suggesting a particular form of bond(age)—as the primary space of life-giving meaning. Its walls confine its inhabitants in the felicitous sense of safekeeping; it is the essential source of order that the organism eats, drinks, breathes, and assimilates. Tellingly, the narrative turning point of the "Sketches"

[23] José Luis Sert, Fernand Léger, and Siegried Giedion, "Nine Points on Monumentality," in Joan Ockman (ed.), *Architecture Culture, 1943–1968* (New York: Rizzoli, 1993), 29.
[24] Sert, Léger, and Giedion, "Nine Points on Monumentality," 30.
[25] Schrödinger expressed these two states of matter with the following "scheme of 'equations'": molecule = solid = crystal; gas = liquid = amorphous. *What is Life?*, 59.
[26] Walter Moore, *Schrödinger: Life and Thought* (New York: Cambridge University Press, 1989), 115.

was the material shortages, culminating in the gas calamity of 1918, that spelled the end of housekeeping and the death of Schrödinger's parents. By this time, however, Schrödinger had left home to pursue his career in science.

The "Sketches" begins with recollections of several of Schrödinger's personal, though not unambivalent, relationships. He recalls his faithless attachment to his friend Fränzel, with whom he studied the work of Richard Semon, whose heterodox views were based on the inheritances of acquired characteristics. Then come two figures who most formidably shaped his intellectual development. The first was Fritz Hasenöhrl, who was Boltzmann's successor at the University of Vienna in 1906. Subject to long bouts of depression, Boltzmann had committed suicide in Duino just weeks before Schrödinger enrolled. It was therefore Hasenöhrl who introduced him to Boltzmann's equation $S = k \log D$, which Schrödinger judged to be the most important perception in physics to date. (Hasenöhrl was killed in World War I. Schrödinger's uneventful military service during the war afforded him the leisure to read Albert Einstein's theories for the first time.) The other figure of consequence was his father, Rudolph, "who in the course of those many years [they] lived together drew [him] into conversations concerning his many interests," including morphology and Darwinism (168). Rudolf's successful linoleum and oilcloth business allowed him to spend much more time at home than most men at the time. The business failed in 1917 due to wartime shortages, which fact he kept hidden from his son.

For the Viennese, the war and its consequences meant that basic needs could no longer be met. In the discussion of order and disorder in *What is Life?*, Schrödinger writes that every process, event, or happening going on in nature means an increase of the entropy of the part of the world in which it occurs. In order to free itself from this fatal increase, the living organism feeds upon negative entropy drawn from its environment. In the "Sketches," hunger is keenly felt. Social life in its customary form came to an end, Schrödinger writes: there was simply nothing to offer guests. The resources of "civilized human surroundings" which gave rise to people of one's kind were no longer available. On balance, the *Gemeinschaftsküchen* (community kitchens) produced a new form of sociability and domestic economy, the women who ran them creating "meals out of nothing" (170). Yet the situation turned from difficult to dire with the enactment of gas rationing, which limited each household to one cubic meter a day. The Schrödingers lived in a "rather valuable building" in Vienna purchased by the maternal grandfather, Alexander Bauer, who rented the top-floor apartment to his daughter and son-in-law. Bauer had not converted his house to electricity, in part because Rudolf had become used to gaslight; thus they depended on gas for heat and light. To make up for the deficit in their daily allotment, Rudolf acquired carbon lamps that he insisted on tending himself. "A dreadful stench spread from his beautiful library, which he had turned into a carbide laboratory," Schrödinger recalls (171). The setting of Rudolf's intellectual life became a literal gas chamber. Rudolf died on Christmas Eve 1919 in his old armchair. Would that James Clerk Maxwell's doorkeeping Demon had allowed out all the noxious gas, thereby maintaining the library's rarified atmosphere and reversing the inevitable, if not fated, course of events.

At the time, Schrödinger was happily occupied at his research post after serving four uneventful years in the army (he spent the last year as a meteorologist), leaving his father "to his own devices." What followed was as unpredictable as the weather patterns he observed during the war years. The rampant inflation of 1920 meant the rapid depreciation of his father's life savings. The proceeds from the Persian rugs that Rudolf had earlier sold, with Schrödinger's consent, "dissolved into nothing." To make ends meet Schrödinger began liquidating the contents of the home. "Gone for ever were the microscopes, the microtome and a good part of his library," which Schrödinger "gave away for a song after his [father's] death." At this moment Schrödinger moved to Jena with his new wife, leaving his mother "to fend for herself," a fact of which he was not proud. She bore the burden alone of packing up and clearing out the apartment after her own father grew anxious over the rent. Schrödinger's father-in-law found a renter in the person of a Jewish businessman working for the Phoenix insurance company, two noted details worthy of a dream narrative. "So mother had to leave, where to I do not know." Evidently Schrödinger interpreted her death a year later in terms of the family's real estate. "Had we not been so blind we would have foreseen… what an excellent source of money the big, well-furnished flat could have proved for my mother had she lived longer" (172). The impossibility of foresight of course coincides with the increased disorder of events.

Schrödinger later made a public expression of what he came to regard as his "neglected duties" toward his parents.[26] Yet it was the lost property, his inheritance, and not the disappearance of his parents—first from view, and then from the world—that continued to trouble him. Schrödinger confided:

> For a long time after my father's death… a nightmare kept recurring again and again: my father was still alive and I knew I had given away all his beautiful instruments and botanical books. What was he to do now that I had rashly and irretrievably destroyed the basis of his intellectual life? (173)

The instruments and books that furnished Rudolf's library and later his carbon laboratory were liquidated. What was solid melted into air. Having set himself the task of explaining the durability of the gene structure, Schrödinger recounts in the "Sketches" how he carelessly gave away part of his own inheritance. Schrödinger was unable to settle properly his parents' real and mortal estates.

The dream narrative is a curious inversion of the harrowing sequence in Freud's *The Interpretation of Dreams* that examines the "most anguishing mystery" which links a father to the corpse of his dead son. Having arranged to have an old man keep vigil over the son's body, the father rests in an adjoining room but leaves the door ajar so that he can look from his room into the next. In fact, the scenario presents a curious mirroring of Maxwell's thought experiment. Freud writes,

> After a few hours' sleep, the father had a dream that *his child was standing beside his bed, caught him by the arm and whispered to him reproachfully: "Father, don't you see I'm burning?"* He woke up, noticed a bright glare of light from the next room, hurried into it and found the old watchman had dropped off to sleep and that the wrappings and one of the arms of his beloved child's dead body had been burned by a lighted candle that had fallen on them.[27]

According to Freud, the dream represents a situation that exists in the present and is perceptible by the senses like an experience in the waking state. The expected perceptual sequence is replaced by the living son who speaks to the father. The watchman (the Demon?) who attends the dead has himself "dropped off to sleep." In this inversion, tantamount to the reversal of death, the desire to see the son again is fulfilled, even if his presence is agony to the father. In Schrödinger's dream-thought, it is the son who is visited by the father. It is the father who returns from death to reproach his son for having dispensed with the instrumental basis of his intellectual life. Schrödinger was not watchful enough; he finally allows, "I should have taken care of him better" (172).

The errant son

The discovery of chromosomes as the decisive factors in heredity, Schrödinger wrote, seems to have given

---

[27] Sigmund Freud, *The Interpretation of Dreams* [1900], in *The Standard Edition of the Complete Psychological Works of Sigmund Freud*, v. 509.
[28] Georges Canguilhem, *A Vital Rationalist*, trans. Arthur Goldhammer (New York: Zone Books, 1994), 319.
[29] Moore, *Schrödinger*, 395.
[30] Canguilhem, *A Vital Rationalist*, 89.
[31] Moore, *Schrödinger*, 16.

society the right to overlook other better-known but equally important factors such as communication, education, and tradition. In other words, development requires "civilized human surroundings." That Schrödinger identifies these surroundings with formal education betrays his ambivalence regarding the proper function of the home. As an example of the role of education he mentions, in passing, the story of the foundling Kaspar Hauser (174). The mysterious origin and death of Hauser have long been the subjects of obsessive documentation. Hauser, a youth of fifteen unable to speak or identify himself in any way, appeared on the streets of Nürnberg in 1828 bearing a letter addressed to a certain cavalry captain detailing his confinement and isolation. When questioned further he simply repeated the cryptic phrase: "Ein Reiter will ich werden, wie mein Vater einer war" (I want to become a horseman, like my father was). The statement's syntax recapitulates the notion of being and becoming that is implicit to the very question of inheritance. For Schrödinger, Hauser's story was proof that even a child deprived of familial bonds—the facts of his parentage were obscure—could be made ready to enter society. Hauser wished to assume his (unknown) father's place in the world, or so he was trained to claim. Yet fantasy and even dynastic intrigue filled the gaps in the foundling's past. Having acquired language and behavioral norms, Hauser was murdered by a person promising to reveal to him his true identity.

Schrödinger averred that the question of nature and nurture was not strictly speaking any of his concern. The question only came to his mind, following as it did his discussion of Hauser, "when I once again recognized how much I gained from the time I spent with my father as a young boy…. If I went into detail here, I should end up telling a very long story" (174). It would also be a very old story; the plot endures while the characters and settings change. Schrödinger's life writings in fact reveal him to be an errant son. As Georges Canguilhem observes, intrinsic to any process of (genetic) communication is the possibility of errancy. An animal is formed by heredity to receive and retransmit certain kinds of information. Yet for life to have meaning, for knowledge of life to be possible, error must be admitted into its plan. Errancy refers to the movement from place to place—often without a plan or itinerary—in order to see things anew. It entails the act of rearranging the outline and contents of spaces and places in order to know them more fully.[28] Canguilhem thus connects the subject's self-formation to dissatisfaction with existing meaning; the subject evolves by moving beyond its pre-adapted sources of self. The errant subject strays from home; he makes mistakes because he does not know where to settle; and in the exchange he comes into possession of self. But at what cost? Schrödinger stood by and watched as his family's home was unmade by the gas calamity. Curiously, while he was writing *What is Life?*, Schrödinger indulged his hobby of making dollhouse furniture with textiles woven on a miniature loom.[29] Was he busy reproducing the elements of his lost home—the Persian rugs, the old armchair in which his father died?

The genetic heritage, Canguilhem writes, "is like a loan, and death is the due date when that loan must be repaid. It is as if, after a certain time, it were the duty of individuals to disappear, to revert to the status of inert matter."[30] For Schrödinger the marvel of life is that this debt could be deferred for so long; this deferral was synonymous with its "gift" for going on. The question "what is life?" is thus inextricable from the query "what is the precious something… which keeps us from death?" Yet the troubling question to emerge from the "Sketches" is what happens when the dead are not kept from the living? After death, Schrödinger's father haunted the unhomely house of entropy, upon the walls of which played the shadowgraphs of familiar life. Apparently the only dream Schrödinger recalled from his childhood involved the frightful appearance of the word *Gefängnis* (prison) on the ceiling over his bed.[31] Schrödinger saw the writing on the walls, so to speak. In the agitated though clairvoyant sleep state he discerned the codescript of the house—the structure of confinement

Fig. 3 Tombstone of Kaspar Hauser, Ansbach Cemetery

32 Jacques Derrida, "Fors: The Anglish Words of Nicolas Abraham and Maria Torok," trans. Barbara Johnson, in Nicolas Abraham and Maria Torok, *The Wolf Man's Magic Word: A Cryptonymy* (Minneapolis: University of Minnesota Press, 1986), xxxvi.

33 Mark Wigley, *The Architecture of Deconstruction: Derrida's Haunt* (Cambridge, Mass.: MIT Press, 1993), 142.

34 Gilles Deleuze, *Expressionism in Philosophy: Spinoza*, trans. Martin Joughin (New York: Zone Books, 1990), 262.

35 Jacques Derrida, *The Work of Mourning* (Chicago: University of Chicago Press, 2001), 154.

Fig. 4 Schrödinger Death Mask

revealed. He becomes a secret sharer in the logic that connects the house, the setting that produces people of our kind—finally the act of edification—as bound to the space of the crypt. The trope of the crypt, the philosopher Jacques Derrida has written, implies a topographic arrangement made to keep (conserve hidden) the *living dead*.[32] As Mark Wigley explains, this arrangement of space is bound up with the double gesture by which "the familiar becomes frightening, the *heimlich* [homely] resonating with what it supposedly excludes, such that what doesn't 'belong in the house' somehow belongs and the unfamiliar remains all too familiar."[33] The discussion of life's code thus leads to other cryptic meanings.

What is Life? is written so as to keep a distance from thoughts of death. From the book's start Schrödinger leads the reader astray with the following passage from

Acknowledgement
This essay was originally inspired by Evelyn Fox Keller, a valued teacher. I would like to thank Meredith TenHoor and Michael Osman for their perspicacious criticisms, which contributed to the strengths of this essay such that they may be; to Sara Eigen the preceding phrase, and more.

Fig. 5 (left and center) Claus de Werve, *Mourners from the Tomb of Philip the Bold, Duke of Burgundy (1342–1404)*, 1406–10; (right) Jean de la Huerta, *Mourner with a Book from the Tomb of John the Fearless, Duke of Burgundy (1371–1419)*, 1443–5

Spinoza's *Ethics* (Pt. IV, Prop. 67): "There is nothing over which a free man ponders less than death; his wisdom is, to meditate not on death but on life." What does it mean to be free? For Spinoza, Gilles Deleuze explains, the free and reasonable man "strives to extricate himself from chance encounters and the concatenations of sad passions, to organize good encounters… all this in such a way as to be affected with joy."[34] The essence of freedom is the capacity to be affected; the free man keeps chance (a corollary of disorder) and the dominion of external forces at bay. Tellingly, Schrödinger begins the "Sketches" with the admission, "I lived apart from my best friend, actually the only close friend I ever had, for the greater part of my life. (Maybe that is why I have often been accused of flirtatiousness instead of true friendship)" (167). Flirtation involves keeping the other at a distance, delaying indefinitely the act of consummation. The work of mourning, in marked contrast, makes the absent present, as friendship is said to do.[35] Had Schrödinger mourned better he might have been moved by the inevitably of death. And what of Eros, the counterpart of Thanatos? Schrödinger concludes the "Sketches" with an avowal of silence:

> I must refrain from drawing a complete picture of my life, as I am not good at telling stories; besides, I would have to leave out a very substantial part of this portrait, i.e., that dealing with my relationships with women. First of all it would no doubt kindle gossip, secondly it is hardly interesting enough for others, and last but not least I don't believe anyone can or may be truthful enough in those matters. (184)

Karl Chu

Metaphysics of Genetic Architecture and Computation

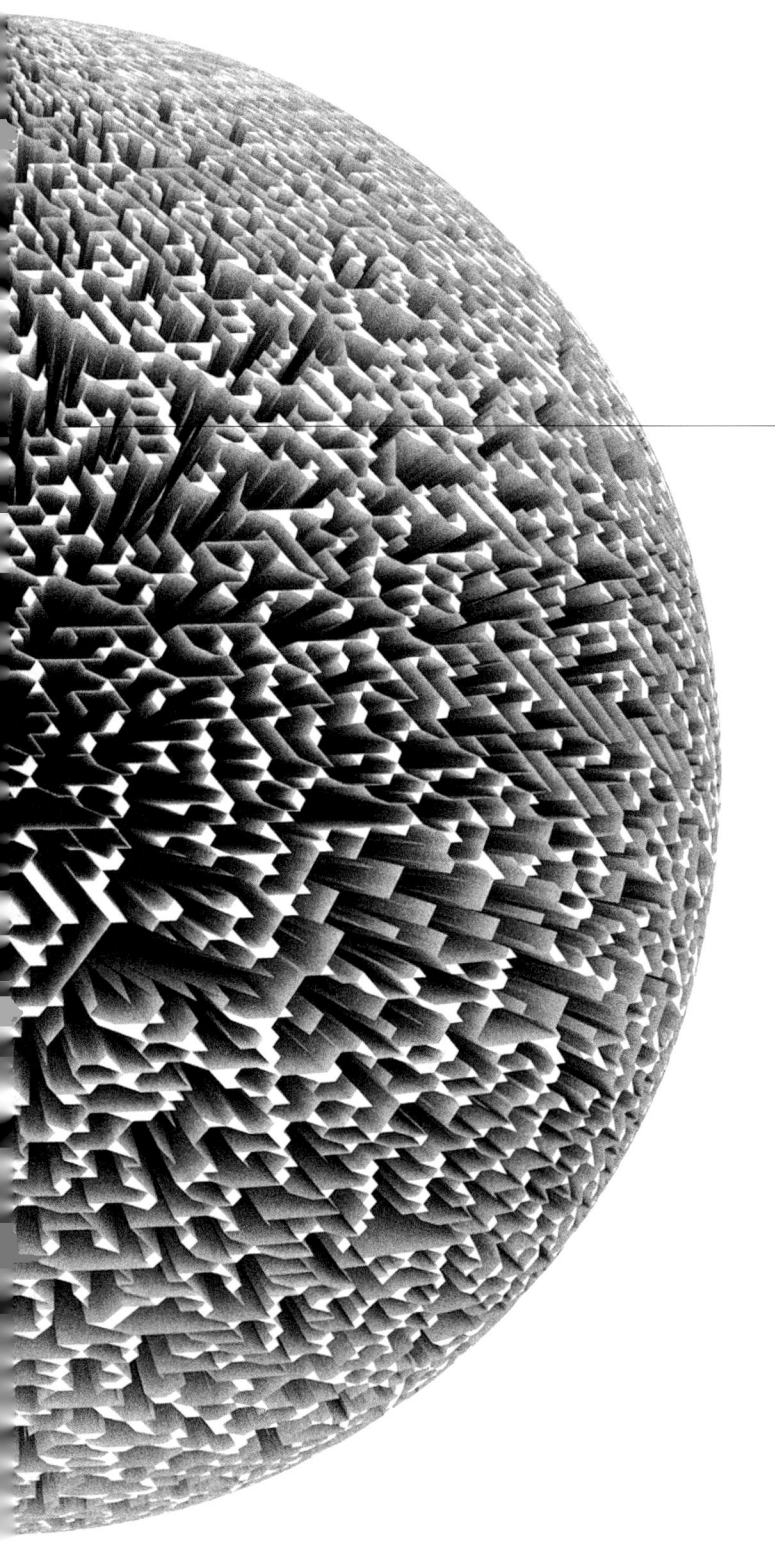
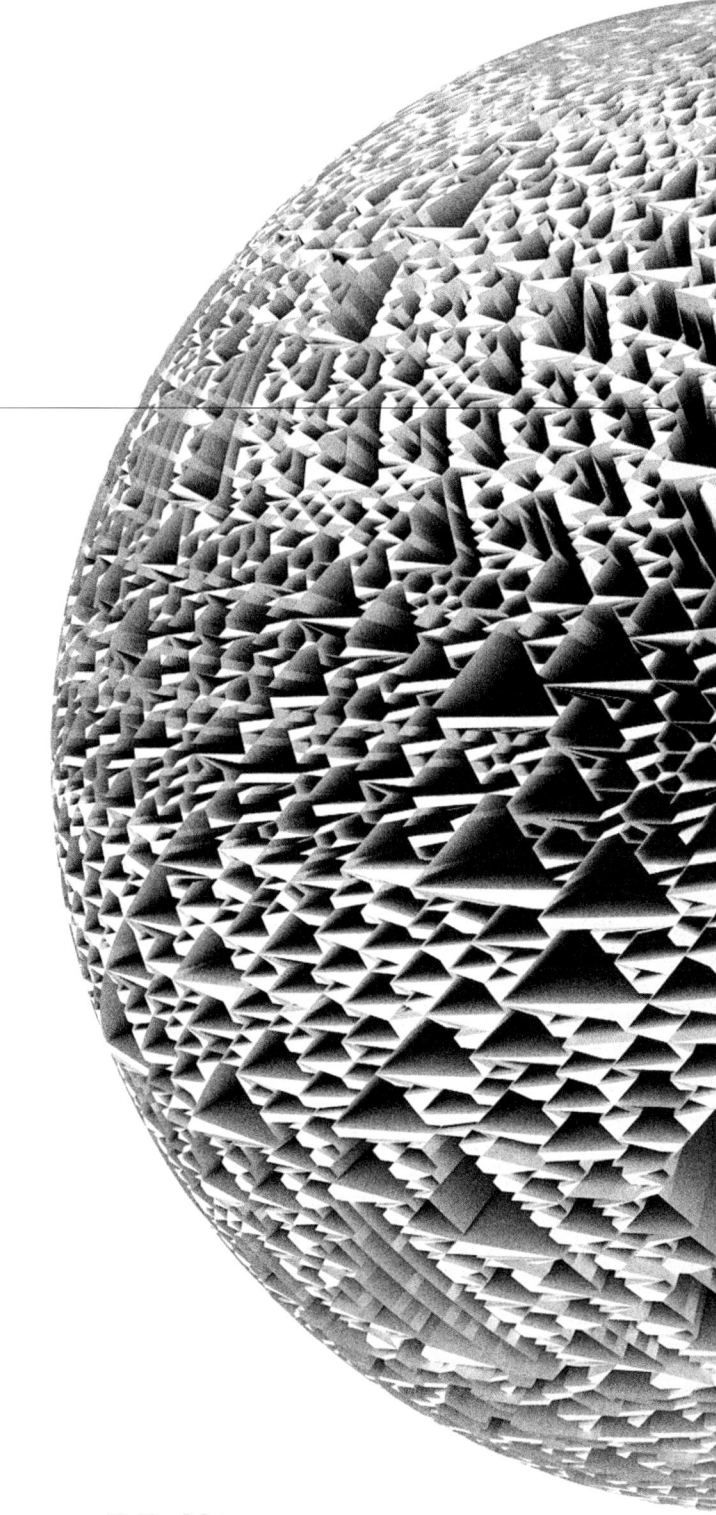

Figs. 1, 2, 3 *ZyZx*, Meta XY. *ZyZx* symbolizes a sampling from the set of configuration spaces of architecture inherent within the universe of cellular automata. Karl Chu would like to thank Chris Sandes for programming cellular automata and Christian Lange for assisting with digital constructions.

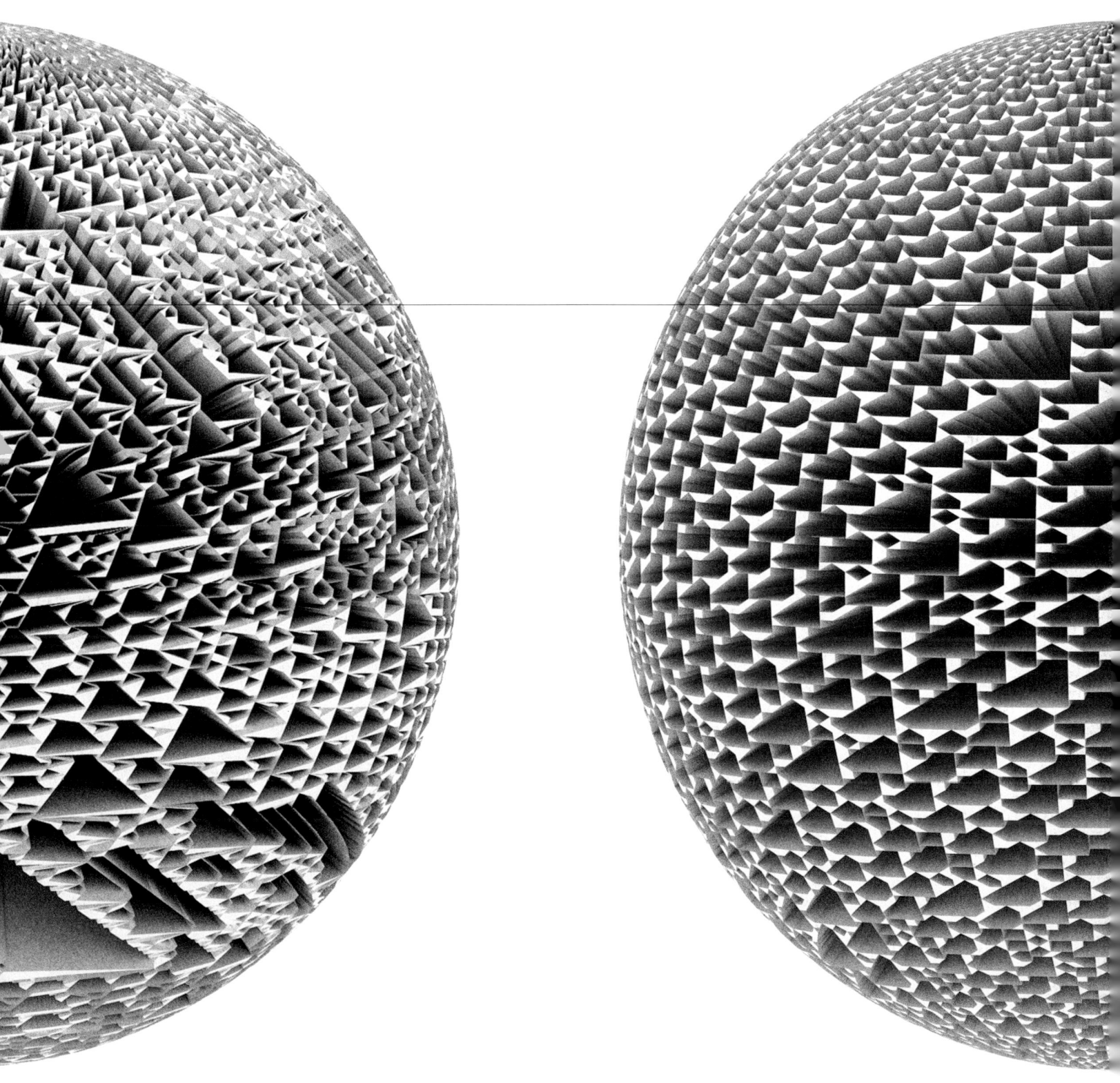

All is algorithm! Gregory Chaitin[1]

With the dissolution of the last utopian project of Man in the name of Communism, the great specter that once haunted Europe and the rest of the world has all but vanished, leaving in its wake an ideological vacuum that is now being filled by the tentacles of globalization with its ecumenical ambition. As humanity has become mesmerized by the triumphant spell of capitalism, what remains less apparent in the aftermath of this dissolution is that the world is moving incipiently toward a threshold that is far more radical and fantastic than any utopic vision since the dawn of the Enlightenment. Once again, the world is witnessing the rumblings of a Promethean fire that is destined to irrupt into the universe of humanity, calling into question the nature and function of life world relations as they so far have existed. These rumblings, stemming in large measure from the convergence of computation and biogenetics in the latter part of the twentieth century, have already begun to invoke gravid visions of the unthinkable: the unmasking of the primordial veil of reality.

The evolution of life and intelligence on Earth has finally reached the point where it is now deemed possible to engender something almost out of nothing.[2] In principle, a universe of possible worlds based on generative principles inherent within nature and the physical universe is considered to be within the realm of the computable once quantum computing systems become a reality. For the first time, mankind is finally in possession of the power to change and transform the genetic constitution of biological species, which, without a doubt, has profound implications for the future of life on Earth. By bringing into the foreground the hidden reservoir of life in all its potential manifestations through the manipulation of the genetic code, the unmasking or the transgression of what could be considered the first principle of prohibition—the taking into possession of what was once presumed to be the power of God to create life—may lead to conditions that are so precarious and treacherous as to even threaten the future viability of the species, *Homo sapiens*, on Earth. At the same time, depending on how mankind navigates into the universe of possible worlds that are about to be siphoned through computation, it could once again bring forth a poetic re-enchantment of the world, one that resonates with all the attributes of a pre-modern era derived, in this instance, from the intersection of the seemingly irreconcilable domains of logos and mythos. Organically interconnected to form a new plane of immanence that is digital, computation is the modern equivalent of a global alchemical system destined to transform the world into the sphere of hyper-intelligent beings.

---

[1] Gregory Chaitin, "Leibniz, Information, Math and Physics" [online text], <http://www.cs.auckland.ac.nz/CDMTCS/chaitin/kirchberg.pdf> (2003), 9.

[2] Stephen Wolfram, *A New Kind of Science* (Champaign: Wolfram Research, 2002), 41.

[3] Alan Turing, "On Computable Numbers with an Application to the Entscheidungsproblem," *Proceedings of the London Mathematical Society*, 2:42 (1936). Alan Turing developed for the first time the conceptual blueprint for an abstract machine noted as the Turing machine in the above mentioned paper.

[4] Stuart Kauffman, *Investigations* (New York: Oxford University Press, 2000), 142–4. Kauffman's concept of the Adjacent Possible was applied in the context of his investigations into the origin of life based on autocatalytic systems, which are derived from random interactions of nodes within Boolean networks.

[5] "Life Is Inevitable in Stuart Kauffman's Creative Universe," *The Paula Gordon Show* [website], <http://www.paulagordon.com/shows/kauffman/> (posted date unknown; accessed February 13, 2004).

[6] Alan Turing developed the Universal Turing Machine, an abstract machine in the logical sense of the term, in response to David Hilbert's call for the resolution of the decision problem, or *Entscheidungsproblem*, in mathematics.

[7] Paolo Rossi, *Logic and the Art of Memory: The Quest for a Universal Language* (Chicago: University of Chicago Press, 2000), 145–94.

[8] John Wheeler, "Information, Physics, Quantum: The Search for Links," in Wojciech Zurek (ed.), *Complexity, Entropy, and the Physics of Information*, proceedings of the SFI workshop of the same title, held May 29 to June 10, 1989 (Redwood City: Addison-Wesley, 1990), VIII. 5.

The power of computation is already evident in the fact that in less than seventy years since the inception of the Universal Turing Machine,[3] it has ushered in the Information Revolution by giving rise to one of the most significant and now indispensable phenomenon in the history of communication: the Internet, or, what could also be characterized as the universe of the Adjacent Possible.[4] Stuart Kauffman defines the Adjacent Possible as the expansion of the networks of reaction graphs within an interactive system into the neighborhood domain of connectivity which until then remains only in a state of pure potentiality. Kauffman suggests, "The Universe has not explored all possible kinds of people, legal systems, economies or other complex systems," and that "autonomous Agents tend to arrange work and coordination so that they are expanding into the Adjacent Possible as fast as they can get away with it."[5] Like every phase transition, the Internet marks a new world order by re-configuring the planet with a virtual, albeit an interactive matrix that is becoming increasingly spatial, intelligent and autonomous: a global self-synthesizing organ bustling with neural intelligence possibly detectable from every corner of the Milky Way and beyond. It is at the level of the construction of possible worlds that the implications for architecture are most pronounced. The thesis that will be advanced at the latter part of this paper is that architecture is becoming increasingly dependent on genetic computation: the generative construction and the mutual coexistence of possible worlds within the computable domain of modal space.

Yet, what is the nature of computation that is destined to change the world including architecture? No instrumental concept or logic of implementation since the invention of the wheel has fostered so much enthusiasm and promise as computation has. Beyond the normative conception of computing machines as mere instruments for calculation, fabrication and communication, it is important to recognize the nature of the underlying ambitions of computation and its relation to architecture. As controversial and provocative as it may seem, the underlying ambitions of computation are already apparent: the embodiment of artificial life and intelligence systems either through abstract machines or through biomachinic mutation of organic and inorganic substances, and, most significantly, the subsequent sublimation of physical and actual worlds into higher forms of organic intelligence by extending into the computable domain of possible worlds. At the most prosaic level however, computation, like natural languages, deals with information in its most general form. Computation functions as manipulator of integers, graphs, programs, and many other kinds of entities. In reality, however, computation only manipulates strings of symbols that represent the objects. It should also be pointed out that, according to the late Richard Feynman, computing systems could be constructed at the atomic scale: swarms of nanobots, each functioning in accordance to a simple set of rules, could be made to infiltrate into host organisms or environments including the human body. In its simplest form, computation is a system that processes information through a discrete sequence of steps by taking the results of its preceding stage and transforming it to the next stage in accordance to a recursive function. Such an iterative procedure based on recursion has proved to be astonishingly powerful and is classified as belonging to a class of machines having universal properties.

It is not surprising that the origin of computation lies in an attempt to embody instrumental reason in an abstract machine[6] along with the attendant drive to encode the logic of life and the world around us in all its manifestation. The quest for a Universal Language[7] which could encapsulate all the attributes and functions necessary to inscribe the form and structure of all computable worlds is becoming one of the most persistent endeavors in the short history of computation. Since computation is about information processing at the most fundamental level, John Wheeler, the prominent American scientist influential to a whole generation of physicists in the latter half of the twentieth century, initiated an information-theoretic conception of the world by stipulating that every item in the universe has at bottom—at a very deep bottom, in most instances—an immaterial source and explanation that is information-theoretic in origin.[8] The fact that computation is a physical process further stipulates the existence of a self-consistent logical loop: the laws of physics define the allowed mechanical operations and the possible activities of a Universal Turing Machine, which in turn determine which mathematical operations are computable and define the nature of solvable mathematics. In other words, the laws of physics generate the very mathematics that makes those laws computable. This discovery of the inextricable linkage that exists between computation and physics has led to the awareness that physical processes are in fact forms of computation, and, nowhere is this understanding made more explicit than in Stephen Wolfram's formulation of the Principle of Computational Equivalence. Wolfram remarks, "All processes, whether they are produced by human effort or occur spontaneously in nature, can be viewed as computations."[9] This proposition reflects a fundamental shift in the way we think about the nature of the physical universe; it is nothing short of a paradigm shift, which would not have been conceivable without an underlying thesis that enables the construction of such a world view: the Church-Turing Thesis as formulated by Alfonso Church and Alan Turing in the early part of the twentieth century. According to Turing, "Every 'function which would naturally be regarded as computable' can be computed by the universal Turing machine."[10] Although the absolute veracity of the thesis cannot be decided by logical means, all attempts to give an exact analysis of the intuitive notion of an effectively calculable function have turned out to be equivalent. Each analysis offered has been proven to pick out the same class of functions, namely those that are computable by the Turing machine.[11]

Parallel to the development of computation is the discovery of the DNA code in the early part of the twentieth century, the significance of which has only begun to be realized with the completion of the Human Genome Project. Finally, with the convergence of computation and biogenetics, the world is now moving into the so-called Post-Human Era, which will bring forth a new kind of bio-machinic mutation of organic and inorganic substances. Information is the currency that drives all these developments and nowhere is this more apparent than in the words uttered by Craig Venter, the ex-CEO of Celera Corporation, which completed the human genome sequence: "The goal is to engineer a new species from scratch."[12]

This statement bluntly announces the unadulterated ambition of the biogenetic revolution. It is only a matter of time before the world will witness bio-machinic mutation of species proliferating into every facet of what so far has been the cultural landscape of humanity. Architects take note: this is the beginning of the demise, if not the displacement, of the reign of anthropology, which has always subsumed architecture. Architecture, especially from the standpoint of its mythical inception, has always been a subset of anthropology: the expulsion of Minotaur, the beast, by entrapping it into the labyrinth built by Daedalus, the mythical architect at Knossos. The potential emancipation of architecture from anthropology is already affording us to think for the first time of a new kind of *xenoarchitecture* with its own autonomy and will to being. In order to break through the barrier of complacency and self-imposed ignorance on the part of the discipline, what is needed is a radicalization of the prevailing paradigm of architecture, beyond retroactive manifestoes, by developing a

[9] Wolfram, Stephen, *A New Kind of Science* (Champaign: Wolfram Research, 2002), 715.
[10] David Deutsch, "Quantum Theory, the Church-Turing Principle and the Universal Quantum Computer," *Proceedings of the Royal Society of London*, A:400 (1985), 3.
[11] Apart from the analyses defined in terms of lambda-definability by A. Church and recursiveness, there are analyses in terms of register machines by J. P. Shepherdson and H. E. Sturgis, E. L. Post's canonical and normal systems, combinatory definability by M. Schönfinkel and H. B. Curry, Markov algorithms, and Gödel's notion of reckonability.
[12] Craig Venter, "Supermicrobe Man," *Wired*, 10:12 (December 2002), 191.
[13] Rem Koolhaas, "Junk Space," *October*, 100 (Cambridge, Mass.: MIT Press, 2002), 175–90.

new concept of architecture that is adequate to the demands imposed by computation and the biogenetic revolution.

Even though architects have incorporated computing systems in the design and construction of buildings and environments, the phase of transmodernity that we are now in is perhaps best characterized by the use of computation still operating under the vestiges of the old paradigm. In other words, architecture has still yet to incorporate the architecture of computation into the computation of architecture. Within the contemporary landscape of architectural discourse there are two divergent trends with theoretical motivations: the morphodynamical and the morphogenetic systems approaches to the design and construction of buildings. These two systems are reminiscent of a strikingly similar problem that exists in modern biology, which is still attempting to synthesize the differences that exist between molecular biology, on the one hand, and developmental biology on the other. What is needed in architecture also is a similar synthesis of the two. After more than half a century of engagement with the avant-garde, the practice of architecture has become increasingly conscious of its embeddedness within the general economy of forces, relationships, and the global economy. The morphodynamical approach, which has spurred two different methodological orientations in dealing with programmatic issues, is the more dominant of the two at the moment. The morphogenetic system is still more or less in its embryonic stage even though it is by far the more fundamental and necessary since it deals with the construction of objects directly. What follows is a brief excursion into conceptual issues that motivate the two approaches in architecture before providing a brief sketch of Genetic Architecture in the latter part of this article.

The opera of globalization

The first and most influential of the two directions within the morphodynamical approach is Rem Koolhaas's reformulation of architecture as the spatial registry for the new world order engendered by International Capital. Long dispensed with the heroic spirit of modernity and the attendant need for salvation, Koolhaas resembles a man who fell to Earth, saturated with the discrete charm of a nihilist who nonetheless preoccupies himself with the problems of the world. He is essentially an idealist wearing the cloak of realism, which allows him to embody the perceptive intelligence of a surveyor with a vision of the world that is at once pragmatic and cynical. Concerned primarily with the organization and modulation of forces operative within the global market economy, his detachment allows him to engage in a mannerist critique of 1) modern architecture by deploying the very language of the modernist ethos that he is critical of, and 2) various pretensions and absurdities of life which find such compulsive expressions within the cultural domain including architecture. A thinly veiled impatience if not a lack of tolerance accompanies this demeanor: "It's the economy, stupid! Get on with infrastructure and the flow of Capital." A realist presentiment that is all the more reasonable when viewed from the standpoint of the practice of architecture embedded within the capitalist system. But, what is left unsaid or remains unthought is that architecture, especially with the demise of the USSR and the subsequent opening of the market economy into Russia and the People's Republic of China, which has embraced the wild and unruly side of capitalism far more than the United States of America, has become the instrument of the ontological destiny of Capital: a truly prolific system capable of transcending national boundaries and ideologies.

The stakes, no doubt, are supremely high. This approach, however, is not without merit. The Koolhaasian outlook calls attention to the proliferation of wastelands and Junk Space[13] as well as to the general economy of abstract machines that regulate monetary flux, systems of production, supply chains, modes of distribution, new markets, shopping, shifts in demography, traffic patterns, etc. We should not overlook the fact

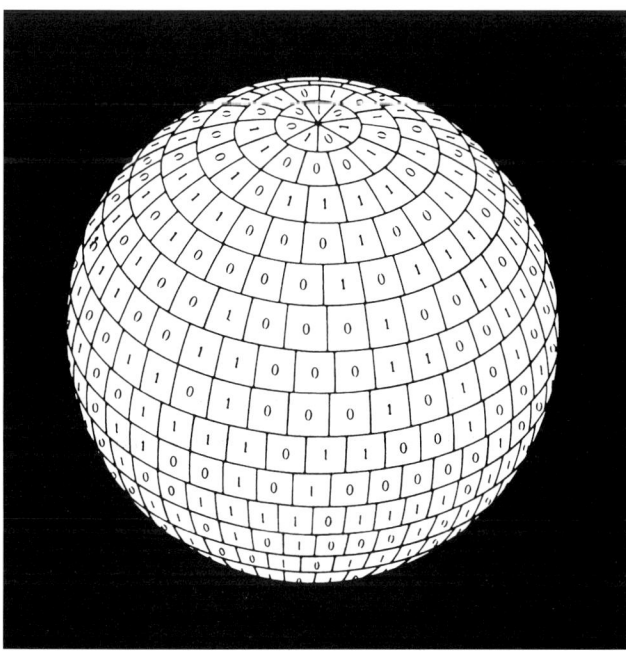

Fig. 4 *It from Bit*. Representation of the Universe in terms of binary digits by John Wheeler

that, unlike real dynamical systems that are found in nature, Koolhaas's framing of architecture as a consequence of the market economy does not lead to the dynamical construction of architecture per se. This approach places emphasis on the performative aspect of cultural programming and alludes, in some rare instances, to an architecture of reactive sublimation. This is most vividly displayed in the compression of Cool Space[14]: the heightened arrest of immanent forces by bracketing the drama of life within the system as a quasi-transcendental zone, at once liminal and erotic, strangely detached and yet simultaneously belonging to the world. Its operative modality: the eye of the architect projecting his cool light, tinged with sublime irony, into the Space of Capital.

With his persistent reminder of the regime of ¥€$ and references to geo-political events as part of the ever-shifting global matrix that governs and constrains the design of buildings, Koolhaas offers a critical realism that deals with the imperatives of the given. Not unlike the art of political dramatization, these social, political and economic issues are framed strategically by Koolhaas in a condensed fashion, with the aim to provoke and shatter the decrepit mind of a stubborn architect who still indulgently holds onto the defunct formalism of the avant-garde. Due in part to his eloquence, which tends to be laconic and pungent, his pronouncements are almost always accompanied by seductive images designed to heighten the surrealism of facts and events. Consequently, they are all the more effective, especially for those architects who have become disenchanted with the avant-garde and who have either lost the desire or are encumbered by the sense of futility in developing new ideas—which in their eyes will inevitably be smoothed over by the capitalist machinery, in framing conditions of possibility or impossibility for the programmatic genesis and construction of architecture within the capitalist system of axiomatization. Given this intention, it is understandable yet unfortunate that such a venue relies exclusively on the default language of modern architecture and its typology with its attendant semiology to organize and frame its dramatic form. By appealing to the generic, Koolhaas takes on an objective stance with a minimalist vocabulary without indulging in extraneous design solutions or idiosyncratic embellishments. The generic affect, especially when subordinated solely to the dictates of the commercial, is liable to be co-opted and blended into what Marshall Blonsky, a professor of semiotics at the New School in Manhattan, refers to as "the indifferent equivalence of everything with everything else, for an audience that has no concern for that

---

14 *Cool Space* is a term that I coined to refer to the cool and translucent nature of minimalist aesthetics.
15 Constance L. Hays, "The Wal-Mart Way Becomes Topic A in Business Schools," *The New York Times*, July 27, 2003, Section 3, 10.
16 Rem Koolhaas, "The New World," *Wired*, 11:6 (June 2002), 115–37.
17 See the cinematic aesthetics of *Alphaville*, directed by Jean-Luc Godard (1965). *Alphaville*, a story which unfolds in a utopian world of the future, is governed by a totalitarian system in which the individual counts for almost nothing, and an alienated society has no use for art, poetry, love, or even thought. People are reduced essentially to the level of robots.
18 Jaegwon Kim, *Supervenience and Mind* (Cambridge: Cambridge University Press, 1994), 92–5.
19 Kim, *Supervenience and Mind*, 101–2.
20 A kynic, stemming from Diogenes, is the provocative but stubborn moralist with a plebian intelligence, who lets out a satirical laughter, unlike the cynic who, according to Sloterdjik, harbors the smile of an enlightened false consciousness on his lip. Peter Sloterdjik, *Critique of Cynical Reason* (Minneapolis: University of Minnesota Press, 1988).

difference, and no discernment of quality" and where "America's least common denominators gathered together."[15] Based on the reductive rationality befitting a bureaucrat, of which Koolhaas is fully aware of the concealment of the irrational by the rational—a very special delirium inherent to the regime of money, according to Deleuze—architecture is now in a position to concentrate, even in the context of his acute awareness of this madness, on modulating the flow of programmatic issues driven by the ever-expanding capitalist system of circumlocution.

As such, the locus of force is situated neither in the material or formal cause but posited exclusively in the efficient cause, i.e., programmatic determinants engendered by the system, which, for Koolhaas, constitutes the fundamental reason for being of architecture. The main interest therefore is not in the formal genesis or in the search for the autonomy of architecture but to grasp the dynamics of the capitalist regime, which comes replete with a new zodiac for a new world order[16] represented by the ever shifting constellation of corporate logos collectively standing in to frame the cosmography of Capital. Machinic assemblages of this regime are then channeled, coalesced and constrained appropriately through a spatial medium charged with a quasi-transcendental aesthetics reminiscent of *Alphaville*.[17] The impotence of architecture therefore is inversely related to the cosmology of the power system that subsumes it; architecture, at best, according to this position, can do nothing more than to invert this inversion through irony while sublimating Junk Space into a flattened and translucent Cool Space. His position is one of reactive sublimation, which contents itself with the mere accomplishment of sublime irony as opposed to getting involved in the messianic projection of possible worlds to come.

The Koolhaasian approach therefore is that of a journalist who relishes an *extensional* description of architecture where the entire universe of relevant objects is captured under the sign of ¥€$. His method is a top-down analysis of the brutality of facts, of the reality of the given based on epiphenomenal causation,[18] which reveals dependency relations that exist at the macro level rather than on the internal structure of causal relations that connect facts and events. It is a version of mereological supervenience,[19] a generalized appeal to the operations of the macro-economy where the characteristics of wholes supervene on the properties and relationships characterizing their proper parts. The alchemical transformations occurring within these objects—the hidden micro-economy of internal relations and interactions that exist at various scalar and specification regimes of matter, energy, and information that lead to complex organizations—remain outside the scope of his surveillance and penetration. Being all too comfortable with the fashionable display of charts and figures, as if they alone adequately explain the inner complexity of the world, Koolhaas seems resigned to making enlightened remarks on just about everything: from Largos to Shanghai via 9/11. Far from being a stalemate, this is only the beginning of the capitalist version of alchemy: the incarnation and mutation of affects produced by Capital into the mind and body of Man as well as into the organic and inorganic substances of reality, an inevitable fatalism that is destined to fundamentally alter the very definition of Man, along with it, the category of the species—*Homo sapiens*. Koolhaas, for the moment, represents an index of consciousness, a critical facet of neo-conservatism which expands architecture outside of its parochial limitations and allows it to be subsumed, undoubtedly at a price, by the restricted economy of Capital.

Finally, accompanied by the ambivalent smile of a kynic[20] who has become adept at playing with the flux of Capital, the message disseminated by Koolhaas is clear: be a capitalist with the moral prerogatives of a skeptic who, in his case, is tinged with a heavy dose of asceticism where the principle of salvation, ever an unacknowledged sentiment which constitutes such a monastic or repressed aesthetics of architecture, converges with that of the accrual of surplus value, neither contradictory nor regrettable especially when it comes to life and architecture. It is this proposition—a massive rhetorical adumbration if not an apologetic for the capitalization of architecture, which unabashedly subordinates, subsumes and suppresses the autonomy of architecture and its internal will to freedom by locking its interiority into the restricted economy of Capital, not leaving any room for the messianic exploration of worlds to come—that is most problematic with this orientation. In other words, it is the dissipation of the will to architecture through a transfusion of that will into the cartography of branding: the end of architecture and the beginning of the presumed enlightened Space of Capital, at least up to the stage of transmodernity. Such is the militant nature of an ontological commitment to naïve realism, an epiphenomenalist drama based on apparent causation that characterizes the work of Rem Koolhaas and his disciples—thoughtful architects who, far from being sleepwalkers from the late modernist era, are nonetheless all too willing and eager to be caught in a uniquely Western version of *feng shui*, albeit without their being aware of it, which literally means *wind and water*—

elements that constitute, in this instance, the fluid dynamics of an esoteric belief system. In other words, it is the *smoothing* of the flow of *oracles* induced by the master into the flow of MM&M—Money, Matter, and Meaning—as if this magnificent confluence is the only theater of the world worth enacting on the plane of consistency which has no place for the irruption of the untimely or the intrusion of the unexpected, notwithstanding the catastrophic events of 9/11, and much less the caesura that momentarily pauses the sound and the fury of everything. This is the Koolhaasian rendition of the Opera of Globalization.

Morphing matter

The second direction within the morphodynamical approach is represented by a host of young architects working in the digital domain. They are concerned with the architecture of so-called soft morphology and, for some, biomorphic representation. Influenced by Greg Lynn's interest in animate form, on the one hand, and, to compensate for the lack of kinematical use of force in Koolhaas on the other, these architects, being playfully enthusiastic with the use of dynamical features such as particle systems and inverse kinematics available within animation software such as Maya, Softimage and Houdini, instantiate interactive morphing based on dependency graphs that are spuriously linked to contextual forces that exist within a given site or condition. Mobility and flow are once again at the top of the agenda. Unaware of the fundamental difference that exists between modeling and simulation, not to mention the occasionally ambiguous relation that exists between representational and non-representational modes of computation, they thrive on the confusion derived from mistaking the behavior of forces enacted within the virtual environment as being identical and isomorphic to the complex behavior of forces and relations that occur in the physical world. In most cases, they are examples of misplaced concreteness staged on a virtual plane of consistency without, on the most part, the necessary rigor required in the modeling of complex adaptive behavior that approximates real world situations. In addition, neither are they involved in the simulation of pure dynamical possibilities, or *bodies without organs*, in the words of Deleuze and Guattari echoing Antonin Artaud, without the attendant trauma of being bondaged to representation. Instead, they are deployments of the same set of animation features that post-production companies, both in Hollywood and elsewhere, use to generate virtual affects for TV advertisements and films, and in a few cases, the manipulation of parametric

21 Stuart Kauffman, *Investigations*, 131.

constraints within engineering software to instantiate complex morphing. Unfortunately, some of these animations, more often than not, tend to lapse into comical display of animated forces represented by the flow of particles as they contort and distort Nurb surfaces enacted within the virtual environment. These contortions are then augmented by narratives already stipulated and rehearsed by Koolhaas.

The characteristic feature of dynamical systems in general is that they are fundamentally not equipped with constructive processes. The formal constitution of these systems is predicated on the quantitative properties and couplings of interacting elements which are construed as *unformed matter* and they fail to represent elements as objects with distinct internal structures that can give rise to behavior. Objects therefore disappear into arrays of structureless variables confined to holding numerical values that quantify properties of an object class. These values represent intensive ordinates that map changes in time, density and space: the frequency of a gene, the concentration of a chemical, the position and velocity of an aircraft, the pressure of a gas, the rate of change in interest rates, the fluctuations of the dollar, the density of population, the earnings of a firm, the rise and fall of stocks, the diagrammatic flow of traffic, etc. As a consequence, interaction is understood as the temporal or spatial change in the numerical value of quantitative variables. This change is captured by a set of (deterministic or stochastic) differential (or difference) equations and the solutions of these equations may then be viewed as a flow in phase space, which then can be characterized as a manifold that governs the set of possible trajectories. In Nature, however, interaction involves objects directly and never by a numerical value describing them. With regard to having too much faith in statistics, a caution by Kauffman made in a different context is appropriate: "there is no finite prestatement of the configuration space of a biosphere."[21] Neither is there one for a truly radical conception of architecture that is open to the future.

Going outside of the framework of conventional dynamical systems requires taking this observation seriously. Given the inherent limitation of dynamical systems, which is an abstraction of one aspect of the behavior of nature, the application of this conceptual apparatus as an expository system for architecture inevitably leads to the assumption that architecture has no interiority of its own since the very notion of interiority presupposes the construction of objects and their genesis over time. The emphasis placed by the dynamical approach therefore is in the interaction of forces within a given context which is consistent with the notion of architecture conceived as an adaptive discipline predicated on weaving, critically or otherwise, into a given fabric of urban condition that is already infused with a set of social, political and economic reality. What is left behind, and this is the crucial point to remember, is the very logic of construction whereby the internal structure of an element or a group of elements causes specific actions to occur, such as the replication, mutation, construction, modification, substitution or deletion of other objects, all of which are part of the grammatical functions of a language that participates in the genesis of an internal *will to architecture*. Unfortunately, some architectural theorists and critics who are vehemently supportive, almost to the point of being militant, of the morphodynamical approach, especially with its appeal to the flow of Capital, are unduly obstinate in avoiding formal issues that are internal to these systems, which, in fact, give impetus to their arguments. Concerned primarily with the inductive use of associative reasoning, the nature and function of metaphoric import that give explanatory power to these concepts, which are derived from the science of dynamical systems, remain largely unthought.

Parallel to this is a corresponding lack of critical stance concerning the hegemonic influence of software systems that are made all too "user-friendly" by software manufacturers. The uncritical use of pre-determined functions within these systems tend to produce architectural affects and morphologies that are recognizably homogeneous and predictable. What is most problematic is the unconscious propagation of a pre-constituted set of functions that invariably lead to architectural traits devoid of any critical import or will to being: the multi-faceted novelty of the ready-made which engenders, through the manipulation of parametric constraints, inexhaustible variations of the same—another newfound lease on life for architecture under the regime of Capital.

The art of rewriting
In contrast to the morphodynamical systems approach to architecture, the morphogenetic orientation has its premise in the idea of an internal principle that generates architectural form and organization. It is an investment of the will to architecture that is clearly lacking in the morphodynamical approach, which depends exclusively on exogenous issues to regulate the composition and packaging of architectural form. Dynamical systems are generative systems endowed with the capacity for self-organization but not self-replication.

They contain neither a description of its logic and

template of its organization nor mechanisms for copying hereditary information onto subsequent generations. In contrast, a genetic system contains a description of itself that is necessary for self-replication. Of the two uses of computation, representational and non-representational, non-representational procedures allow for the development and emergence of forms that are intrinsic to genetic systems. The representational concept of modeling instead relies on references that exist outside of the computational process, such as in computer simulation. In non-representational modeling, there is no a priori reference to any pre-existent model or condition that exists outside of itself; it models its own reality by exploring generative possibilities inherent within an axiomatic rule set. It is the purest form of information processing that is based on inherent possibilities and limitations.

Among the few architects[22] who are involved in the morphogenetic approach, there have emerged three complementary directions: 1) a genetic hermeneutics of architecture as represented by Peter Eisenman, 2) algorithmic architecture explored by Cecil Belmond, John Frazer, and a few others who rely on fractal systems, Lindenmayer systems, and genetic algorithms to generate recursively defined geometric objects, and, 3) a genetic monadology of architecture, which takes on *symbiogenesis* as the *modus operandi* for the construction of possible worlds. As it is presented here, this last approach is implicitly related to the first and explicitly connected to the second.

All these approaches take as their central idea the concept of *rewriting*. The difference in the interpretation and use of this concept essentially differentiates Eisenman's methodology and the other two positions which are based on recursion. Even though Eisenman does not rely on formal axioms, he can be considered a precursor to the morphogenetic orientation. His early interest in the deep structures of Chomsky's grammar is indicative of his later but abiding interest in the interiority of architecture and the autonomy of the generative, twin concepts that are fundamental to the development of a theory of genetic architecture. It must be mentioned that Chomsky's grammar paved the way for Aristid Lindenmayer to develop a mathematical theory of plant formation called Lindenmayer System, or simply, L-system, which is based on the logic of string rewriting: a technique for defining complex objects by successively replacing parts of a simple initial object using a set of *rewriting rules*.[23] Genetics also presupposes the concept of rewriting within its system. Eisenman has introduced a less formal concept of rewriting: the diagram. The

---

22 John Frazer, *An Evolutionary Architecture* (London: Architectural Association, 1995). Some of the engineering work done by Cecil Belmond relied on fractal systems.
23 Aristid Lindenmayer and Przemyslaw Prusinkiewicz, *The Algorithmic Beauty of Plants* (New York: Springer-Verlag, 1990), 1.
24 Betty Rojtman, *Black Fire on White Fire* (Berkeley: University of California Press, 1998), 1.
25 Rojtman, *Black Fire on White Fire*, 1.
26 Ernst Haeckel's well known assertion that "Ontogeny is the short and rapid recapitulation of phylogeny" is based entirely on mechanical causes which are physical-chemical in nature. His position, unfortunately, led him to the ideology of National Socialism in Germany. In the case of Eisenman, there is no appeal to such mechanical causes or physical substances that provide the basis for such recapitulation. It is purely a hermeneutical gesture that attempts to address the interiority of architecture through the diagram, which has none of the absolute certainty that Haeckel implied with his assertion. Stephen J. Gould, *Ontogeny and Phylogeny* (Cambridge: Belknap Press, 1977), 76–85.

difference in the two conceptions of rewriting is fundamental: the one that I am proposing is formal, which is based on *recursion*, and Eisenman's version is founded upon hermeneutical inscription. This distinction essentially differentiates Eisenman's approach, which I am referring to as a *genetic hermeneutics of architecture*, derived from exegetical procedures, and a *monadology of genetic architecture* that I am proposing, which is an extension and transformation of Leibniz's *Monadology*, albeit without his theogony. From a philosophical point of view, both approaches operate in the void opened up by the absence of the Word, in the fertile space that is now being traversed by computation which, as mentioned earlier, is involved in the search for the code of existence—even in the oblique sense that it has imparted to architecture since time immemorial.

Archaeology of the future
Peter Eisenman's architecture over the last thirty years consistently relies on some form of generative process, at times highly idiosyncratic, to arrive at architectural form. Although Eisenman deploys morphing techniques in some of the projects done in the last few years, what is significant is that he is motivated by the desire to uncover a phenomenology of interiority and autonomy within the discipline of architecture by inscribing his own theoretical work within the same tradition in order to disclose the nature of that autonomy that he so wishes to perpetuate. This is a move that is not without a degree of paradoxical relation to its subject matter. Correspondingly, he is consciously involved in the chain of interpretation that includes dialogical relations with certain select architects from history. His work therefore can be characterized as a genetic hermeneutics of architecture. In contrast to genetic systems, a genetic hermeneutics is a generative modality based principally on the interpretation of the sense of interiority embedded within a series or tradition. By subsequently re-investing the results of its interpretation back into the structure, it attempts to maintain and further propagate the unfolding of the series. This move allows him to acquire a dimension of singularity and autonomy with regard to the series. However, the condensation and perpetuation of this series, which constitute the history of architecture, is done without the benefit of any appeal to formal logic or axiomatics. Correspondingly, a genetic hermeneutics of architecture is grounded in the tradition of interpretation which attempts to decipher and unfold an original presence whose inexhaustibility is both testified and investigated by the exegetical tradition. The paradigm for such a hermeneutical approach is offered by Bette

Rojtman in her study on Jewish hermeneutics. In her book *Black Fire on White Fire*, Rojtman recounts and situates the origin of the infinite series propagated by textual exegesis as follows:

> The Torah that God gave to Moses opens with the second letter of the alphabet, the 'beth' of plurality. The Law of truth, the charter of the world's foundation, is thus presented first of all as disseminated 'Word' at the heart of the unique.

This is the original scene of inscription that deliberately sidesteps any coincidence and instantiated "a deep rent in the fabric of an absolute pronouncement, it marks the entire range of history to come, the place allowed for the living within an essential Word."[24] Furthermore, "Exegesis repeats this paradox by positing a true univocal meaning that nevertheless opens out toward the world and 'plays' between writing and orality, between the interpreted word and the transmitted word."[25]

Let it be stated without too much preamble that Peter Eisenman's architecture must be understood as a similar attempt to situate architecture as part of the inner unfolding of an exegetical tradition and the hermeneutical role that the architect plays within such a process, which is highly nuanced, complex and synthetic without being dialectical. To judge his architecture outside of the context of the tradition of interpretation is to miss a fundamental thesis of his work: architecture is a form of inscription or *rewriting* situated at the intersection of a past which constitutes its tradition and possible futures. It is mediated, at this juncture, by the diagram which folds and unfolds the textual tradition of architecture, an archaeology of the future that resembles an arithmetical series: infinite but secretly calculated and, in the case of Eisenman, mediated by an active renewal of signification in the very act of inscribing the diagram—writing that opens up the futurity of writing.

The diagram therefore re-presents by rewriting traces of the interpreted word and the transmitted word. It is at once diachronic and synchronic with regard to the simultaneous registration of latent trajectories that eventually unfold into the configuration space of buildings. This is the genetic aspect of Eisenman's theoretical work which, in the process of unfolding, gives structure and organicity to the interiority of architecture, a singularity that, by virtue of its reference to an original presence, is endowed with the imperatives of a messianic force directed toward the future unfolding of the world. Ontogeny, in this context, is understood as the development of an organ of architecture by recapitulating the traces of interiority that constitutes the lineage of a phylogenetic branch.[26] Herein lies the logic of the infinite series, a genetic hermeneutics of architecture engendered by languages of the unsayable. The spirit of the exegetical tradition is the call to read the unwritable and follow the movements of the hidden traces of interiority, which is virtually identified with the logic and structure of the series itself. As can be seen, the theoretical position taken by Eisenman is profound even though its archaeological dimension is less than transparent in his built projects. At the same time, it is extremely fragile, given the context of globalization where the specificity of an exegetical tradition is already threatened by the capitalist system of axiomatization. If Eisenman offers a genetic hermeneutics of architecture by tapping into the lineage of a phylogeny with an interiority of its own, the concept of genetic architecture that is offered here will implicate Eisenman's phylogenetic deferrals into the distributive networks of computing systems, which may allow for the rhizomatic proliferation of a jungle, at once superposed onto and co-extensive with the desert of existence: a monad.

Monadology of genetic architecture

Having identified some of the salient features that are integral to dominant trends within contemporary architecture as well as the nuanced relations that each of these trends have with regard to the phenomenon of globalization, which is increasingly augmented and driven by the gift of Promethean fire that is now saturating the cultural universe of humanity with all forms of transgenic mutation, we are now in a position to articulate a more comprehensive theory of architecture, one that is adequate to the demands imposed by the convergence of computation and biogentics in the so-called Post-Human Era: a monadology of genetic architecture that deals with the construction of possible worlds. As we now approach what Ray Kurzweil refers to as the Singularity,[27] the myth of matter, which underlies most theoretical and practical discussions of architecture, is about to be displaced by the myth of information. Contrary to Mies van der Rohe's oft-quoted remark that architecture is the art of putting two bricks together, the emerging conception is that architecture is the art of putting two bits together, at least bits that are programmed to self-replicate, self-organize and self-synthesize into ever new constellations of emergent relations and ensembles.

The use of the term *monadology* is based on the fact that genetic architecture is an extension and transformation of some of the propositions, especially those that define attributes and properties of relationships among monads, contained in Gottfried W. Leibniz's

---

27 Ray Kurzweil, "The Singularity" in John Brockman (ed.), *The New Humanists: Science at the Edge* (New York: Barnes & Noble, 2003), 215–32.
28 Chaitin, "Leibniz, Information, Math and Physics."
29 Juan Alvarez de Lorenzana, "The Constructive Framework and the Evolutionary Systems," in Stanley N. Salthe, *Development and Evolution: Complexity and Change in Biology* (Cambridge, Mass.: MIT Press, 1993), 298–9. Note: de Lorenzana's deployment of these principles is, *prima facie*, not based on computation. I have instead chosen to interpret these principles as being applicable to monadology of genetic architecture based on recursion.
30 Martin Davis, *The Universal Computer: The Road From Leibniz to Turing* (New York: W. W. Norton, 2000), 180–7.
31 William Poundstone, *The Recursive Universe: Cosmic Complexity and the Limits of Scientific Knowledge* (Chicago: NTC / Contemporary Publishing, 1985). See also: <http://www.zyvex.com/nanotech/selfRepJBIS.html#vonNeumann Architecture>.
32 John Divers, *Possible Worlds* (London: Routledge, 2002).

Monadology, albeit without its theogony, into an architectural theory of world making. *Monadology* is one of the earliest attempts in sketching out a *system of principles* that generalizes the nature of the world from an abstract point of view; it shares conceptual properties that are now deemed to be fundamental to the science and philosophy of computation. Even though Leibniz was impeded by the lack of conceptual and technical resources at the time, his ideas nonetheless paved the way for subsequent development of computation and, according to Gregory Chaitin, Algorithmic Information Theory[28] in the twentieth century. Leibniz's *Monadology* is arguably the earliest endeavor to propose what is now known as an open-source architecture based on the principles of philosophical genetics: the principle of generative condensation, the principle of combinatorial expansion, and the principle of the conservation of information.[29] *Monadology* is a metaphysical treatise; Leibniz defines each monad as a metaphysical point, an irreducible concept of an atomic entity that is endowed with an immaterial substance. Contrary to Leibniz and without the reference to God as the supreme creator of monads, a computational theory of monadology would instead qualify each monad as one *bit* of information at the most irreducible level, and by extension, a unit of self-replicating system. It is based on this conception of a monad as a minimal unit of self-replicating system that a monadology of genetic architecture is developed here.

Historically, genetic architecture can be seen as an extension and transformation of utopic ideas implicit within the avant-garde to create new worlds by drawing on new sciences and technologies. Genetics is a name coined by William Bateson in 1905 to encompass the whole of the study of heredity but the term *gene* was introduced by the Danish botanist Wilhelm Johannsen, also around the same time, to account for the units within sex cells that determine the hereditary characteristics. The meaning of both terms, genetics and gene, are sufficiently abstract and general enough to be used as concepts that have logical implications for architecture without being anchored too explicitly to biology. Implicit within the concept of genetics is the idea of replication of heritable units based on some rule inherent within the genetic code, and embedded within the mechanism for replication is a generative function: the self-referential logic of recursion. Recursion is a function or rule that repeatedly calls itself or its preceding stage by applying the same rule successively, thereby generating a self-referential propagation of a sequence or a series of transformation. It is this logic encoded within an internal principle which constitutes the autonomy of the generative that lies at the heart of computation.

Even though *genetic* is a term derived from biology, it is used here as a generic concept based on the interconnected logic of recursion and self-replication whose philosophical underpinnings go far beyond the confines of molecular biology. It should therefore be noted that genetic architecture is neither a representation of biology nor a form of biomimesis; instead, its theoretical origins, insofar as genetic architecture is concerned, can be traced to John von Neumann's invention of the cellular automaton and the so-called "von Neumann Architecture" for self-replicating systems. From the early stages of the development of modern computing systems, the idea of self-replication was put forward by John von Neumann.[30] Even though he participated in discussions leading to the development of the first electronic computer ever built—the ENIAC—von Neumann eventually came up with what is now known as the von Neumann Architecture—the prototype for modern computing systems with its stored memory program. The von Neumann Architecture managed to address the idea of a machine that could manufacture itself: a robot that self-replicates and self-constructs copies of itself.[31] This is a notion that lies at the heart of biology: the essence of self-reproduction is organization—the ability of a system to contain a complete description of itself and use that information to create new copies. The von Neumann Architecture for a self-replicating system is the ancestral and archetypical proposal which consisted of two central elements: a Universal Computer and a Universal Constructor. The Universal Computer contains a program that directs the behavior of the Universal Constructor, which, in turn, is used to manufacture both another Universal Computer and a Universal Constructor. Once finished, the newly manufactured Universal Computer was programmed by copying the program contained in the original Universal Computer, and program execution would then begin again. The von Neumann Architecture therefore is a precursor to the architecture of a genetic system.

While most experiments done so far using various kinds of algorithmic systems tend to be reductive and literal in their appropriation of manifest identity or self-expression contained within these systems, genetic architecture has a two-fold ambition: co-evolutionary construction of complex ensembles or possible worlds[32] (*partial universes* in the language of set theory) based on *symbiogenesis*, and disclosure of the sublime *other* within the *same* without identity. The first ambition is concerned with the development of a general theory of world making based on symbiogenesis: co-construction of possible worlds by autonomous agents within a symbiosis. A symbiosis is an ecology where different agents and organisms interact and live in close proximity with each other. In biology, long-term stable symbiosis that leads to evolutionary change is called symbiogenesis.[33] Here, symbiosis is conceived in terms of a world generated and constructed through viral dissemination: the clustering and mutation of genomic spaces engendered by viral agents. With the capacity for genetic propagation that is neither intrinsically good/bad nor primarily destructive in its function, as it is commonly understood, an architectural virus is a parasitical unit of self-replicating system, a micro-computational monad with built-in mechanisms for absorption and conversion of a given host organism—be it virtual or actual—into a new state of affairs or a possible world. It is predicated on the logic of micro-intervention that leads to macro-transformation at various scalar and specification regimes of transaction, mutation and organization. Viruses usually operate collectively as a distributive system within a symbiotic whole—swarms of infectious monads infiltrate into a given host environment and genetically propagate each of its built-in function(s) in order to alter, modify and transform the information content of both the intertextual as well as the intratextual networks of host organisms. In the process, viruses re-configure and re-organize the metabolism of a host organism into a new organizational entity with a different set of interstitial vestibules and vestigial traces, which, in turn, establish conditions of possibility for further transformation and differentiation into future organisms. New forms of power structures and organizations have shown to emerge through viral interventions that are symbiotic in nature. Even though viral interaction is aleatory in scope, it is deterministic in function. Consequently, autocatalytic reactions of viruses could lead to the conjunctive synthesis of emergent morphology that is fundamentally cohesive. A viral theory of architecture therefore is based on the premise that collective transformation derived from distributive systems whose internal elements or population is embedded with a high degree of generative autonomy could potentially lead to the emergence of a new kind of possible world, one that is intrinsically democratic in its performance and aspiration. The meaning of globalization is radically incomplete and inadequate without an architectural theory of viral infection.

The concept of *world* is a philosophical abstraction transcribed into the idea of a computational entity, which can be scaled to any desired level of manifestation.

---

[33] According to Lynn Margulis and Dorion Sagan, these mergers, long-term biological fusions beginning as symbiosis, are the engine of species evolution. See: Lynn Margulis and Dorian Sagan, *Acquiring Genomes* (New York: Basic, 2002).
[34] *Physiovirtual* is a word that I coined, for lack of a term, to address the inextricable linkage and dependency of the physical with the virtual.
[35] Eric Steinhart, "Digital Metaphysics," in Terrell Ward Bynum and James H. Moor (eds.), *The Digital Phoenix* (Oxford and Malden: Blackwell, 1998), 117–34.
[36] Simulated annealing, neural nets, genetic algorithm and genetic programming all fall under the category of evolutionary algorithm.
[37] See Ray Kurzweil's *The Age of Spiritual Machine* (New York: Viking, 1999).
[38] Wolfram, *A New Kind of Science*, 392.

As such, it does not presuppose any a priori reference to size or scale. In a general sense, a *world* can be thought of as an emergent phenomenon, an *inconsistent multiplicity*, with its own symbiosis at different scalar and specification regimes of organization. At the level of architecture, a world is an heterogeneous ensemble generated by the symbiotic cooperation of freedoms between monads and human societies. Each monad can be a genotype, a unit of self-replicating system or a phenotype as a collective ensemble with a global morphology. As genotypes, monads exist on the plane of content, and as phenotypes, they are emergent morphology on the plane of expression engendered by massive clusters of micro-monadic interactions. As such, monads exist at various scalar and specification regimes of organization: an object, an aggregation of objects, a building, a group of buildings, a proto-species of genetic architecture, a bionic being, a *physiovirtual* environment, etc.[34]

genotypes → **computation** → phenotypes

the plane of content → **computation** → the plane of expression

Computation is the medium for *in vitro* fertilization of genetic architecture; computing systems are mechanisms in which things build other things. Such things are essentially processes and functions that generate symbolic strings within a computing machine. A string is a list that represents a grouping of atoms such as $((a_1, a_2, a_3)(b_1, b_2 (c_1)))$ where the symbols 'a,' 'b' and 'c' are *elements* which can also take the role of *functions* within a system of combinatorial interactions based on recursion. As mentioned before, at the core of genetic computation is a recursive engine that calls itself repeatedly; at the heart genetic architecture is an algorithm that constitutes its internal principle. An algorithm is a software program that is more than an instruction set; it should also be understood as a dynamic rational pattern. Software programs may be exceedingly complex but at the level of hardware, only a few operations are repeated over and over again. Programs therefore are orderings of *abstract transformations of abstract states of affairs* and their executions are series of *concrete transformations of concrete states of affairs* that constitutes *histories*. According to Eric Steinhart, "The set of all executions of a program is its 'extension'. As a set of histories, the extension of a program defines its 'nature'. A program is true of a thing exactly to the extent that its nature is co-extensive with the nature of the thing."[35] As opposed to a clockwork or a steam engine, computation is inherently constructive: it is a formal system that enables symbolic structures to build further symbolic structures in a consistent way; these symbolic structures have information content that convey the internal structures of objects.

Given the nature of computation, what is needed in architecture is a theory of the construction of objects in a many-body dynamical setting. It allows for the co-construction of possible worlds based on symbiotic corporation of viral agents within the Sphere of Hypervirtuality: the global network of computing machines that constitute a monadic organism. The infrastructure of the global system is mirrored and nested within each monad or computing system. Complex organization emerges from the interactions and the synthesis of combinatorial activities within such a constructive dynamical system. It is within such a setting that interactions of symbolic strings can be performed in a manner that lead to the construction of complex symbolic strings, which can then be mapped into geometric expression. It is in this sense that a universal computing system or a network of computing engines can be thought of as a cohesive monad. Although emphasis is given to an internal principle, an organization has many *generators* which are either subsets of an axiom or a compilation of axioms which together constitute the logic of an internal principle. In general, a genetic or an evolutionary algorithm is a well-defined mathematical procedure that generates contingency via some chance process and sifts it via some lawlike process.[36] Even though evolutionary algorithms constitute the mathematical underpinnings of Darwinian theory, most of these systems, so far, are incapable of generating specified complexity without having to smuggle in fitness criteria from the outside. Defining fitness is tantamount to bringing in pre-existing notions of specified complexity: it requires the input of intelligence from outside of the system. This may change in the future, however.[37] Wolfram has gone so far to say that the Darwinian approach to natural selection, contrary to accepted wisdom, reduces rather than generates complexity.[38]

At the crux of the problem lies the efficacy and power of genetic codes. Leibniz's Principle of Sufficient Reason provides the basis for comparing two contemporary approaches, which appear, on the surface, to be diametrically opposed to each other: Wolfram's theory of cellular automaton and Chaitin's Algorithmic Information Theory. Leibniz stipulates that for every truth whatsoever, there is a sufficient reason for its being so rather than otherwise. Wolfram's idea of the physical universe as generated by a simple set of cellular automaton rule affirms Leibniz's stipulation. Chaitin, based on the idea of program-sized complexity, suggests that it is theoretically impossible to prove the absolute sufficiency of an algorithm. Since computation is about the ordering of information, Chaitin's formulation of Algorithmic Information Theory establishes close connection between the physics of entropy, which is a probability measure of the amount of disorder or randomness within a system, and information. Chaitin remarked that while his own research deals with software "complexity," Wolfram is concerned with hardware "simplicity."[39]

Echoing Leibniz's Principle of Sufficient Reason,[40] Wolfram remarks that the existence of such a simple program "would validate the idea that human thought can comprehend the construction of the universe."[41] Wolfram's use of cellular automata is perhaps the clearest, purest and most effective in exposing the unadulterated behavior of generative systems: one dimensional cellular automaton. Based on his experiments, Wolfram arrived at the counter-intuitive notion that simple rules can generate complex outcomes, and the physical universe is one such outcome[42]: a totally deterministic system without randomness. Any random phenomenon that we see in nature, according to Wolfram, is merely pseudorandom.[43] In other words, it is the clearest example of the Principle of Sufficient Reason manifested through cellular automaton. The formal sufficiency of reason behind a rule set, Wolfram argues, cannot be given ahead of time due to computational irreducibility:[44] there is no way to predict the outcome of computational processes ahead of time by traditional methods based on mathematical formulation; the only way to find out is to let the system run and then wait to see what the results are.

Gregory Chaitin, on the other hand, formulated the Algorithmic Information Theory[45] based on program-size complexity. In consonant with Wolfram's computational irreducibility, the following set of diagrams illustrates his thesis:

> The basic idea of algorithmic information theory (AIT) is that a scientific theory is a computer program, and the smaller, the more concise the program is, the better the theory!
>
> [...] The central idea of algorithmic information theory is reflected in the belief that the following diagrams all have something fundamental in common. In each case, ask how much information we put in versus how much we get out. And everything is digital, discrete.

39 Gregory Chaitin, "On the Intelligibility of the Universe and the Notions of Simplicity, Complexity and Irreducibility" [online text], <http://www.umcs.maine.edu/~chaitin/bonn.pdf> (2002).
40 The Principle of Sufficient Reason stipulates that for every truth whatever, there is a sufficient reason for its being so rather than otherwise. See section 32 in Nicholas Rescher, *G. W. Leibniz's Monadology* (Pittsburgh: University of Pittsburgh Press, 1991), 116.
41 Wolfram, *A New Kind of Science*, 465.
42 Wolfram, *A New Kind of Science*, 23–41.
43 In addition, Wolfram arrived at the provocative insight that computation will eventually dispense with Calculus once and for all since computational processes, especially cellular automata, can emulate any thing that exists in nature without having to rely on differential equations.
44 Wolfram, *A New Kind of Science*, 737–49.
45 Chaitin, "Leibniz, Information, Math and Physics."
46 Chaitin, "On the Intelligibility of the Universe and the Notions of Simplicity, Complexity, and Irreducibility."
47 Gödel came up with his monumental treatise titled, "The Theory of Incompleteness and Undecidability," in 1931 for his PH.D. thesis. The theory is in response to David Hilbert's call for the completion of the entire field of mathematics once and for all. Alan Turing later provided a constructive interpretation of Gödel's results by placing them on an algorithmic foundation: there are numbers and functions that cannot be computed by any logical machine.
48 Gregory Chaitin, *The Limits of Mathematics* (London: Springer-Verlag, 1998), 1–27.
49 Chaitin, "On the Intelligibility of the Universe."
50 Chaitin, *Exploring Randomness*, 21.
51 Zurek (ed.), *Complexity, Entropy and The Physics of Information*, 137–48.
52 Krzysztof Czarnecki and Ulrich W. Eisenecker, *Generative Programming: Methods, Tools, and Applications* (Upper Saddle River: Addison-Wesley, 2000).

Shannon information theory (communications engineering), noiseless coding:

> encoded
> message → **decoder** → original message

Model of scientific method:

> scientific
> theory → **calculations** → empirical/ experimental data

Algorithmic information theory (AIT), definition of program-size complexity:

> program → **computer** → output

Central dogma of molecular biology:

> DNA → **embryogenesis/ development** → organism

Turing/Post abstract formulation of a Hilbert-style formal axiomatic mathematical theory as a mechanical procedure for systematically deducing all possible consequences from the axioms:

> axioms → **deduction** → theories

Contemporary physicists' efforts to find a Theory of Everything (TOE):

> TOE → **calculations** → universe

Leibniz, *Discourse on Metaphysics*, 1686:

> Ideas → **Mind of God** → the World

In each case the left-hand side is smaller, much smaller, than the right-hand side. In each case, the right-hand side can be constructed (re-constructed) mechanically, or systematically, from the left-hand side. And in each case we want to keep the right-hand side fixed while making the left-hand side as small as possible. Once this is accomplished, we can use the size of the left-hand side as a measure of the simplicity or the complexity of the corresponding right-hand side.[46]

Building on the results of Gödel and Turing's analysis on the logic and limitations of computing programs,[47] Chaitin makes the provocative assertion that the mathematical universe is intrinsically random and infinitely complex. There are mathematical truths that are true for no reason; they are true by accident.[48] Therefore, there is no hope of ever compressing the entire universe of mathematics by an elegant code as Hilbert suggested.[49] He proposed a definition of a random sequence as one that cannot be algorithmically compressed: the shortest description of a random sequence is simply the sequence itself. On the other hand, Chaitin's program-sized complexity enabled him to discover a real number for the Alan Turing's halting probability: Ω, whose numerical value is maximally unknowable.[50] "Ω is the probability that an arbitrary computer program will eventually halt. Ω is computable in a weak sense, but its binary digits or bits are algorithmically random and cannot be distinguished from the result of independent tosses of a fair coin," remarked Chaitin. Ω has no pattern or structure. What is interesting is that Ω shares two apparently irreconcilable properties: "algorithmic randomness" and "computable enumerability." Related to this, Charles Bennett has coined the term *logical depth* to designate the problem of time-complexity involved in computation.[51] Since randomness pervades everywhere in mathematics as well as in nature, there is no choice but to add new axioms to an existing set of axioms within a program in order to generate specified complexity. Even if there exists such a Principle of Sufficient Reason, it is theoretically impossible to prove that a particular program in question is, in fact, the shortest string or the most efficient and optimal one.

Given such a situation, Chaitin's discoveries necessitate the principle of combinatorial expansion on the grounds that no software program is ever complete or absolutely decidable with regard to its potential affects. In other words, a genetic program is an open-ended system that can incorporate new axioms and fitness criteria into its existing matrix of axioms in order to generate specified complexity. Ideally, a generative program should be a self-reproducing and self-organizing system with the capacity to generate and evolve other self-reproducing programs.[52] Furthermore, this principle is reflected yet on another level in the concept of the Adjacent Possible: a multiplicity that grows through viral dissemination and mutation over time. The Adjacent Possible is bidirectional: expansion into the networks of interiority as well as extending into the global matrix outside of a monadic organization or agency. In addition to combinatorial activities and synthesis of symbolic strings within a computing environment, it also applies to the infiltration of nanobots[53] into the body of Man. Everything that is both inside and outside of the body becomes intertwined to form a social organon: an interconnected plenum that forms the world-wide Web of Existence. In other words, genetic architecture is that aspect of process cosmology which involves the generative construction and weaving of *physiovirtual* environments, each of which is a world unto itself. In other words, the principle of combinatorial expansion is essentially about part/whole relationships where the increase in magnitude of the whole is a function of the multiplication of parts.

In this respect, there are two kinds of aggregation with regard to combinatorial expansion: the first is a heap or a grouping with no internal connection; the second is an organized clustering of units having a regulatory network of some kind. An interconnected aggregation of computing monads is a set of entities that continuously regenerates itself by transformation pathways; the matrix that provides connectivity is irreducible. A monadic ensemble can be either one of these two kinds of aggregation or a combination of both. A point to note is that monads are patterns that supervene on other patterns. Each monad is a fractal system and the clustering of monads thereby leads to the emergent patterns of organization. These patterns, in turn, supervene onto other patterns in order to arrive at the autogenetic construction of a monadic ensemble or a possible world: proto-species of genetic architecture. Such a possible world of architecture can be a complex object or building, evolutionary games, interactive virtual environments, etc. The complete overall coordination of monadic agents are so many representations of one single complex world system, each depicting this common universe from its own point of view. Clearly, there is nothing more fundamental to the construction of possible worlds than the principle of the conservation of information.

Given the abstract nature of genetic architecture, it would be helpful to illustrate the concept of genetic space by providing a glimpse into the sublime world of a fiction that has inspired many a theoretician involved with the phenomenon of computation: *The Glass Bead Game* by Herman Hesse. *The Glass Bead Game* can be interpreted as the embodiment of the ambitions of computation. By encapsulating the logic of the universe, which Wolfram is currently attempting to do, it exemplifies the fulfillment of instrumental reason in a monadic *organ*. As a novel, it clearly establishes precedent for the concept of the world understood as a simulacrum, which

---

53 Kurzweil, *The Age of Spiritual Machines*, 139–40.
54 *The Matrix* (1999), directed by Larry Wachowski and Andy Wachowski, is the story of a world generated by computation and the protagonists who try to escape from the hegemonic control of the system. The story however distinguishes the real world from the virtual world.
55 *eXistenZ* (1999) is directed by David Cronenberg. It has a plot that seems to blur "what's real and what's not real?" The world of *eXistenZ* is in the future, and it is about a video game controlled by a joystick that looks something like an internal organ. You interface directly with the game by inserting a umbilical cord like tube into your "bio-port," a small hole in the small of your back. Once plugged in, the game takes you to a virtual reality without leaving the confines of your own room.
56 Hermann Hesse, *The Glass Bead Game: Magister Ludi* (New York: Bantam, 1972), 6.
57 It should be noted that such a monadic system does not necessarily entail a despotic regime built up on a hierarchical system as implied by Deleuze. It is more the case that monadic systems of organization are intrinsically free and self-organize themselves without dependency on a given hierarchical system.
58 David Deutsch, *The Fabric of Reality* (New York: Allen Lane, 1997), 3.
59 Deutsch, *The Fabric of Reality*, 3.
60 Deutsch, *The Fabric of Reality*, 132.
61 Rudy Rucker, *Infinity and the Mind* (Princeton: Princeton University Press, 1995), 194.

can be reproduced ad infinitum. It is therefore not surprising to find resonance of this idea in such sci-fi films as *The Matrix*[54] and *eXistenZ*.[55] Bear in mind that this quotation is interpreted as an extrapolation of a possible world based purely on the metaphysics of computation.

> All the insights, noble thoughts, and works of art that the human race has produced in its creative eras, all that subsequent periods of scholarly study have reduced to concepts and converted into intellectual property—on all this immense body of intellectual values the Glass Bead Game player plays like the organist on an organ. And this organ has attained an almost unimaginable perfection; its manuals and pedals range over the entire intellectual cosmos; its stops are almost beyond number. Theoretically this instrument is capable of reproducing in the Glass the entire intellectual content of the universe.[56]

The Glass Bead Game is a magisterial exposition of a fictional world by Herman Hesse, who was unmistakably influenced by Leibniz among others. The Game, of course, is an idealization of a possible world in which the logic of universal computation is embedded and folded into its matrix of social organization: the embodiment of machinic intelligence into the social organon whose internal organ(s) could model the behavior of itself as well as the entire universe. Leibniz was careful to acknowledge the incompleteness and imperfection of monads with regard to the embodiment of absolute reason. The *organ* in Hesse's novel however is endowed with the capacity to engender the entire intellectual content of the universe. It exemplifies, in fictional form, the fulfillment of the dream of instrumental reason couched in the organic, albeit musical body of a *socius* or social body-with-organs, in contradistinction to Deleuze and Guattari's notion of body-without-organs.[57] *The Glass Bead Game* is an example of a world order that has completely saturated the information content of the entire universe into its system of organization and transformation. The premise of the story lends support to John Wheeler's argument that the world, at a very deep bottom, has an immaterial source and explanation that is information-theoretic in origin. As such, the *organ* in *The Glass Bead Game* is a universal computing system with built-in genetic properties whose theoretical orientation, albeit augmented by Kurt Gödel's Theory of Incompleteness and Undecidability, is central and necessary for a philosophical genetics of architecture.

The basis for such an *organ* is not without theoretical support, at least in principle, from the science of computation: the Church-Turing Hypothesis as mentioned earlier. This hypothesis as proposed by Turing, according to David Deutsch, a physicist working on quantum computation, is "a quasi-mathematical conjecture that all possible formalizations of the intuitive mathematical notion of 'algorithm' or 'computation' are equivalent to each other."[58] This is a non-physical view that has been re-formulated by Deutsch as a physical principle. Correspondingly, Deutsch reframed it as the Church-Turing Principle: "Every finitely realizable physical system can be perfectly simulated by a universal model computing machine operating by finite means."[59] Deutsch further re-interprets the above interpretation by calling it the Turing Principle, which states that, "There exists an abstract universal computer whose repertoire includes any computation that any physically possible object can perform."[60] This is an astonishing proposition that is founded on the paradigm of quantum computation as opposed to the classical model of computation which is based on the Universal Turing Machine. The Turing Principle establishes the equivalence between the universe generated by the laws of physics and the universe engendered by the laws of computation, as implied by the Principle of Computational Equivalence. In other words, the universe is a computational monad. So are the outputs of genetic architecture.

As a compliment to this co-evolutionary construction of possible worlds, the second ambition of genetic architecture deals primarily with sublimation. Sublimation is a high level notion that has, at this stage, no clearly defined relation to computation. Monadology of genetic architecture seeks to accomplish this by sublating factual as well as counterfactual states of affairs into a phenomenology of non-objective being. In other words, it is the condensation and the figuration of anonymity which points to the sublime threshold as represented by the noumenal *it* of existence. Sublimation, therefore, is about the overcoming of manifest identity contained within an object/species by further disclosing the *other of itself* within itself. Another way of understanding the paradox of the *other* within the *same* is from the principle of genetic formation of sets[61] in set theory: no set is a member of itself. The universe of set theory, like architecture, is a *Many* that does not allow itself to be thought of as a *One*. Architecture, seen in this light, is conceived as a *quasi-transcendental* notion, an indefinable singularity that is in excess of the set of all possible worlds. As a global concept that signifies an inconsistent multiplicity, *architecture* is pure excess to every specific appropriation of architecture. Every instance of architecture is already implicated in a quasi-transcendental appropriation of the *other*, understood as the Absolute, which, paradoxically, is co-extensive with the *same*. The other is pure excess within the Absolute, which, in principle, cannot be totalized by the same. The reality of nonobjective being situated at the sublime threshold is arrived at by means of a negative dialectics that progressively engage in the transformation of affects produced at every stage of developmental organization. In so doing, the logic of sublimation enables architecture to overcome semiological references to identity, objects and meaning.

> the plane of
> content → **sublimation** → the plane of
> nonobjective
> being

Finally, in the attempt to develop a new metaphysics of genetic architecture, we should not lose sight of the fact that what was originally a metaphysical desire to attain omniscience through abstract reasoning has now acquired the garment of the Emperor's new clothing: the instrument of geo-political power and globalization through genetic computation. Computation can be considered genetic to the extent that it is based on the logic of recursion and recursive functions are self-referential procedures that call themselves over and over again, thereby engaging in the propagation of hereditary characteristics inherent within a system. Let it suffice for the moment to say that computation is not only the medium but the power behind the message. The Nietzschean will to power has become synonymous with the power of computation, which can also be translated as the computation of power. Computation therefore is not merely another technological innovation but ultimately a consequence of the metaphysical desire to uncover the Code of Life, and along with it, the invention and the construction of abstract machines that could engender possible worlds. Given this orientation, computation is now increasingly looked upon as the reality engine channeling out that most abstract of immaterial substances—information—into the world. Such an outlook, as provocative and controversial it may seem, points to the undeniable fact that information occupies a far more fundamental position than the other two parameters of physical existence: energy and matter.

Correspondingly, value will be defined in terms of information. Since the concept of value is intimately connected to the source and sustenance of power, it is being defined not in terms of quantity but instead in

---

62 Kevin Kelly, "God is the Machine," *Wired*, 10:12 (December 2002), 180–5.
63 Frank Tipler, *The Physics of Immortality: Modern Cosmology, God and Resurrection* (New York: Doubleday, 1995). See also David Deutsch's interpretation in *The Fabric of Reality*, 347–59.
64 See Jorge Luis Borges, "The Library of Babel," in Donald A. Yates and James E. Irby (eds.), *Labyrinths: Selected Stories and Other Writings* (New York: New Directions, 1964), 51–8.
65 Kurzweil, *The Age of Spiritual Machines*, 119.
66 Friedrich Wilhelm Joseph von Schelling, *The Ages of the World* (Albany: SUNY Press, 2000), 4.
67 Kauffman Stuart, *At Home in the Universe: The Search for Laws of Self-organization and Complexity* (New York: Oxford University Press, 1995). See also Mark Buchanan, *Nexus: Small Worlds and the Groundbreaking Science of Networks* (New York: W. W. Norton, 2002).
68 Howard Bloom, *The Global Brain: The Evolution of Mass Mind from the Big Bang to the 21st Century* (New York: John Wiley & Sons, 2000). Even though Bloom was concerned with the general interconnected nature of knowledge, culture and history from pre-historic times to the present without emphasizing the mediation of networks enabled by computation, what is significant here is the interconnected nature of a global organic intelligence embedded within the virtual matrix, of which the Internet is an early precursor.
69 Kurzweil, *The Age of Spiritual Machines*.

terms of "logical depth" and "algorithmic complexity." In other words, value is a function of how difficult it is to generate the information that is deemed desirable. In this context, nothing is more desirable than the Code of Life, which could at least give the illusion of determination and control of infinite life: the potential fulfillment of the dream for immortality itself. As such, one of the latent ambitions of capitalism is to put into motion the value of Information Capital as that which gives sustenance to the capitalist system of axiomatization. The new locus of power therefore resides within the code. In the midst of the resurgence of what could be considered a logocentric world view, now increasingly understood as an algorithmic conception of reality, all signs are now pointing toward a renewed metaphysics where the plane of immanence is being re-defined in terms of the domain of the computable. Correspondingly, the transcendent dimension of alterity beyond being is that which is beyond the pale of computation: the radically non-computable as demarcated by the principles of computation. Given the power and promise of computation, some have gone so far as to literally identify God with the Machine, albeit a universal computing system, as Kevin Kelly did,[62] which is profoundly misplaced. Be that as it may, this lends further support to the fact that at the heart of computation lie the yearnings of a metaphysical desire,[63] which is inexhaustible.

As mentioned before, one of the ambitions of computation is in establishing conditions of possibility for the embodiment of information simultaneously both inside and outside of our bodies by virtue of being interconnected to the matrix of the social organism at large. Consequently, it would require us to re-conceptualize architecture from one that depends predominantly on the construction of hardware as container and modulator of events and activities to that of intelligent network systems which carry as well as engender bionic information recursively. In this regard, the provocative but insightful question raised by Borges, "Is the book in the library or the library on the book?"[64] calls into question the possible inclusion of one in the other in a manner that defies common sense if not wisdom. Notwithstanding the metaphysical and theological implications inherent in Borges's interrogation, the question discloses the fundamental problem of representation: the ancient antinomy that exists between theory and practice, on the one hand, and the Cartesian split of the mind and body, on the other, is now couched in the form of the difference between software and hardware, and the privileged position that software has over hardware. Finally, after having ushered in the dawn of a new era by computation, speculations such as those once entertained by medieval monks concerning the number of angels that can dance on the tip of a pin no longer appear to be as strange, bizarre and esoteric as we once thought, for the simple reason that all the information content contained in all the books that have ever existed since time immemorial could be compressed, in principle, onto the size of a thing that is at least as small as the tip of a pin.[65]

Unlike preceding attempts at overcoming this dichotomy, which tend to privilege materialist/phenomenological conceptions of the body and its mobility, the reality of simulation promises to eliminate this dilemma with a vanishing mediator by blurring the boundary between the two with feed-back and feed-forward mechanisms, thereby weaving all the nested interconnections of both domains to form a singularity, a virtual monad or an incomplete totality. Lurking within these symbiotic correspondences is the age-old metaphysical desire that drives the phenomenon of computation from its very inception: the search for the *code* that would contain a maximum of possible affects or possible worlds. Lest we forget Schelling's precaution that "the world is not a riddle whose solution could not be given with a single word,"[66] a premonition that is finally confirmed in Chaitin's Algorithmic Information Theory, the physical and logical limits of computation will nonetheless temper and constrain this insatiable desire for omnipotence and total communion with the Absolute. Despite the limitations, and lest we also forget that we are all travelers in the nocturnal abyss of the intergalactic space on a miniscule planet we called Earth, this ambition is now being fueled by the spell of instrumental reason which has taken on the scope of a tragic euphoria, or tragic transport, that seems limitless with regard to its possibilities.

In the meantime, as computing machines are weaving the global network of communication and exchange into an inexorable matrix via the Internet, capitalism is being transformed into a demiurgic system that is destined to become virtually intelligent and alive. Kauffman and others have shown that when the connectivity of nodes within a network reaches a critical threshold or singularity, it takes on an emergent behavior that is akin to an organic entity.[67] Such a global application of neural network systems derived from biocomputation will invariably lead to what at the present seems unthinkable: the emergence of a global brain[68] or intelligence with an internal will to being:[69] a self-organizing and self-synthesizing monad. Consequently, capitalism is in the process of being sublimated from a restricted economy to a general economy predicated on the transvaluation of all values into the value of Information Capital.

The Principle of Computational Equivalence implies that the physical universe is a simulacrum engendered by computation. With the eventual proliferation of bionic beings and proto-species of genetic architecture populating the Sphere of Hypervirtuality, where the Internet will eventually be transformed into a self-synthesizing and self-organizing organ, virtual artifacts and ghostly phantoms will co-evolve with human societies in a symbiotic cooperation of freedoms. Long after she has departed from this material world, her DNA patented, encrypted and transcribed into digital archives, Madonna—the material girl—will most likely continue to sing and dance, at various scalable regimes of organization and transmutation, with all her provocative passion and seductive gestures augmented by her perpetually renewed sense of immortality. This phenomenal performance, however, will neither take place solely in the corporeal library of Borges nor represented in the incorporeal pages of the book of simulacra, but somewhere in-between—a phantasmagoric chamber of bionic proclivities that would be indistinguishable, if not undecidable, from the global Sphere of Hypervirtuality: an *interconnected but discrete plenum*,[70] which will be propelled, sustained and modulated by the evolutionary dynamism of a demiurgic capitalism that is poised to flourish, with all the vicissitudes that accompany a fantasmatic dramatology of a brave new world, on the horizon of expectation. Welcome to monadology of genetic architecture on the Turing Dimension.[71]

---

[70] Sander Olson, "Ray Kurzweil: Technologies of *The Matrix* Could Soon Be Real" [online text], <http://www.geek.com/news/geeknews/2003Mar/bch20030305018948.htm> (2003).

[71] Karl S. Chu, "The Turing Dimension," in Frédéric Migayrou and Marie-Ange Brayer (eds.), *ArchiLab: Radical Experiments in Global Architecture* (London: Thames & Hudson, 2001), 490–4.

Fig. 5 *Outside-in*, collage by Meta XY

Sylvia Lavin

What Color is it Now?

To walk into most architecture schools today is to be overwhelmed by the color blue: cathode ray blue in particular. Its omnipresence is not just because of the many ubiquitous monitors actually aglow, but because the aura of the monitor is preserved at all costs. Even when the monitors themselves are a distant memory, banished as an irritant to final reviews (too new, too slow, too prone to crashes, too few) their color stains the proliferating 11x17 prints that paper the walls. Various Photoshop filters transform each sheet into a pixel in a collectively fabricated virtual image of blueness that is saturating architecture with an atmospheric perspective. This haze at once reflects the popularity of blue in the modern period but equally reveals that in its effects, cathode ray blue works more as an impression than a pigment, more to produce mood than meaning. None of the many available analytiques of color, which range from the psycho-physiological to the phenomenological, from the semiological to the classification of color as a social practice, are adequate for understanding these effects: the impulse to codification fails to suggest how and why cathode ray bluism is not a color but is the very affect of contemporary architecture.[1]

While architecture has always had color, coloration today is both uniquely determinant and oddly vague. That color can form a common bond between such polar opposites as the "War on Terror's" chromometer of anxiety and Karim Rashid's lavender dish soap demonstrates that color is urgently everywhere, yet apparently—even appealingly—insignificant. While Bush's "Red Alert" and Rashid's cucumber liquid couldn't be more different as colors, each is part of a system that is both totally dependent on color and in which color is increasingly detachable from signification. Rashid's color

[1] There is a massive literature on the history and theory of color that is beyond the scope of this essay. Nevertheless, it is essential to acknowledge Mark Wigley, *White Walls, Designer Dresses: The Fashioning of Modern Architecture* (Cambridge, Mass.: MIT Press, 1995). In this most important recent addition to architectural discourse on color, Wigley insists that we recognize whiteness in modern architecture as a color. My argument relies on the repressed ideational importance of color to modernism that Wigley so convincingly presents to further explore the manifest affective role of color in contemporary design practice.

Fig. 1 Panelite™ PE/RX-blue, 2003

Fig. 2 Karim Rashid, Method™ Home Dish Soap, 2003: Mint, Cucumber, Mandarin and Lavender

Fig. 3 U.S. Department of Homeland Security, Homeland Security Advisory System, 2001

2 Sylvia Lavin, "The Temporary Contemporary," in Noah Biklen et al. (eds.), *Perspecta 34: Temporary Architecture* (Cambridge, Mass.: MIT Press, 2003), 128–38.
3 See Benjamin Bucloch, "The Primary Colors for the Second Time: A Paradigm of Repetition of the Neo-Avant Garde," in *October*, 37 (Summer 1986), 41–52.

of "minty freshness" does not rise to the occasion of a meaning, and Bush's palette of fear barely compensates, with a surprising lack of irony, for the fact that real information about terrorism is the one thing that nobody has. Although more present today than in the past, color can no longer be invoked in its historical role as a perfect and universal semiological system, as it was by heraldry, traffic lights, and the Pompidou center.

Yet if the meaning of color is less significant today than in the past, its effects have become more significant than ever. And one of the effects produced by color is the effect of today. Color is a key producer of what Baudelaire described as presentness, of what I have called contemporaneity, todayness, or the now.[2] For Baudelaire, the key indicators of presentness were the mannerisms of everyday life and fashion in particular. The more extreme the expression of these qualities—and both the "War on Terror" chromometer and Rashid's soaps are extreme uses of color in their way—the more presentness was invoked. Thus, for Baudelaire, the prostitute was an exceptionally contemporary figure because she was exaggeratedly mannered and overdressed. Now, color has taken on the valence of the present. Color, for example, was the first indication that even *The New York Times* was to devote more and more attention to capturing "today:" soon to follow the introduction of color images was a proliferation of sections including "Circuits," "House and Home," and "Sunday Styles"—all devoted to versions of Baudelaire's idea of presentness. Bold type announcing the day's breaking news no longer suffices in the quest for presentness, not even in daily newspapers, which, with their early editions and late editions and extra editions, once were the timekeepers of currency. Now, today is as much a color as it is anything else.

Modernity is full of blueness: from the primary blue of De Stijl to International Klein Blue to the Beatles and the Blue Meanies. My concern here is not a history of color or its genealogy or even the overdetermined compulsion to repeat a particular palette.[3] Rather, my concern is for the effectivity of color and the relation between color understood as a field of effects and color understood as a producer of contemporaneity. Cathode ray blue makes contemporary an historic mixing of architecture, technology and effect. High modernism relied on this mixture most notably in relation to glass (which, as an aside, it generally registered as an absence of material and especially of color). But modernist effects were rarely meant to produce the prostitute's presentness, her enticingly contemporary duration, or her tempting flicker of provisionality. Rather, modernist

Fig. 4 Yves Klein, *Untitled Blue Monochrome (IKB)*, detail, 1959

effects were intended to produce truth and transcendence, which for the most part explicitly required the elimination of color of all kinds. In the Crystal Palace, perhaps the most historic locus of the architecture of technological effects, color, and blue in particular, literally evaporated. As a visitor described it, "If we let our gaze travel downward it encounters the blue-painted lattice girders… they are interrupted by a dazzling band of light… which dissolves into a distant background where all materiality is blended into the atmosphere."[4]

The Crystal Palace was enormously "effective," a tour de force of dazzlement, and it certainly manifested the zeitgeist, but it did not effect contemporaneity.[5] Zeitgeist was understood as a mysterious yet reliable force that permeated everything with the aura of modernity. Although some things were thought to have more zeitgeist than others, it was nevertheless a unifying principle. All things had zeitgeist at least to some degree, and it was a moral imperative to reveal the zeitgeist when it was hidden. The Crystal Palace was a special effects machine, but what it effected was revelation, truth, and an atmosphere that invoked the constant present of nature. The Crystal Palace sought to produce a *Deus* from its *machina*, the eternally unfolding spirit of modernity itself.

Contemporaneity, by contrast, has no depth in which to hide things and is itself not hidden. It lies on the surface of things, and that is why today it is precisely the bluish haze of the Crystal Palace that is of interest. It is the blue of the girders, the blues in the glass, the blues in the atmosphere that form a continuous surface of the many different material conditions that together produce the effects of the Crystal Palace. And this atmospheric perspective, from a contemporary point of view, is manifestly constructed rather than natural, temporary and fluctuating as a condition, and provisional in its claims. On the one hand, blue itself, because of its association with modernity, technology and atmospherics, is a critical factor in these effects.[6] But on the other hand, these effects are not reducible to the color blue since any hue (although some would do it better than others) could theoretically be made to coagulate multiple materials and surfaces. A contemporary reading of color must emphasize this combination of associative and affective operations and must resist the pull toward making an updated color code, since all such codes have been different versions of the same quest for true color. Architecture can no longer be true blue, nor can it invoke the sparkle producing fairies that were said to be the cause of the Crystal Palace's effects during the 19th century. Instead, color must be reframed as a material instrument of effects.

---

4 Sigfried Giedion, *Space, Time and Architecture: The Growth of a New Tradition* (Cambridge, Mass.: Harvard University Press, 1967), 252.

5 This aspect of the Crystal Palace has generally been discussed in the context of the technological sublime.

6 On the particular identification of blue with modernity, see Michel Pastoureau, *Blue: The History of a Color* (Princeton: Princeton University Press, 2001).

7 On the concept of cunning, see Jeffrey Kipnis, "The Cunning of Cosmetics," in *El Croquis*, 84 (1997), 22–9.

8 On the history of polychrome in architecture, see David Van Zanten, *Architectural Polychromy of the 1830's* (New York: Garland, 1977). For an analysis of modernity's repression of color in architecture, see Wigley, *White Walls*.

9 For an extensive bibliography on color in art, see John Gage, *Color and Culture: Practice and Meaning from Antiquity to Abstraction* (London: Thames and Hudson, 1993).

10 For a brilliant analysis of this debate, see Jacqueline Lichtenstein, *Couleur éloquente: Rhétorique et peinture à l'age classique* (Paris: Flammarion, 1989).

11 I first developed aspects of this argument for a conference on drawing: "Ways of World Making," organized by Jeffrey Kipnis at the Wexner Center for the Arts in January 2001.

Fig. 5 Thomas Nelson & Sons, *Nave and Crystal Fountain – Crystal Place*, 1867

Color can emphasize how design performs and make design sensible to contemporaneity. Indeed, a contemporary observer of a current nexus of technology, architecture, and effect might write, "If we let our gaze travel along the not quite default blue ribbon of Diller & Scofidio's Eyebeam Atelier winning competition entry, its notional specificity oscillates with an affective sensibility that together produce the atmosphere of contemporaneity." On the one hand, Diller & Scofidio rely on a set of cultural associations between blue and currency, and perhaps above all on the fact that cathode ray blue and its chromatic progeny are manifestly technological colors. While the cathode ray is not itself new, the current proliferation of its blueness is aligned with the computer screen and thus supposedly with technologies of more recent vintage. On the other hand, the modes of cathode ray blue production, from TV monitors, to luminol testing, to Adobe Photoshop, rely on indirection and on the effect of luminescence, rather than on the (false) indexicality of blue. Neither the particular color, which is notational and thus arbitrary, nor its cultural associations, which are ideological and specific, produce contemporaneity. Rather, it is the oscillation itself that effects presentness. Diller & Scofidio's Eyebeam vibrates with both the signs and the swagger of Baudelaire's hyper-present and ever-cunning prostitute.[7]

Color offers architecture the means to act as the binder of a sensibility of the now. Ironically, understanding the relation between color and contemporaneity requires working through rather old, indeed ultimately antique discourses on color. Despite architecture's long and well-known problem with polychromy, the discipline has in fact succeeded in largely ignoring the issue of color as such.[8] But in the art historical and rhetorical discourses, the relation between color and affect and thus the relation between color and sensibility have been elaborately debated.[9] And it is through a consideration of the relationship between color and affect that an understanding of the role of color and the sensibility of presentness can be developed.

The primary art historical formulations on the subject took place in the context of the debate between *colore* and *disegno*, a conflict over whether painting should be organized around meaning or affect.[10] This dialogue began while art theory and architecture were still intermingled and the disciplines not fully differentiated, yet architecture seems to have studiously avoided engaging the question. In fact, whether buildings have been colored or not, the discipline of architecture conceives of itself in relation to design, which is to say in relation to the logic of the drawing, of the line and of the code, all of which are historically and discursively pitted against color. Architecture so sided with *disegno*, so aligned its discipline with the regulations of design, that the possibilities of *colore* barely inflect the field, even when its buildings have been significantly colored. But the long tradition in architecture of subjugating color to meaning does not preclude the possibility of developing for architecture a less "meaningful" but more effective sense of what it can do in and through color. It only makes the embrace of the sensibility of color more new.

When we speak in English of the primary activity of the architect, we speak of the act of design. And when we do so, we tend to forget that the first definition of the Italian word *disegno* (from which the English "design" derives) is "drawing," the noun. While it is possible to use the verb *disegnare* in Italian to refer to a larger and more conceptual domain than the physical act of making a drawing, generally Italian uses the term "to project" where we "design," and uses "design" when we "draw." This is an oblique piece of evidence but it nevertheless suggests architecture's deep investment in drawing as well as the discipline's basic alignment with the conceptual apparatus of *disegno*. Although architectural drawings have always been made—Egyptian and Greek clay tablets depicting temple plans and urban organizations exist—drawing did not become a constituent part of the discipline until the invention of perspective.[11] In fact, the development of architectural drawing coincides with the birth of perspective in the Renaissance, and ever since that coincidence, perspective and architectural drawing have been seen as inexorably linked and indeed

Fig. 6 Titian, *Portrait of a Man*, c. 1510

as virtually synonymous. From the moment that Brunelleschi made his gadget depicting the Florence Baptistery with such thrilling verisimilitude that it made people gasp, perspective as drawing began to determine the parameters of what the architectural drawing could be in the future and, by extension, what architecture could be. Most importantly in this context, by hitching its future to design, architecture became colorless; in fact it became against color.

The over-determination of architecture by design is characterized by two trajectories that were coterminous for Brunelleschi but that progressively diverged as the uses of drawing proliferated. The world that was captured by Brunelleschi's device was both real and ideal. On the one hand, Brunelleschi's drawing subjected the real world of Florence to the strictures of mathematical regularity, and thereby inaugurated a certain form of the pursuit of realism in architectural drawing. On the other hand, the same mathematical regulation permitted the drawing to be received not as a representation of reality but as the manifestation of an idea conceived, however divinely, by the architect. It was this ideality that was used to authorize architecture's entry into the world of the liberal arts and thus to equate the architect with the visionary artist.

The provocation of this conflict internal to the origins of perspective relatively quickly gave way to isolating the two trajectories. Thus, the intellectual nature of perspective gave architecture the capacity to envision new worlds with the authority of the ideal in the technical sense of the term and this idealism undergirds much visionary drawing, whether rendered in perspective or not. At the same time, perspective forever yoked architectural drawing to the rules of mathematical accountability, and thus the drawing became, as importantly as it became the vehicle of imagining, the legal instrument of the profession. The whole apparatus of working drawings, construction documents, and so forth, even though not drawn in perspective (in fact usually perspective is explicitly forbidden), can be traced to the faith in perspective's capacity to constitute the real. Perspective is in that sense a perfect example of an ideological instrument, because it offers itself as a means of representation that is so complete that it spans the spectrum from the real to the ideal and can even engulf drawings not explicitly rendered in perspective.

As the development of digital drawing seems to be continuing the will to perspective by dividing itself between the professional labors of CAD on the one hand, and the voluptuous fantasies of Maya on the other, it might be productive to think that the collapse of *disegno*

12 Franciscus Junius, *De pictura veterum* (Amsterdam, 1634); trans. as *The Painting of the Ancients* (London, 1638).
13 Sylvia Lavin, *Quatremère de Quincy and the Invention of a Modern Language of Architecture* (Cambridge, Mass.: MIT Press, 1992).

14 On the cloud and perspective, see Hubert Damisch, *A Theory of Cloud: Toward a History of Painting*, trans. Janet Lloyd (Stanford: Stanford University Press, 2002); and Hubert Damisch, *The Origin of Perspective*, trans. John Goodman (Cambridge, Mass.: MIT Press, 1994).

into perspective was not the only possibility for architecture. And for the sake of my argument, let us equate this opposition with the limitation of architecture not to black and white but to green—the code color for "in the nature of materials" and thus for reality—and pink—the proverbial rose-colored glasses. In painting, by contrast, the question of drawing was framed quite differently. There, drawing, or rather *disegno*, was not dominated by controversies between the real and the ideal but rather was concerned with drawing as a mode of imitation, of which there were many kinds. *Disegno* was primarily differentiated from *colore*, which was understood as a technique of affect rather than of mimesis. From the 16th century on, as the relative merits of Michelangelo and Titian, Poussin and Reubens, Ingres and Delacroix were debated, *disegno* and *colore* were compared as modes of pictorialism. *Disegno* was linked primarily to a representational and narrative-driven paradigm, whether hyperrealistic or super-idealized, while *colore* was associated with the world of affect and sensation. It was thus color that was said to make "painting seem alive" and that could "commonly ravish our sight with the bewitching pleasure of delightsome and stately ornaments."[12] While it was precisely the intoxicating quality of color that led theorists to be afraid of its charms, as they feared a seductive temptress, one wonders what might have happened to architecture had it succumbed to the temptation and allowed its "design" to engage the antithetical pleasures of depiction not authorized by perspective.

For its own purposes—entry into the liberal arts, establishing a base in professionalism, guaranteeing the permanent monumentality of its built output—architecture remained largely contained within what we could call intra-drawing issues, leaving matters of color to the side. The theoretical underpinnings of the late 18th and 19th century architectural discussions about polychromy, for example, stem primarily from a concern with the representation of antiquity: for Quatremère de Quincy, color is a sign of classicism, and in that sense Quatremère is concerned with color as a component of imitation rather than with its affective role.[13] And while arguments about the polychrome condition of ancient statues of Athena would seem quite distinct from the use of color by Le Corbusier, for example, the theoretical underpinnings are related. For Le Corbusier, color is used as a notational system and as a means of formal codification. Modernism in general used color to clarify and elucidate both the formal and technical aspects of its kit of parts. It can therefore be argued that both Quatremère and Le Corbusier used color for representational rather than affective purposes and thus produced colored "designs" rather than designed in color.

Because architecture pressed even color into the service of *disegno*, imagining architectural design in color is, by disciplinary definition, a transformational proposition. *Colore* can as a result be used to reconfigure the origins of architectural "design" in perspective and to loosen the grip of *disegno* on the discipline. More specifically, color can be made to emerge as having increasingly become a tool in the production of architectural presentness. Color, for architecture, is the equivalent of the cloud for Brunelleschi: the key to the code that is itself not codified.[14] While the cloud is understood to have made Brunelleschi's perspective contraption appear to capture reality, the cloud also permitted perspective to capture contemporaneity: as the cloud passed over the mirror, the movement of time was registered. Through that animation, the image of the Baptistery could not belong to the timelessness of art but nor, since it was an image, did it return to the simple temporariness of the real. Instead, the animate cloud gave presentness to the Baptistery.

Temporality, and thus the form of presentness that generally goes by the name "modernity," first became of concern in relation to color when artists sought to distinguish historical or visionary events from current events. *Grisaille*, a monochrome palette of greys, was used during the Renaissance to signify the pastness of antiquity while polychromy was reserved specifically for the depiction of the present. While *grisaille* thus used color to indicate a form of contemporaneity, it did so by symbolizing modernity not by considering the use of color in relation to effects, whether of contemporaneity or of other kinds. On the other hand, time and color, even monochromy in particular, came together in what was perhaps the first attempt to identify architecture as a

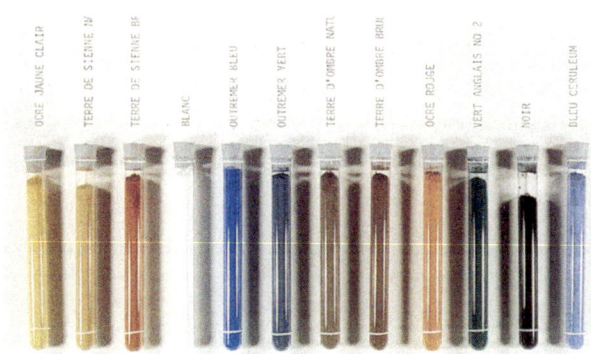

Fig. 7 The initial products of Le Corbusier's color palette, from the collection of Arthur Rüegg

Fig. 8 Julien Guadet, *Un hospice dans les alpes*, section of chapel, 1864

15 Heinrich Wölfflin, *Renaissance and Baroque*, trans. Kathrin Simon (Ithaca: Cornell University Press, 1964), 34–6.

field of special effects. For Wölfflin, most notably, the chiaroscuro that was generated by the dynamics of light moving across a variegated surface gave Baroque architecture its "painterly" as opposed to linear quality. Painterliness was thus characterized for Wölfflin by atmospheric effects rather than by modes of imitation and was intensified by animation rather than by chromatic polemics: the dynamics of a small range of tones were more effective in his view than extreme variations in color, or mere colorfulness. "Vitality," "incidental effects," "broken surfaces," and "atmospherics" rather than a specific palette were the techniques he identified as being able to engage architecture in the speculative and effective terrain of *colore*.[15]

The discussion of Wölfflin could profitably be extended to such topics as Boullée and the architecture of shadows, but it is perhaps more productively troublesome to consider the more normative types of Ecole de Beaux-Arts drawings. From the *envois* to the *concours*, the Ecole was the context for some of architecture's most colorful moments. Despite this apparent vibrancy, one of the Ecole's main preoccupations was codification of all kinds, and the use of color was no exception. The traditional Beaux-Arts drawing relies on the color of antiquity, the color of building materials, the color of drawing pigments, and yet in keeping with the Ecole's injunction against the illusionism of perspective, the drawings eschew the temptations of *colore* through their very colorfulness. The only exception is in the treatment of *poché*, one of the greatly undervalued even if incidental inventions of the Ecole: *poché*, a terrain that is neither real nor ideal but virtual, was generally rendered by atmospheric washes. Like the cloud, the fleshy pinks of *poché* seem to come out of the conceptual blue to give these drawings neither verisimilitude nor idealism but rather effect.

Color is not merely a palette or a pigment. When engaged with the territory of effects, color is today's prostitute. The more effective the color the more able it is to convey the presentness that was once her purview, and the way color is used rather than which color is selected is of the most consequence when you are a streetwalker. Color becomes contemporary as it moves away from indexicality, symbolism, codification, and ideation because this move away from signification allows color to register traces of a much more complex series of historically specific conditions and forces: those of technology, sensibility, capital, taste, materiality, manufacture. In other words, when working through the field of effects, color can do more to engage contemporaneity than when it works through the structures of meaning.

Fig. 9 Dominic Crinson, Jafleur wallpaper pattern, 2003

Two distinct techniques in the use of color are proving to be most effective in giving freshness to architecture today: what I will call Wallpaper Color and the Hyperpainterly. Wallpaper Color works through extreme scale, environmental saturation, and the hypergraphical. Sometimes incorporating pattern, Wallpaper Color is always flat and superficial. It is not in the nature of materials, but rather acts as a varnish suffusing architecture with ambient effects. Wallpaper Color immerses the viewer in the atmospheres of dimensional chromaticism but does not give up notational clarity altogether. This inherent contradiction can be seen in the mid-century collaborative project by André Bruyere and Fernand Leger, the Village Polychrome, which used Wallpaper Color to elide architecture with painting and landscape even though paint charmingly codified notions of formal propriety. The use of supergraphics in postmodern architecture by figures such as Charles Moore and Venturi, Scott Brown employed Wallpaper Color to deliberately disobey formal codification while retaining an emphasis on legible signage. These examples under-

Fig. 10 Fernand Léger and André Bruyère, Project for Village Polychrome, Biot, France, perspective for a villa with three workshops, 1953

Fig. 11 Barbara Stauffacher / MLTW Architects, Supergraphics for Sea Ranch Athletic Club, Sea Ranch, California, 1963–6

score one of the most important effects of Wallpaper Color, the movement of architecture away from the design of space and toward the production of zones or environmental moods.

The Hyperpainterly focuses on the surface effects of animate color in the production of contemporaneity. Like Wallpaper Color, the Hyperpainterly works through extreme scale and environmental saturation. But unlike Wallpaper Color, the Hyperpainterly does not rely on graphic or uniform color. Instead, the Hyperpainterly is a flavor and additive that gives vibe to the surface through patterned shifts and tonal variations of color. If Wallpaper Color manages notational codification, the Hyperpainterly manages affective codification, avoiding a too obvious and limiting reliance on associations between color and feelings. Herzog and De Meuron use the Hyperpainterly to produce what could be called the atmospherics of impressionism, for example. But Herzog and De Meuron eliminate the sentimental and naturalistic associations of the impressionist color palette to retain only its cloudy indeterminate quality. A collabora-

Fig. 12 Herzog & De Meuron, Institute for Hospital Pharmaceuticals, Rossettiareal Basel, Switzerland, 1995–8

tive proposal for the Caltrans Headquarters submitted by Rem Koolhaas and John Baldessari transfigures Los Angeles into a mechanically mobilized form of pointillism: individual trucks painted in different colors acted like semi-autonomous pixels, colonizing the city each day in a variegated pattern with their mood-inducing colors. Frank Gehry's work is perhaps the most directly linked to Wölfflin's notion of coloristic painterliness as the titanium of Bilbao or Disney Concert Hall exaggerates the monochromatic chiaroscuro effects of Wölfflin's Baroque architecture. The iridescent pink of the Canadian Winery gives this research even greater intensity. The Hyperpainterly puts architecture in the mood of today.

Wölfflin might have waxed rhapsodic about cathode ray blue, but not because it proved architecture's modernity by technological affiliation. That CRB can be used nostalgically should not be overlooked. The many efforts to use monitors simply because they refer to the culture of TV and thus must be new are a depressing reminder of how difficult it is to engage the mood of today and how much easier it is to slip on the look of yesterday's modernism. Rather, Wölfflin's emphasis on the animated chromaticism of chiaroscuro provides an unsuspected link between Brunelleschi's cloud, the haze of the Crystal Palace and architecture's current bluish luminosity, and opens for color new terrain within the field. As I am framing them, these examples constitute a reading of color that provokes disciplinary transformation, intermingles technological and atmospheric perspectives, and relies on animate visualities to create a

[16] See Reyner Banham, "The Great Gizmo," in *A Critic Writes: Essays by Reyner Banham* (Berkeley: University of California Press, 1996), 109–18.

Fig. 13 Rem Koolhaas and John Baldessari, Caltrans District 7 Headquarters competition entry, Los Angeles, California, 2001

mood that registers presentness. When cathode ray blue is understood thus to suffuse architecture—as do Wallpaper Color and the Hyperpainterly—the color becomes instrumental in making architecture an agent of contemporaneity.

Colore may always have belonged properly to the field of effects rather than to the field of signification, but it has not always had the effect of the now. In the modern period, the period that invented the problem of the now, color has become increasingly embedded in issues of technology, mass culture and the global market. Many lament the age of authentic color when architecture was always in some sense green—in the nature of materials (and their various colors). But the redness of brick or the whiteness of whitewash, while perhaps full of eternal values of some kind, have none of the timeliness of avocado Formica or the Pantone chip *du jour*. Color's mediation by color experts, industrial trends, and the mechanisms of designed obsolescence urgently engage the now. By virtue of the material, technical and cultural emulsion through which it operates, color is the most implicated phenomenon in architecture's current *effectiveness*. And like Banham's gizmo, while some colors may require significant investment to produce, generally speaking their deployment is still seen as cheap, below the radar, stealthy even.[16] In that sense, effects have taken over as techniques in the production of political and cultural change once accorded to technology. Effects are the new instruments of power, and one of their most significant powers is the production of the sensibility that is today.

Jonathan Massey

New Necessities

Fig. 1 Claude Bragdon, photographed in 1897

1 For an overview of Bragdon's career, see Blake McKelvey, "Claude F. Bragdon, Architect, Stage Designer, and Mystic," *Rochester History*, 29:4 (October 1967), 1–20.

Architectural ornament played a key role in the representation of power within sixteenth- and seventeenth-century court societies. Ornamental magnificence displayed the position of its bearer along a scale that ran from commoner to king. In absolutist France, this representational system was codified through the architectural doctrine of *convenance*, usually translated as "appropriateness" or decorum. Treatise writers such as Philibert de l'Orme, Pierre Lemuet, and Michel de Fremin instructed architects on the proper use of the orders and other marks of architectural distinction to accurately represent the client's status. The design code of *convenance* was one of many ways that aristocratic society regulated self-presentation. Informal behavioral codes were buttressed by legislative codes: sumptuary laws regulated ornamentation in dress, dishware, coaches, and domestic furnishings such as cabinets and draperies.

Architectural modernism emerged from the breakdown of this doctrine of *convenance*. Beginning with eighteenth-century "revolutionary architects" such as Etienne-Louis Boullée and Claude-Nicolas Ledoux, new criteria such as utility, convenience, economy, and functional expressiveness began to displace the representation of social status through gradations of magnificence. These criteria, which reflected the values of a rising middle class, eventually became normative for twentieth-century architectural modernism. One index of this transformation is the changing status of ornament: a central *ancien régime* technique of adequation between social structure and architectural representation, ornament became by the turn of the twentieth century a vestige of outmoded economies to be eliminated or sublimated into forms suitable to disinterested aesthetic appreciation.

Modernist Aesthetic Discipline

It is customary to understand this transformation as a process of autonomization wherein architecture sought out laws of expression internal to the discipline rather than given by social and political structure. Such an interpretation misrecognizes the nature of power in liberal modernity, however. This essay draws on the work of Jürgen Habermas and Michel Foucault to suggest that architectural modernism did not so much make architecture independent of social structure as develop new techniques of regulation appropriate to liberal society. Through a case study of the system of "projective ornament" developed in 1915 by American architect Claude Bragdon, it argues that early-twentieth-century modernisms reconstituted *convenance* based on new social ideals and modalities of power. Bragdon's modernist ornament aimed to persuade individuals to conform voluntarily to practices in line with what Bragdon saw as social necessities. An examination of his use of a sumptuary rhetoric to regulate architectural ornament reveals parallels to the strategies that more influential modernists such as Hermann Muthesius and Adolf Loos used to eliminate or sublimate ornament. Examining these stances toward ornament as instances of sumptuary regulation suggests that modernist architectural discourse reflects both the rise of the public sphere as an arena of political deliberation and the operation of the modality of power that Foucault characterized as "discipline."

Projective ornament

Claude Bragdon (1866–1946: Fig. 1) was a Rochester, New York, architect and critic who contributed to the development of modernism by developing a distinctive mode of progressive architecture.[1] Bragdon's career spanned many fields, from architecture and theater design to writing, publishing, and the graphic arts. In the 1890s, after apprenticeships with the Buffalo firm Green and Wicks and New York architect Bruce Price, Bragdon opened a practice in Rochester, where he was active in Arts and Crafts circles. His designs for posters and magazine covers distinguished him as a graphic artist, and his journalism soon gained him a reputation as one of America's foremost architecture critics. As a supportive critic, then as editor of the republished *Kindergarten Chats*, he was a leading interpreter of Louis Sullivan to professional and general audiences from the turn of the century into the 1930s. Bragdon developed professional and personal ties not only to Sullivan, but also to Frank Lloyd Wright, Ralph Adams Cram, Bertram Goodhue, Irving K. Pond, and Lewis Mumford. As one of Rochester's leading architects, he built many houses and significant public buildings, including police stations, a YMCA, a Chamber of Commerce, and a new terminal for the New York Central Rail Road. At the end of World War I, Bragdon closed his architectural practice to pursue writing and stage design. Moving to New York, he established himself as a practitioner of the modernist staging technique known as the New Stagecraft. Bragdon's theater work extended into the 1930s, and his writing continued up to his death in 1946. His major books on architecture are *The Beautiful Necessity* (1910), *Projective Ornament* (1915), *Architecture and Democracy* (1918), and *The Frozen Fountain* (1932). In addition to these, Bragdon published many books and articles on mysticism, Theosophy, the new woman, and the fourth dimension of space.

Beyond advocating modernism in his architectural criticism, magazine pieces, and books, Bragdon created in 1915 a modernist ornamental canon he called "projective ornament"[2] (Figs. 2 and 3). He developed projective ornament as a comprehensive response to modernity, a "new generalization" reflecting developments in science (theorization of n-dimensional space); technology (exploitation of invisible wavelengths for representation and communication); and society (the vastly enlarged scale of social organization in an expanding industrial economy). By folding these and other factors into his system of ornament, Bragdon sought to create a single ornamental language suitable to the full range of modern programs and contexts.

Bragdon based projective ornament on his conviction that the key to modernity lay in recognition of the fourth dimension of space. One of the great accomplishments of nineteenth-century mathematics had been G. B. F. Riemann's 1854 reconceptualization of space as a manifold that could possess a variable and potentially infinite number of dimensions.[3] Riemann's theorization of n-dimensional space challenged the authority of Euclidean geometry and laid the groundwork for the later discoveries of Hermann Minkowski and Albert Einstein. At the same time, his work inspired a large parascientific literature that posited a fourth spatial

2 Bragdon's system of ornament is presented in Claude Bragdon, *Projective Ornament* (Rochester: Manas Press, 1915). For a detailed examination of projective ornament, see Jonathan Massey, "Architecture and Involution: Claude Bragdon's Projective Ornament 1915–1946" (PH.D. dissertation, Princeton University, 2001).

3 Riemann's June 10, 1854 lecture "Über die Hypothesen, welche der Geometrie zu Grunde liegen," which first presented his theory of n-dimensional space, was published in *Abhandlungen der Königlichen Gesellschaft der Wissenschaften zu Göttingen*, 13 (1868). It appeared in an English translation by William Kingdon Clifford as "On the Hypotheses which Lie at the Bases of Geometry," *Nature*, 8 (1873), 14–17, 36–7. For an overview of changing theorizations of space, see Max Jammer, *Concepts of Space: The History of Theories of Space in Physics*, 3rd edn. (New York: Dover, 1994).

4 The best account of the discourse of the fourth dimension of space and its significance for modern art is Linda Dalrymple Henderson, *The Fourth Dimension and Non-Euclidean Geometry in Modern Art* (Princeton: Princeton University Press, 1983; forthcoming in an expanded second edition).

Tetrahedrons: Tesseracts: Icositetrahedroid

Pentahedroids: Tesseracts

dimension as the explanation for occult phenomena and mystical experiences. Popularized as a discourse of the fourth dimension of space, Riemann's discovery became a vehicle for social critiques and spiritual visions, including those of Theosophy, the "spiritual science" that had emerged in the 1870s as one of the many new religions of the era.[4]

Bragdon was a leading American advocate of Theosophy, and he based his approach to virtually every issue on Theosophical doctrine, even if he frequently reinterpreted it creatively to engage other thought systems and cultural domains. During the 1910s and 1920s, he promulgated a spiritualized conception of the fourth dimension that echoed nineteenth-century Protestant visions of the City of God. Building on Theosophical doctrine, he claimed that the fourth dimension was a physically real space within which humanity would realize millennial dreams of harmony and transcendence. Bragdon created projective ornament in large part to disseminate this "higher space theory." Many of his techniques for generating projective ornament patterns consisted of projections and "unfoldings" of four-dimensional geometries—ways of translating them into more familiar three- and two-dimensional spaces.

By introducing viewers to Bragdon's spiritualized concept of "higher space," projective ornament would advance humanity toward its transcendent future.

Projective ornament combined three kinds of patterns. One was based on what Bragdon called "magic lines in magic squares." These are the lines created by tracing in ascending numerical order the numbers in a "magic square," an arrangement of sequential numbers into a square, each column, row, and diagonal of which sums to the same number. Tracing the "magic lines" of different magic squares, Bragdon created patterns he then used as templates for ornamental figures and decorative fields (Fig. 4). A second basis for the patterns of projective ornament was graphic projection of the Platonic solids. Bragdon produced two-dimensional projections of these three-dimensional solids in two ways: by "unfolding" them onto a plane, much as one might flatten a cardboard box by cutting it at certain vertices and unfolding it; and through axonometric projection (Fig. 5). The third basis for the patterns of Bragdon's system of ornament was an extrapolation of the second: simulated axonometric projections of "hypersolids," the four-dimensional correlatives to the Platonic solids. Four-dimensional "polyhedroids" such as

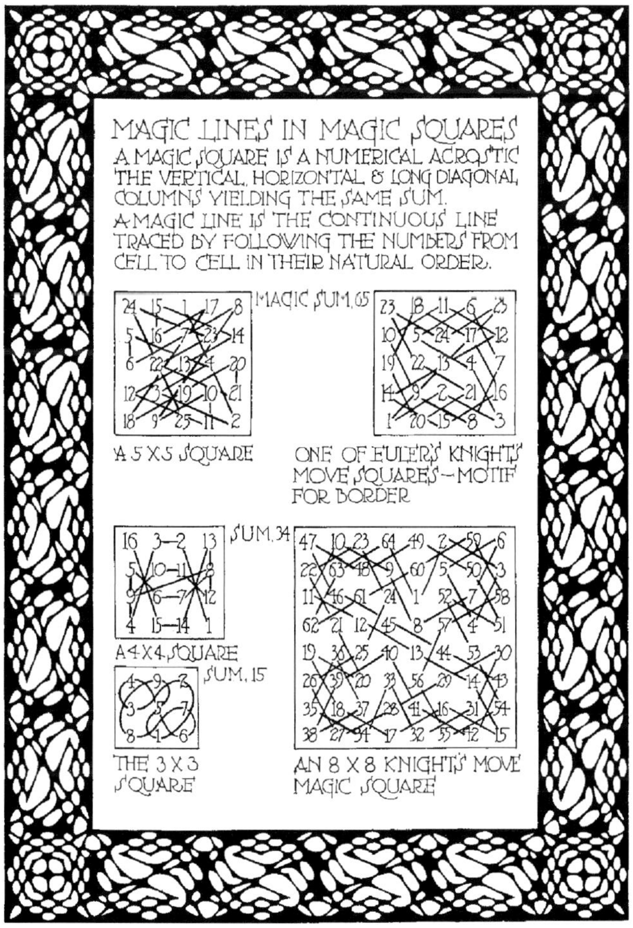

Fig. 2 (left) Claude Bragdon's projective ornament designs
Fig. 3 (center) Projective ornament patterns applied to interior paneling, trim, and textiles
Fig. 4 (right) One of Bragdon's explanations of the process for generating magic lines from magic squares, framed by a projective ornament pattern based on magic lines

the tesseract, the four-dimensional extrapolation of the cube, could be described mathematically and geometrically, but they could not be built or seen. To make these sublime shapes visible, after a fashion, Bragdon followed conventions of mathematical representation and extrapolated from conventional axonometric projection. He projected the additional dimension along a fourth axis, thereby representing the "fourth perpendicular"—the hypothetical direction in which four-dimensional spatial extension was to be found. This technique generated graphic figures that simulated axonometric views of four-dimensional hypersolids (Fig. 6).

By selectively accentuating and repeating elements of these different patterns and projections, Bragdon turned them into ornament (Fig. 7). He hoped that exposure to projective ornament would habituate viewers to seeing space as a series of dimensional translations: from the two-dimensional space of the picture plane, to the three-dimensional space of bodies and buildings, to the four-dimensional space of democratic and Theosophical communion. This dimensional sequence reflected Bragdon's familiarity with Plato's cave allegory. Projective ornament was intended to help people confined to the "cave" of three-dimensional space—

Fig. 5 (left) Three-dimensional polyhedrons, projected and unfolded into two dimensions
Fig. 6 (center) Selected four-dimensional polyhedroids, projected into two dimensions and translated into ornament
Fig. 7 (right) Projections and magic lines translated into ornament through selective manipulation, repetition, and filling

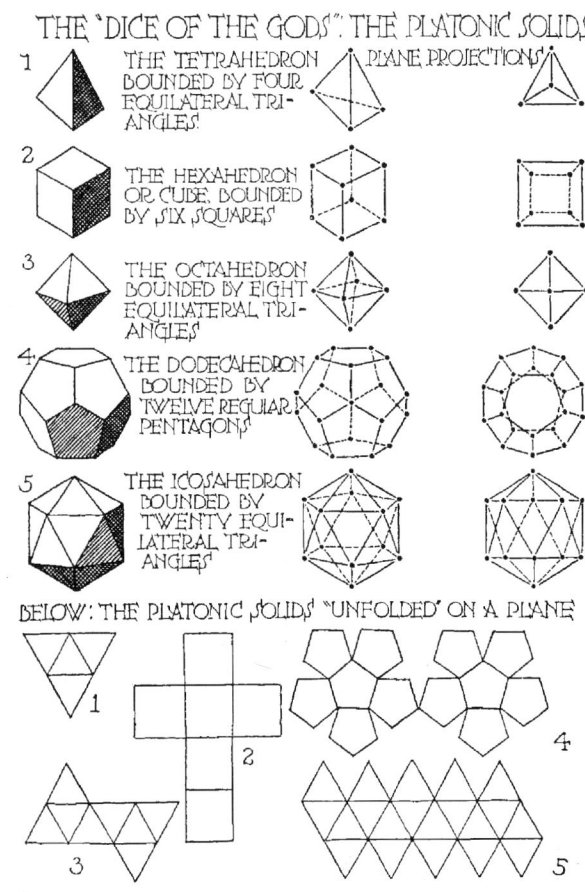

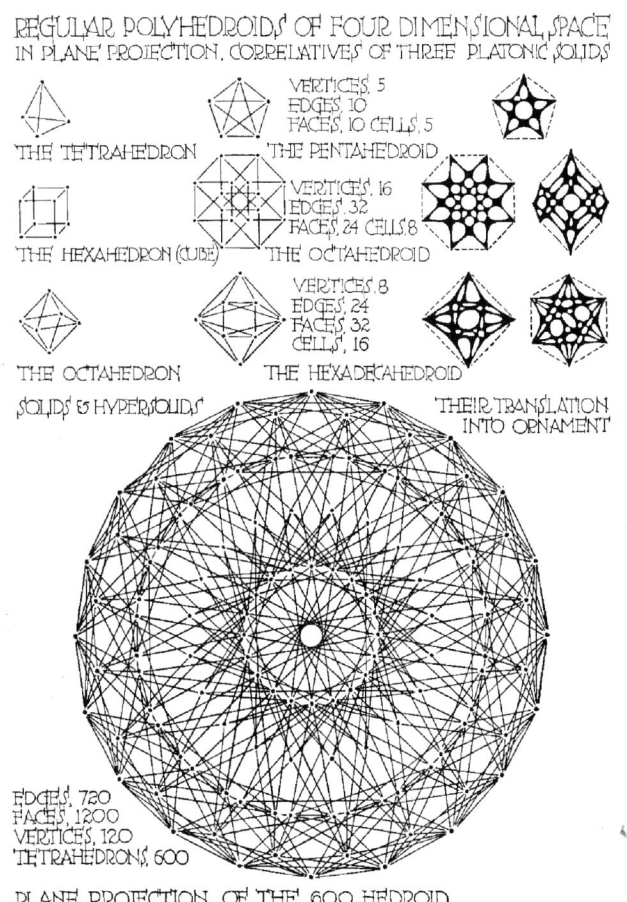

prisoners of phenomenality—recognize their deception and break out into the lightful realm of ideas: the fourth dimension.

Within this mystical framework, projective ornament addressed the more mundane problems of Progressive Era American society. One of Bragdon's primary aims in creating a universal ornament was to integrate a society divided by distinctions of class, language, and national origin. Discomfited by the class antagonisms of industrial society, Bragdon criticized liberal modernity for being excessively individualistic and materialistic. He took these distinctions to jeopardize social coherence and democratic political traditions. In response, he enlisted architecture in the construction of a common culture. Approaching architectural progressivism in communicative terms, Bragdon envisioned projective ornament as a universal architectural "form-language" to replace the ornament of the historical architectural styles. In its project of simplifying and abstracting ornament to broaden its intelligibility, projective ornament was an architectural analogue to language reforms such as Basic English, Simplified Spelling, and Esperanto. Universal ornament would turn architecture from a technique of differentiation and distinction into one of integration.

Abstraction played a fundamental role in Bragdon's architectural reform project. Ornament marked stylistic difference by deploying a specialized vocabulary of forms associated with a particular period and place, and often by representing regionally specific foliage. By abstracting ornament into geometric patterns and regular arabesques, Bragdon sought to make it universally legible, requiring neither special linguistic competency nor culturally particular knowledge. He resorted to geometry not only to visualize dimensional sequences but also because, as a formal manifestation of mathematics, it was universally intelligible to human reason.

The geometric basis of projective ornament also marked Bragdon's search for an impersonal mode of architectural expression. The individualism of his mentor Sullivan and rival Wright struck Bragdon as a misguided expression of the individualist ethos of liberal modernity. Bragdon saw the rigorous objectivity of geometric form as a more suitable basis than individual *virtù* for an egalitarian and assimilationist architectural mode. Geometry and regularity provided design strategies that were "objective" rather than "subjective." Bragdon developed techniques to express this "objectivity" in graphic terms: crisp black-and-white linework

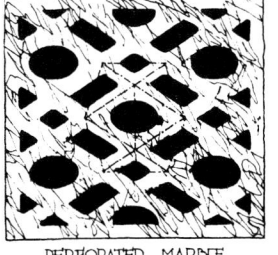 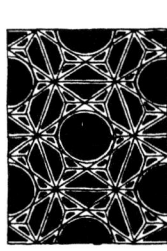 

THE CHARACTER OF ORNAMENT DETERMINED BY THE NATURE OF THE MATERIAL EACH OF THESE DESIGNS HAS THE SAME MATHEMATICAL "WEB" THE ICOSAHEDRON

Fig. 8 A projective ornament pattern based on the icosahedron, interpreted in three different materials: perforated marble, leaded glass, and brick

gave his drawings an impersonal cast. The linear forms of projective ornament could be translated into building materials such as brick, tile, and textile without the personalizing effect of handicraft (Fig. 8).

Bragdon's impersonal universalism was based on his sense that industrial capitalism was at odds with the realization of democratic social ideals. The specialization and differentiation at the core of industrial process seemed antithetical to democratic egalitarianism, as well as to the viability of the shared public discourse necessary for deliberative self-government. But Bragdon's universalism also manifested his commitment to Theosophy. By fusing the cosmology of ancient Eastern sacred texts such as the Upanishads and the Bhagavad-Gita with the discoveries of modern Western science, Theosophy proposed to reintegrate science with religion and create a worldwide "brotherhood of man." The impersonality and universalism of projective ornament reflected Bragdon's Theosophical convictions.

Projective ornament reflected on the problem of consensus in democratic society by constructing an allegory of voluntary conformity. Bragdon's ornamental designs were structured by the tension between geometric crystals and sinuous arabesques, which reflected a political allegory rooted in nineteenth-century architectural theory and practice. In *The Seven Lamps of Architecture* (1849) and elsewhere, English critic John Ruskin had opposed the social consequences of industrialization by exalting the carved ornament of medieval churches for its representational naturalism, which reflected the carver's apprenticeship in imitating the perfection of God's creation, and its handicraft imperfections, which registered the integration of design and execution prior to the division of labor. Ruskin had made this interpretation the basis of an allegory wherein Gothic naturalism reflected the political freedom enjoyed within Christian humanist society, while the stylized geometry of Islamic architecture represented its antipode: "Oriental despotism" (Fig. 9).

This allegory provided Bragdon with a way of engaging the political context of Progressive Era America. The problem of balancing individual liberty against collective needs, a permanent dilemma of democratic society, was a particular focus of Progressive attempts to reform the city and its governance. *Architectural Record* editor and *New Republic* founder Herbert Croly spoke for many reformers when he argued in 1909 that "a more highly socialized democracy is the only practical substitute on the part of convinced democrats for an excessively individualized democracy."[5]

Croly and many other progressives saw the "socializa-

---

5 Herbert Croly, *The Promise of American Life* (New York: Macmillan, 1909).
6 Bragdon, *Projective Ornament*, 63–4.

Fig. 9 *The Vine, Free and in Service*: one of Ruskin's representations of the contrast between freehand naturalism and geometric stylization, which he associated with the supposed contrast between Christian freedom and Islamic "despotism." John Ruskin, *The Stones of Venice* (London, 1851–3)

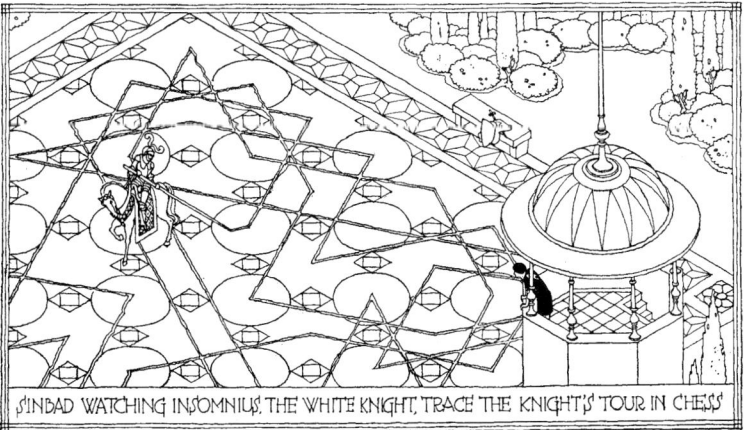

Fig. 10 In this allegorical drawing, one of a series depicting the education of the architect in Bragdon's 1932 treatise *The Frozen Fountain*, the architect's drawing hand (here allegorized by the knight's stylus/lance) follows a pattern already established by the invariant geometric order of a notionally Islamic garden. See also the pattern derived from the 3 x 3 square in the lower left-hand corner of Fig. 2

tion" of the polity in largely pragmatic terms: as a matter of shifting control over governance from the electorate toward technocratic commissions, boards, and bureaucracies. Bragdon, by contrast, saw the socialization of democracy in cultural, subjective, and spiritual terms. For him, it consisted of encouraging citizens to transcend ego and merge with the *demos* or "spirit of the people." Bragdon's ornament reflected this political goal. Reversing the poles of Ruskin's architectural ethic, Bragdon attempted through ornament to socialize unruly individualism and transform industrial capitalist fragmentation into democratic brotherhood. Accordingly, the patterns of Bragdon's ornament disciplined the free-growing arabesque to the rigorous objectivity of the geometric crystal. These designs of curved lines yielding to geometric frames figured the reconciliation of individual will to the demands of social order. They symbolized Bragdon's application of a dose of "Oriental despotism" to a society in which, he felt, Christian humanism had been co-opted by laissez-faire capitalism (Fig. 10). Bragdon sought to endow his ornament with the beauty of "exquisite acquiescence": individual will yielding to the demands of social necessity.[6] Projective ornament was charged with the rhetorical task of persuading willful individuals to yield gracefully to the demands of social order.

Bragdon's term for this graceful yielding was "Beautiful Necessity." It was a phrase he adopted from Ralph Waldo Emerson's 1860 essay "Fate," an analysis of the opposition between a materialist discourse of determinist heredity and the notion of individual free will. Fate and free will, Emerson claimed, are always in tension; their antinomy defines the parameters of human action. Emerson attempted to harmonize opposing points of view that he felt emphasized too strongly either the freedom of individual action from the heritage of the past or the limitation imposed by genetic and cultural heritage. The main thrust of his essay, however, was against the materialist discourse of social Darwinism. Emerson concluded "Fate" with a sermonic exhortation to sacralize the "Beautiful Necessity" that human freedom is not at odds with natural law:

> Let us build altars to the Beautiful Necessity, which secures that all is made of one piece; that plaintiff and defendant, friend and enemy, animal and planet, food and eater, are of one kind…
> Let us build to the Beautiful Necessity…which rudely or softly educates [man] to the perception that Law rules throughout existence, a Law which is not intelligent but intelligence—not personal nor impersonal—it disdains words and passes under-

standing; it dissolves persons; it vivifies nature; yet solicits the pure in heart to draw on all its omnipotence.[7]

In Emerson's figure of the "Beautiful Necessity," Bragdon saw a harmonious reconciliation of the polar opposition between individual and society that dominated Progressive Era politics and culture. Whereas Emerson's main objective had been to reassert the power of human action and thought in the face of a social discourse that used science to legitimize social hierarchy, Bragdon's aim was to regulate what he took to be the excessive individualism of his era by exalting the principle of free will yielding to the constraints of an egalitarian social order. The title of Bragdon's 1910 treatise evoked his assertion that "Art is at all times subject to the *Beautiful Necessity* of proclaiming the *world order*."[8] Projective ornament was an "altar" of the kind Emerson had exhorted his readers to build: it sacralized the mathematical laws that for Bragdon characterized the natural "world order." The magic line figure that graced the dust jacket of the book (a knight's tour pattern) gave formal expression to Bragdon's ethos of "exquisite acquiescence" (Fig. 11). Contrasted with the freehand naturalism of Ruskin's nature studies, it emphatically posited that—for the twentieth century, at least—study of nature would reveal an impersonal order to which all things must conform.

Fig. 11 The dust jacket of the fourth edition of *The Beautiful Necessity*, published by Alfred A. Knopf in 1939

Sumptuary regulation

We can recognize in Bragdon's concept of "Beautiful Necessity" a modern instance of the perennial Western use of rhetorics of need to regulate desire. Bragdon's ethos of "exquisite acquiescence," had precursors in classical, Renaissance, and early modern traditions of regulating luxury in service of political goals. Within the Western tradition, sumptuary codes since antiquity have regulated consumption to maintain particular aspects of social order.[9] Sumptuary laws regulate luxury by identifying some desires as excessive and thus illegitimate. In the name of the public good, they regulate expressions of private desire.

Sumptuary determinations of the distinction between socializing and sociopathic desires have been shaped by broader discourse about luxury that has drawn and redrawn distinctions between needs and desires. In *The Idea of Luxury*, Christopher Berry reviews some of the changing frameworks within which luxury has been conceptualized and regulated. The regulation of consumption in ancient Rome, he explains, operated in the name of republican polity: "Luxury was a political question because it signified the presence of the poten-

---

7 Ralph Waldo Emerson, *Essays and Lectures* (New York: Literary Classics of the United States, 1983), 967–8.
8 Claude Bragdon, *The Beautiful Necessity* (New York: Knopf, 1922), 9.
9 For a survey of Western sumptuary regulation, see Alan Hunt, *Governance of the Consuming Passions: A History of Sumptuary Law* (New York: St. Martin's Press, 1996).
10 Christopher J. Berry, *The Idea of Luxury: A Conceptual and Historical Investigation* (Cambridge: Cambridge University Press, 1994), 63.

11 In addition to Berry, see Diane Owen Hughes, "Sumptuary Law and Social Relations in Renaissance Italy," in John Bossy (ed.), *Disputes and Settlements: Law and Human Relations in the West* (Cambridge: Cambridge University Press, 1983), 69–100; and Catherine Kovesi Killerby, *Sumptuary Law in Italy, 1200–1500* (Oxford: Clarendon, 2002).
12 Quoted in Daniel L. Purdy, *The Tyranny of Elegance: Consumer Cosmopolitanism in the Era of Goethe* (Baltimore: Johns Hopkins University Press, 1998), 99.
13 Quoted in Hughes, "Sumptuary Law and Social Relations in Renaissance Italy," 77.

tially disruptive power of human desire, a power which must be policed."[10] Within this republican ethos, desires stimulated by luxury were seen to subvert good social order because they emphasized the pursuit of selfish pleasures that could jeopardize commitment to the public good. In Medieval Europe luxury was generally viewed within a Christian ethics that conflated it with lechery: terms such as the French *luxure* and the Latin *luxuria* signified both luxury and sexual lasciviousness. Renaissance attitudes toward luxury revived elements of the Roman tradition and commingled them with medieval Christian views. The Renaissance civic humanist tradition saw luxury as a corruption of resources that should instead support the independence a citizen needed to act virtuously in the polis.[11]

Attitudes toward luxury found expression in sumptuary laws that at various times regulated what individuals could wear and eat, what kinds of furnishings they could possess, and how they could conduct funerals and weddings. The quantitative high point of sumptuary law occurred in the absolutist societies of the sixteenth and seventeenth centuries. These regimes greatly increased the number and degree of sumptuary distinctions in order to clarify individuals' standing within a minutely graded prestige economy. Absolutist sumptuary laws sought, in the words of one preamble, to preserve the visible differences in rank "which God and all propriety requires, without which also the political harmony and the commonwealth of continued well-being would no longer exist"[12] (Fig. 12).

In modernity the political implications of luxury were redefined in terms more often economic than moral. The centralization of political authority that had begun under the princely courts of the sixteenth and seventeenth centuries continued with the rise of large, imperial nation-states. Mercantilist economists and social thinkers such as Adam Smith elaborated a political economy of luxury based on criteria of economic well-being and national prosperity within the context of global trade. The emergent mercantile ethos can be discerned in the language of sumptuary codes from maritime trading cities such as Venice and Genoa beginning as early as the fourteenth century. Preambles to sumptuary codes, which frequently attempted to spell out the rationale for legislation, began to include managing investment among their stated motivations. A Venetian law of 1360, for instance, proclaimed, "Our state has become less strong because money that should navigate and multiply... lies dead, converted into vanities."[13]

Later mercantile doctrines increasingly assessed luxury consumption within a framework of economic

Fig. 12 Clothing as an index to social position: depictions of the attire proper to individuals of different social stations in late-17th-century Nuremberg

well-being. Because it stimulated consumption, luxury could be justified if it promoted a positive balance of trade, which mercantilists considered to yield positive social well-being. In other words, a new discourse reconstituted the distinction between necessity and luxury in terms based on the new political criterion of national political economy.

As the transition from caste to class society gained momentum, regulation of consumption was liberalized in parallel with political liberalization. With some exceptions, such as restrictions on drug consumption, modern sumptuary regulation is typically conducted through economic incentives. Complex and precisely calibrated tax codes encourage some kinds of consumption and discourage others by assessing them at different rates.

Necessary luxury

Architectural ornament enjoyed a relative freedom from this tradition of legislative regulation. Medieval and Renaissance sumptuary codes typically focused on the ornamentation of clothing and on the ways a family observed weddings and funerals, occasions that had a public character in an age of large families acting in a corporate manner within small cities and city-states. Absolutist codes concerned not only dress but also the trim and decoration of carriages, as well as furnishings and draperies.[14]

In *ancien régime* society, architectural representation was regulated less through legal codes than by professional codes such as the doctrine of *convenance*. *Convenance* was a body of principles for ensuring that the design of houses conformed to the ranked display of prestige through which power in court society was articulated.[15] The classical orders, linked to degrees of ostentation and sumptuousness, marked social distinction within a system of representation based on gradations of prestige. *Hôtels particuliers* were built and designed with the client's particular family or "house" in mind, and architects made each hotel's form and ornamentation conform to the social status of its occupants. This system not only expressed the distinction between those of noble and common birth; it also articulated gradations within the nobility. Nobles of the sword or the robe, of royal or of merely aristocratic rank, the *Encyclopédie* notes, are figures "who, not holding the same rank in society, should have habitations fitted out so as to mark the superiority or inferiority of the different orders of the state"[16] (Fig. 13). The authors of the *Encyclopédie* wrote of aristocratic *hôtels particuliers* that "the character of their decoration requires a

---

14 See Johanna B. Moyer, "Sumptuary Law in Ancien Régime France, 1229–1806" (PH.D. dissertation, Syracuse University, 1996).
15 See Norbert Elias, *The Court Society*, trans. Edmund Jephcott (New York: Pantheon, 1983 [1969]); Werner Szambien, *Symétrie, gout, caractère: Théorie et terminologie de l'architecture à l'âge classique, 1550–1800* (Paris: Picard, 1986); and Peter Kohane and Michael Hill, "The Eclipse of a Commonplace Idea: Decorum in Architectural Theory," in *Architectural Research Quarterly*, 5:1 (2001): 63–77.
16 Quoted in Elias, *The Court Society*, 59.
17 Quoted in Elias, *The Court Society*, 58.
18 Max Weber, *Wirtschaft und Gesellschaft* (Tübingen: J. C. B. Mohr, 1922), 750; quoted in Elias, *The Court Society*, 38.
19 Elias, *The Court Society*, 63.
20 Jürgen Habermas, *The Structural Transformation of the Public Sphere: An Inquiry into a Category of Bourgeois Society*, trans. Thomas Burger and Frederick Lawrence (Cambridge: Polity Press; Cambridge, Mass.: MIT Press, 1989 [1962]), 27.
21 Immanuel Kant, "What Is Enlightenment?" (1784), in Kant, *Foundations of the Metaphysics of Morals and What is Enlightenment?*, trans. Lewis White Beck (New York: Bobbs-Merrill, 1959), 85–92: 87.
22 Roger Chartier, *The Cultural Origins of the French Revolution*, trans. Lydia G. Cochrane (Durham and London: Duke University Press, 1991), 26.
23 Sylvia Lavin, "Re Reading the Encyclopedia: Architectural Theory and the Formation of the Public in Late-Eighteenth-Century France," *Journal of the Society of Architectural Historians*, 53:2 (1994): 184–92.

beauty fitting the birth and rank of the persons who have them built; nevertheless they should never exhibit the magnificence reserved for the palaces of kings."[17]

The principles of *convenance* remind us that in *ancien régime* society luxury consumption was itself a form of necessity. Court society was a prestige economy in which the display of wealth was a crucial part of maintaining status. According to Max Weber, "'Luxury' in the sense of a rejection of the purposive-rational orientation of consumption is, to the feudal ruling class, not something 'superfluous,' but one of the means of its social self-assertion."[18] This changed in capitalist modernity, as decisions of expenditure and investment came to be based on their impact on capital accumulation. The bourgeois ethos of economic rationality advocated keeping consumption below income level so that surpluses could be invested to generate increased future income. It stimulated a canon of behavior quite different from that of the prestige economy of court society, in which expenditures for display were considered necessary even when they exceeded incomes and so led to financial ruin. As Norbert Elias explains, "In a society in which every outward manifestation of a person has special significance, expenditure on prestige and display is for the upper classes a necessity which they cannot avoid."[19] For a society of necessary luxury, architectural ostentation is not superfluous but essential.

Despite its consonance with other forms of *ancien régime* sumptuary regulation, *convenance* was not a legal code such as those that regulated ornament in dress, dishware, coaches, furnishings, and other cultural domains. It was instead a professional ideology, a code of decorum formulated by architects and knowledgeable amateurs, such as the Abbé Cordemoy, and disseminated through treatises and other written commentaries. In this sense, *convenance* was a liminal regulatory device between absolutist and republican societies. Although its principle of graduated social representation through controlled magnificence was typical of court society, its form and mode of operation were characteristic of postrevolutionary "professional-bourgeois" society. In operating through the public sphere, using published discourse as its mode of codification and public opinion as its mode of enforcement, the doctrine of *convenance* reflected the rise of the bourgeois public sphere. It helped to inaugurate the modern "publicity of representation" that Jürgen Habermas has identified as a primary form of political decision-making in liberal societies.

As Habermas argued in his 1962 book *The Structural Transformation of the Public Sphere*, liberal modernity is characterized by the emergence of the public sphere as a middle-class arena for political participation through discussion and debate, conducted in such new institutions as salons, cafés, and clubs, as well as newspapers and other print publications. As a domain distinct from both the court and the larger populace, the public sphere afforded members of the middle class an arena within which to formulate shared opinion about matters of common concern. In this new realm of "private persons come together as a public," participants' status was bracketed, so opinions were assessed more for their reasoning than for the prestige of their advocates.[20] In this way, the bourgeois public sphere provided an autonomous venue for the "public use of one's private reason" that Immanuel Kant identified as the primary technique of enlightenment.[21] The consensus formed by public sphere discourse—public opinion—acquired authority as enlightened thought, a category that in theory represented the consensus humanity at large would reach if it had the means and opportunity for collective reasoning.[22]

The rise of the public sphere as a domain of ideas autonomous from social hierarchy contributed to the emergence of new criteria for judging works of art and architecture. Among the subjects of debate in salons, coffee houses, and periodicals were paintings, sculptures, and buildings. Architecture criticism, like criticism of art and literature, represented the application to architecture of the new standards of rational evaluation.[23] Rather than being judged for its consonance with religious faith or scientific truth, art began to be judged

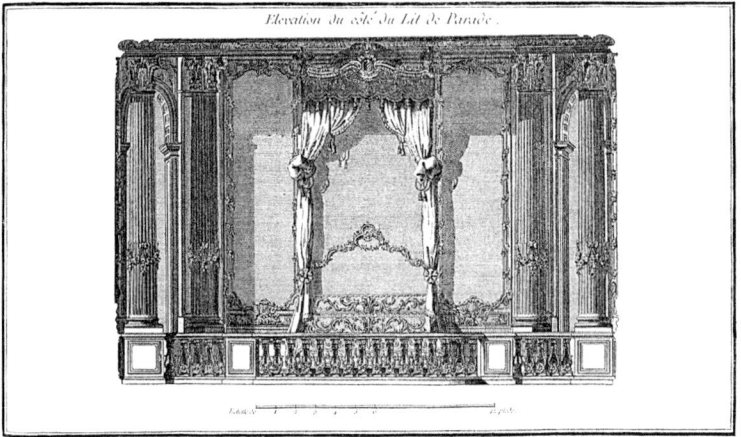

Fig. 13 Ornamental magnificence as an index of social position: section of the royal audience chamber at the Palais Royal

in aesthetic terms—that is to say, for its evocation of disinterested pleasure in the observer. The disinterest through which Kant characterized the emergent practice of aesthetic judgment was one aspect of the bracketing of status in the bourgeois public sphere. The autonomy of art—its judgment and creation according to independent, internal standards—was linked to the political, economic, and moral autonomy of the middle class.

The decline of sumptuary law was part of this process of autonomization. The rise of a new political and economic rationality eroded the social importance of luxury. As capitalist economic rationality became normative, prestige expenditure gave way to investment in productive enterprise.

Architectural modernism emerged out of this rewriting of the representational contract between architecture and society, in part by creating a new framework for the use of architectural ornament. The beginnings of modernist reduction of ornament are usually traced to the shift in French architectural theory from the discourse of *convenance* to that of *caractère*.[24] Some of the designs of Ledoux, Boullée, Lequeu, and others began to replace *convenance* with new modes of representation and communication that reflected the emergent liberal society. Such "revolutionary" architecture minimized ornament to cultivate such new representational techniques as Ledoux's *architecture parlante* and Boullée's experimental sublimes (Fig. 14). Over the course of a century and more, aristocratic and bourgeois modes of architectural representation competed with one another and with alternative approaches: a project such as Charles Garnier's Paris Opera vividly demonstrates the continuing emphasis on magnificence even in buildings that celebrated the expanding bourgeoisie. Early-twentieth-century modernism can be seen as the hegemony of the values that emerged during the earlier Revolutionary moment. In pursuit of architectural autonomy, mainstream modernism eliminated or sublimated ornament by treating the building as a work of art to be appreciated in aesthetic terms rather than read as a sign of its inhabitants' social position within a caste society.[25]

We tend to understand the decline of sumptuary law and the rise of aesthetic autonomy as a liberatory process. But it would be a mistake to think of the aesthetic as an autonomous zone of freedom from sumptuary regulation. As the case of Bragdon suggests, modernist architectural discourse developed new ways of drawing the distinction between luxury and necessity. It also developed new ways of regulating those practices it considered luxurious or excessive.

---

24 See Marc Grignon and Juliana Maxim, "Convenance, Caractère, and the Public Sphere," *Journal of Architectural Education*, 49:1 (September 1995), 29–37.
25 See Michael Osman et al. (eds.), *Perspecta 33: Mining Autonomy* (Cambridge, Mass.: MIT Press, 2002), especially the essays by Hubert Damisch and Anthony Vidler.
26 Nancy Fraser, "Rethinking the Public Sphere: A Contribution to the Critique of Actually Existing Democracy," in Craig Calhoun (ed.), *Habermas and the Public Sphere* (Cambridge, Mass.: MIT Press, 1992); reprinted in Bruce Robbins (ed.), *The Phantom Public Sphere* (Minneapolis: University of Minnesota Press, 1993), 1–32: 7.
27 Lavin, "Re Reading the Encyclopedia," 185.
28 See Thorstein Veblen, *The Theory of the Leisure Class: An Economic Study in the Evolution of Institutions* (New York: Macmillan, 1899). Elias notes that the sumptuary practices Veblen described as "conspicuous consumption" are distinct from those of court society. Conspicuous consumption describes ostentation that expresses an ethos of wealth, whereas the ostentation of court society is bound up in an ethos of caste and is a more central technique of power.

Extensions and critiques of Habermas' account of the public sphere have suggested that the bourgeois public sphere was not only a liberalizing counterweight to absolutist authority, but also a technique of exclusion that exercised new forms of control over public discourse. Scholars such as Joan Landes, Mary Ryan, and Nancy Fraser have argued that the bourgeois public sphere was constituted by exclusions based on gender, class, and other social criteria. It was always in competition with a range of "counterpublics" formed by different constituencies and operating through varied styles of political behavior and norms of public speech. As Fraser puts it, "the bourgeois public was never *the* public."[26] By recognizing only certain forms of discourse, the normative public sphere limited participation to those educated in those kinds of literacy; by recognizing only certain contexts for debate, it limited the impact of those excluded from those domains based on sex, race, or class. Even a principle such as that of bracketing status to diminish "irrational" authority differentials could function repressively, by excluding some styles of comportment and discourse. In this view, the public sphere analyzed by Habermas—bourgeois, masculinist, and highly literate—was a way for a segment of the middle class to contain the authority of these other publics.

The hegemonic dimension of the bourgeois public sphere identified by Fraser and others can be discerned also within architectural discourse. Sylvia Lavin suggests that as Enlightenment architectural theory "began to focus on providing the means for normalizing and codifying individual aesthetic response and for envisaging the production of a coherent body of public opinion on matters hitherto considered to be largely subjective" it created "an aesthetic discourse through which taste was regulated."[27]

This recognition helps to make sense of modernist approaches to architectural ornament. Around the turn of the twentieth century, new rhetorics of "necessity" emerged to discipline consumption and expression by regulating ornament. Bragdon's development and discussion of projective ornament is a case in point. Bragdon approached ornament as a terrain of negotiation of the relation between luxury and necessity, private desire and public good. His decision to focus on ornament was strategic: ornament was a terrain in flux. The bourgeois productivist ethos was eroding its rationale, yet ornament persisted as a site where capitalist class distinctions were articulated through the new practice of conspicuous consumption.[28] In the hope of eliminating this site of invidious distinction, Bragdon made ornament the site for deployment of a new necessity. With projective ornament, Bragdon created something paradoxical within the traditional theory of *convenance*: a universal ornament suitable to all classes and building types. Yet in its antagonism to luxury and ostentation, projective ornament reasserted the tradition of sumptuary regulation—now in the service of bourgeois and egalitarian rather than aristocratic ends.

Middle-class decorum
Bragdon's approach represents a minority position within early-twentieth-century modernism. Projective ornament never acquired the universal currency for which it was intended. Yet Bragdon's alternative modernism yields insights into mainstream modernism. If we compare Bragdon's ornament reform to those of Hermann Muthesius and Adolf Loos, for instance, we can see that even radically divergent approaches to ornament shared the basic aim of sumptuary law: to regulate expression in the name of social order.

German architect, writer, and government minister Muthesius (1861–1927) shaped modernist thinking in German-speaking countries through publications in which he advocated the practical informality of nineteenth-century English and Scottish houses as a model for the renewal of twentieth-century German building practice (Fig. 15). In his 1902 treatise *Style-Architecture and Building-Art*, Muthesius railed against the aristocratic pretensions of the German middle class,

Fig. 14 Autonomous architecture: Ledoux's Shelter for the Rural Guards project for the ideal city of Chaux, 1771

which produced a "sham culture" manifest especially in the taste for rich ornament. Muthesius characterized the modern lack of decoration as a quintessentially "*burgerlich*" trait, part of the middle-class rejection of aristocratic "pomp and need for representation."[29]

Muthesius associated extravagance in architectural decoration with other kinds of excess. In a section on "Dress and Dwelling" he emphasized the bourgeois basis of nineteenth-century "transformations toward simplicity and unconditional functionality." "Today's clothing," Muthesius proclaimed, "is the same for all the classes of society: its singular characteristic is that it defines in every respect the middle-class ideal, whereas in the eighteenth century the particular customs, way of life, and clothing of the highest class set the standard."[30] The turn-of-the-century "unornamented dress and topcoat" was the epitome of modernity because it exemplified "the tendency toward the strict matter-of-fact, in the elimination of every merely applied decorative form, and in shaping each form according to demands set by purpose."[31] Muthesius discerned the same tendency in dwellings, where reforms "strive to increase the amount of light and air, to design strictly functional rooms, to avoid all useless appendages in the decoration, to eliminate heavy, unmovable household furnishings, and to strive for an overall sense of brightness and impression of cleanliness. These reforms," Muthesius asserted, "follow the same tendency as our clothing, the closer dwelling that envelops us."[32] In both cases, the necessity of representation within the courtly prestige economy had been replaced by a functionalist necessity.

Like Muthesius, Moravian-born Viennese architect Loos (1870–1933) criticized as "philistine sham" the aristocratic pretensions of his middle-class compatriots, particularly in his 1898 series of weekly reviews of the Vienna Jubilee Exposition in the *Neue Freie Presse*, subsequently gathered into the 1921 collection *Spoken into the Void*. Like both Muthesius and Bragdon, Loos wrote in service of a social reform project pursued through cultural revitalization. Loos's work was a concerted campaign to strip the ornament from language, from dress, and from dwelling. Instead, he advocated "correct form, solid materials, precise execution"[33] (Fig. 16). His essay "Men's Fashion" characterized good taste in men's clothing in a way that anticipated Muthesius's conflation of functional utility with good taste. Loos opened his essay with a review of the modern liberalization of sumptuary regulation: "Our century has done away with dress code regulations. Everyone now enjoys the right to dress as he pleases,

---

29 Hermann Muthesius, *Style-Architecture and Building-Art: Transformations of Architecture in the Nineteenth Century and Its Present Condition*, introd. and trans. Stanford Anderson (Santa Monica: Getty Center for the History of Art and the Humanities, 1994 [1902; rev. 1903]), 53.
30 Muthesius, *Style-Architecture and Building-Art*, 79.
31 Muthesius, *Style-Architecture and Building-Art*, 79.
32 Muthesius, *Style-Architecture and Building-Art*, 79.
33 Adolf Loos, *Spoken into the Void: Collected Essays 1897–1900*, trans. Jane O. Newman and John H. Smith (Cambridge, Mass.: MIT Press, 1982 [1921, rev. 1931]), 9.
34 Loos, *Spoken into the Void*, 11.
35 Loos, *Spoken into the Void*, 14.
36 Adolf Loos, "Ornament and Crime" (1908), in Ulrich Conrads (ed.), *Programs and Manifestoes on 20th-Century Architecture*, trans. Michael Bullock (Cambridge, Mass.: MIT Press, 1970 [1964]), 19–24.

37 Massimo Cacciari has argued that Loos was less an agent of capitalist rationalization than its most profound critic: the disjunctive synthesis of his houses proclaimed the impossibility of dwelling in fragmented, disenchanted modernity and so developed a radical critique of modern rationalization. See Massimo Cacciari, *Architecture and Nihilism: On the Philosophy of Modern Architecture*, trans. Stephen Sartarelli (New Haven: Yale University Press, 1993). While I admire the subtlety and eloquence of Cacciari's interpretation, it seems to me that Loos's criticism of modernity coexisted with a fervent embrace of rationalization. If the absence of ornament from Loos's interiors and exteriors signified his rejection of the "false synthesis" imposed by Secession members, it also proclaimed his positive affirmation of the bourgeois productivist ethos of renunciation and rationalization. Loos's strenuous advocacy of modernization in his journalism is among the most impassioned modernist expressions of the professional-bourgeois ethos of rationality. Likewise, it is possible to read Loos's sartorial stance as an instance of the defensive use of fashion as "a veil and a protection for everything spiritual and now all the more free," in the words of Georg Simmel (Simmel, "Fashion," *International Quarterly*, 10, trans. unknown [New York: 1904], reprinted in Donald N. Levine [ed.], *Georg Simmel on Individuality and Social Forms* [Chicago: University of Chicago Press, 1971], 294–323: 312). Yet even if we read Loos's middle-class masculine fashion ideal as a mask that protects his "soul" from metropolitan depredations, it is also true that he advocated that fashion ideal as a repressive discipline vis-à-vis Secessionist "aesthetic dress."

Fig. 15 A minimally ornamented Scottish house exterior advanced by Muthesius as a model of middle-class decorum

Fig. 16 The minimally ornamented exterior of Loos's Müller House (Prague, 1930)

even like the king if he wants."[34] The trouble, he went on to say, was that too many Germans and especially Austrians took advantage of that freedom by adopting distinctive, aristocratic, "artistic" clothing styles. Loos had nothing but disdain for these dandies and their outfits: "double-breasted waistcoats and checked suits with velvet collars!... a jacket with blue velvet cuffs!"[35]

Loos took such extravagances of personality in clothing as markers of an evolutionary lag. He associated them with the financially reckless expenditures of courtly prestige economy. This was a more pressing issue in Vienna, where the Habsburgs still held court in the Baroque splendor of the Hofburg, than in more metropolitan cities such as London or New York, where the ethos of investing capital for productive return had more fully taken root. Loos also saw "artistic" garments as breaches of sexual decorum, public eruptions of a sensuality that had to be kept private—had to be bracketed—in order to sustain the rational exchanges of liberal bourgeois society. He applied a similar logic to architecture, identifying cultural advancement with the elimination of decoration from objects of everyday use, among which he included buildings.

The continuity between Loos's militation against architectural ornament and older traditions of regulating ornament to maintain social order is especially clear when we set Loos's attitude toward architectural ornament in the context of his broader lifestyle principles. His criticisms of ornamental cookery ("I eat roast beef") and of ornamentation in clothing ("Anyone who goes around in a velvet coat today is not an artist but a buffoon or a house painter") established a continuum between his views on ornament in architecture and in other domains of culture.[36] The common basis of these views was the conviction that ornament was wasted labor-power: hours of human labor spent ornamenting clothing and buildings should rationally have been directed toward modernizing Austro-Hungarian society. The investment of time and money in ornament, like the continuing rule of the Habsburg family over the Austro-Hungarian empire, was for Loos a vestige of prestige economy inhibiting a modernization that was already far advanced elsewhere, particularly England and the United States. Loos's hostility to ornament stemmed from his application to Austrian society of an analysis based on the productivist ethos of capitalist modernity.[37]

The terms in which modernists such as Muthesius and Loos sought to regulate ornament suggest that architectural modernism reflected not the decline of sumptuary regulation but its reformulation in liberal terms. Modernism revived the regulatory role of ornament, but in the service of bourgeois ideals such as functionality, universality, and economic productivity. At the same time, modernism developed new modes of codification and enforcement: while earlier sumptuary regulation had operated through legislation, in modernity a proliferating discourse about ornament instead mobilized public opinion as a regulatory device.

Aesthetic discipline

We can understand the reformatting of sumptuary regulation exemplified by Loos, Muthesius, and Bragdon as an example of the rise of the disciplinary modality of power that Michel Foucault argued characterizes liberal modernity. In his studies of medicine, penology, and sexuality, Foucault contended that in liberal societies power was generally not centralized, as it had been under monarchical sovereignty, but dispersed across the whole of society. New practices such as individuated incarceration, clinical medicine, nationalized schooling, and military drilling implemented a set of disciplines that drew individuals into their own self-regulation. By training bodies and minds in particular ways, modern institutions instilled in their subjects a discipline that led them to conform voluntarily to social imperatives.[38]

In this analysis, the separation of public and private identified by Habermas as a constitutive dimension of liberal modernity did not create a domain of autonomy wherein subjects were free from regulation. Instead, that separation extended the reach of power into more areas of life through new techniques of social control. The liberal ethic of personal freedom emerged in tandem with newly internalized modes of regulation. As David Halperin puts it, liberal power, "far from enslaving its objects, constructs them as subjective agents and preserves them in their autonomy, so as to invest them all the more completely… The state… can safely leave [its subjects] to make their own choices in the allegedly sacrosanct private sphere of personal freedom which they now inhabit, because within that sphere they *freely and spontaneously* police both their own conduct and the conduct of others."[39]

Foucault's argument that power in liberal modernity is dispersed across the whole social field through practices of self-regulation is corroborated in the case of sumptuary regulation by historians such as Alan Hunt. In his history of sumptuary regulation, Hunt claims that modernity has been characterized by "a general expansion of discipline and surveillance" that has suffused the private sphere with more indirect forms of sumptuary regulation.[40] Now spread across a range of both public and private forms of governance, sumptuary regulation

---

38 See Michel Foucault, *Discipline and Punish: The Birth of the Prison*, trans. Alan Sheridan (New York: Pantheon, 1978 [1975]), especially part 3, "Discipline," 135–228. See also Foucault, "The Subject and Power," in Hubert L. Dreyfus and Paul Rabinow, *Michel Foucault: Beyond Structuralism and Hermeneutics*, 2nd edn. (Chicago: University of Chicago Press, 1983), 208–26; and Foucault, *The History of Sexuality*, I: *An Introduction*, trans. Robert Hurley (New York: Pantheon, 1978 [1976]).
39 David M. Halperin, *Saint Foucault: Towards a Gay Hagiography* (Oxford: Oxford University Press, 1995), 19.
40 Hunt, *Governance of the Consuming Passions*, 378ff.
41 Purdy, *The Tyranny of Elegance*, 91.
42 Purdy, *The Tyranny of Elegance*, 217.
43 Purdy, *The Tyranny of Elegance*, 117.
44 Purdy, *The Tyranny of Elegance*, 193.

Fig. 17 Bourgeois and aristocratic modes of representation in clothing, as depicted by Bruno Paul in his drawing "A Conflict of Fashion," published in *Simplicissimus* in 1902. Reproduced from Adolf Loos, *Spoken into the Void*

operates through dispersed forms of pressure, from workplace dress policies and grooming codes to practices of self-governance shaped by broadly shared social expectations about proper dress and demeanor.

Daniel Purdy has further developed this Foucauldian analysis of modern sumptuary regulation in *The Tyranny of Elegance*, his study of the rise of fashion discourse in German-language magazines during the last decades of the eighteenth century. Purdy argues that social consensus on taste operated as a form of discipline working through the diffuse mechanisms of public opinion about what constituted good taste in clothing.[41] The new middle-class fashion discourse taught consumers to judge sartorial detail according to functional rather than representational criteria. The use of clothes as signs of identity within court society was replaced by a use of clothes as part of "an economic and political calculus of production,"[42] expressed through an "aesthetic of sartorial understatement"[43] that minimized ornament. Under the new productivist dispensation, the primary message of clothes was "the absence of any message not justified by necessity."[44] Restraint in dress signified willing espousal of the modern ethos of fiscal restraint and reinvestment of surpluses in productive enterprise. The seemingly autonomous aesthetic attitude toward clothing was a form of middle-class discipline (Fig. 17).

Purdy's interpretation is a useful key to reading the attitudes of Loos and Muthesius toward clothing—and also toward architecture. Loos recurrently linked rejection of ornament in dress and decoration to the rise of aesthetic judgment. Asserting bourgeois values in a society still dominated by the court and its prestige economy, Loos insisted that the aesthetic attitude toward clothing, furniture, food, and architecture was the attitude appropriate to modern middle-class society. "Absence of ornament has brought the other arts to unsuspected heights," he claimed in "Ornament and Crime" (1908), describing aesthetic perception as the sublimation of sensuous pleasures that in less modern societies had been gratified by ornament. These views constructed close links between economic rationalization and aesthetic appreciation. The elimination of ornament, Loos suggested, would advance modernization both directly, by redirecting capital from investment in display to investment in production, and indirectly, by disseminating the aesthetic attitude toward works of art that supported such a redirection of investment. Loos's sartorial ethos is a quintessential modernist expression of the aesthetic discipline that Purdy reconstructs. "[W]hat does it mean to be dressed well?" Loos asked. "[It] is a question of being dressed *in such a way that one*

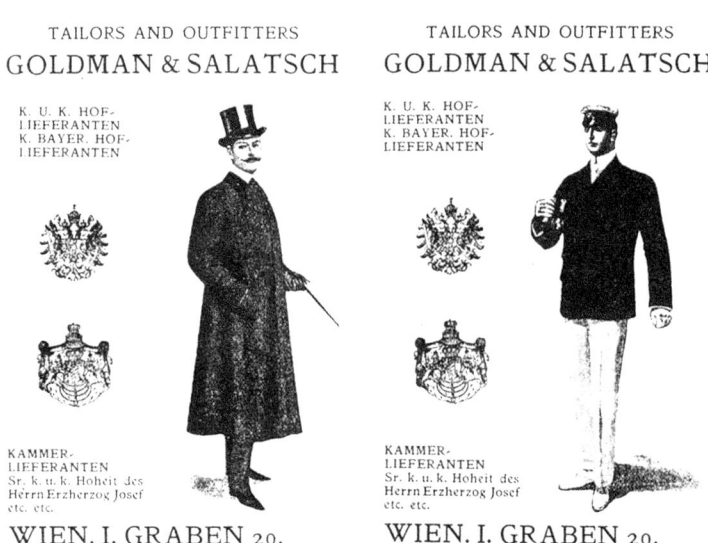

Fig. 18 (left) "Uniforms, compulsory and voluntary," from Goldman & Salatsch advertisements printed in Loos's journal *Das Andere*

Fig. 19 (right) Differential modernization expressed in middle-class clothing: a drawing by Thomas Theodor Heine, captioned "Herr and Frau Schmidt look like this when they travel to London… and like this when they return after a week there as Mr. and Mrs. Smith," published in *Simplicissimus* in 1902. Reproduced from Adolf Loos, *Spoken into the Void*

stands out the least…. In good society, to be conspicuous is bad manners."[45] For Loos, the acme of good society was to be found in London, where the black business suit was a kind of middle-class uniform, one of the bracketing devices sustaining public sphere discourse (Figs. 18 and 19).

The relation between elimination of ornament and the formation of the modern middle-class individual as an autonomous agent of aesthetic judgment is especially clear in Muthesius's text, which establishes strict parameters for the "free" exercise of judgment. Muthesius claimed:

> The wind that today blows across our culture is middle class, just as today we all work, just as everyone's clothing is middle class, just as our new tectonic forms… move in the track of complete simplicity and straightforwardness, so also we want to live in middle-class rooms whose essence and goal is simplicity and straightforwardness. No limits are set to good taste within these forms of straightforwardness; indeed here it can be engaged more genuinely than in the worn out, ostentatious cramming of our houses today.[46]

Muthesius's rhetoric confirms that modernist sublimation of ornament constructed aesthetic judgment as a disciplinary technique.

As with Loos and Muthesius, Bragdon's ornament reform was part of a broader lifestyle reform. Bragdon advocated and followed such new lifestyle practices as vegetarianism, yoga, meditation, and renunciation of alcohol and tobacco. His ornamental designs and his

45 Loos, *Spoken into the Void*, 12.
46 Muthesius, *Style-Architecture and Building-Art*, 94.
47 See Muthesius, *Style-Architecture and Building-Art*, 99; and Loos, "Ornament and Crime."

Fig. 20 (above) One of Bragdon's renderings showing potential applications of projective ornament

Fig. 21 (below) "The Audience Chamber," a rendering—possibly of a design for the stage—from Bragdon's 1918 book *Architecture and Democracy* (New York: Knopf, 1918), 111

renderings of the use of projective ornament featured selected signifiers of luxury remotivated to mark a new hierarchy: the spiritual hierarchy of dedication to Theosophy and its universalist and objectivist ideals. Projective ornament, intended to become a universal ornament for spiritual democracy, in the short term distinguished adepts within the new regime of Theosophical faith and spiritual democracy. Bragdon articulated his commitment to the rule of the *demos* and his Theosophical faith in the existence of an inflexible higher ruling power through figures of authority drawn from caste societies: in his renderings, spiritual adepts are often distinguished by the trappings of aristocratic or priestly authority (Figs. 20 and 21).

Bragdon's use of attributes of royal and priestly luxury, like his emphasis on ornament generally, is an instance of sumptuousness deployed in the service of sumptuary goals. It echoes the Renaissance espousal of civically endorsed splendor (such as official robes), a tradition that Bragdon mobilized against the use of splendor for purposes of conspicuous consumption. The emphasis on ornament and other marks of distinction in Bragdon's work signals his desire for a society based on a hierarchy of spiritual progress toward transcendence of self, rather than on distinctions of nationality, class, or culture. Bragdon's use of markers of luxury to signify spiritual advancement inverts the sumptuary codes of Loos and Muthesius. For them, the uniform of bourgeois dress and deportment or conduct signified membership in a middle-class aristocracy of good taste.[47] Whereas Loos and Muthesius constructed a productivist discipline through sublimation of ornament, Bragdon developed an idealist, counter-productivist discipline to which ornament, as something that answered to a "higher" necessity than those of function and economy, was central.

Modernist convenance
In the trajectory of architectural modernism after the First World War, Bragdon's approach to social regulation through ornament lost out to a mainstream stance derived from the ideas of Muthesius and Loos. A productivist "necessity" became hegemonic within architectural approaches to ornament, much as the bourgeois public sphere acquired hegemony over other modes of publicity.

More important than these discrepant outcomes, though, is the fact that the very different projects of Bragdon, Muthesius, and Loos exemplify a single mode of discursive regulation. Despite their diverging approaches to ornament, all three shared the premise that regulating ornament was a way of regulating individual expression in the name of social order. For all three of these men, ornament was a means of disciplining expression and consumption—a site of what we might call bourgeois *convenance*. In light of this analysis, it seems significant that Bragdon, Muthesius, and Loos were not only architects, but also journalists. They used the discursive public sphere to mold opinion on ornament and decorum, consumption practices, and ways of life.

The liberal regime of social control through public opinion and self-regulation is useful in describing not only the new meaning of clothing in bourgeois modernity, but also the new framework for the understanding and practice of architectural ornament. The modern recoding of sumptuary law from prohibitions on display to tax-code incentives did not mean that the regulation of display declined. Architectural ornament, like clothing

[48] Regarding the modernist white wall as an aesthetic sublimation of ornament, see Mark Wigley, *White Walls, Designer Dresses: The Fashioning of Modern Architecture* (Cambridge, Mass.: MIT Press, 1995).
[49] Marc Grignon and Juliana Maxim, "*Convenance, Caractère*, and the Public Sphere."

and domestic furnishings, shifted from reflecting an economy of symbolic prestige to reflecting an economy of productive labor. Regulation of ornament took on a more pervasively negative character, and it moved from a specifically legislative to a more generally discursive arena, operating through the rule not of law but of public opinion. Sumptuary regulation moved from legislative codes to the more diffuse codes of middle-class deportment and professional ideology.

We tend to think of the aesthetic, and of "autonomous architecture," as the liberation of art from its subservience to religious and political orders. But it is worth remembering that the aesthetic of artistic autonomy served the particular sociopolitical order of bourgeois modernity. Modernist "autonomous architecture" served social and political ends *inasmuch as* it was destined for aesthetic appreciation. The formation of an autonomous architecture predicated on aesthetic appreciation entailed the deployment of a new discipline that mobilized the dispersed and diffuse power of public opinion to re-regulate consumption and expression. Black suits and white walls can both operate as repressive bracketing techniques.[48]

Marc Grignon and Juliana Maxim have characterized the highly articulated doctrine of *convenance* as an attempt to stabilize the representation of status in a period of transition from caste to class society.[49] If we focus on the mechanism more than the content of sumptuary regulation, however, we may come to see the doctrine of *convenance* as not just as the final product of the classical system, but also the beginning of modern discursive regulation. *Convenance* was not only "crepuscular," as Grignon and Maxim judiciously observe, but also auroral.

Acknowledgement
I am grateful to Lauren Kogod for commenting on the essay and sharing her expertise on Muthesius.

Felicity D. Scott

When Systems Fail

On October 29, 1975, *The Architecture of the Ecole des Beaux-Arts* opened to the public at New York's Museum of Modern Art.[1] Almost eight years in preparation, Arthur Drexler's spectacular exhibition of large-scale, nineteenth-century student watercolor drawings and renderings from the Parisian Ecole des Beaux-Arts had a catalyzing effect on the architectural community, opening up debates on topics ranging from modernism and functionalism to eclecticism, ornament, postmodernism, semiotics, drawing techniques, as well as architectural pedagogy and historiography.[2] Drexler's provocation would continue to resonate with contemporary concerns and to proliferate debate as the reception of the exhibition prompted not only scholarly research and polemical exchanges but, to his avowed surprise, a revivalist recuperation of historical form. It is primarily on account of this connection to historicism that the exhibition became a notorious landmark in architecture's postmodern turn, a notoriety exacerbated by its presentation within an institution that had both codified modern architecture for an American audience in the early 1930s and sponsored its ongoing legacy.[3] Yet if MoMA's Beaux-Arts show was (and still is) understood to demonstrate the discipline's turn away from modernist abstraction and the machine aesthetic toward an embrace of historical and semantic referents (a paradigm that would dominate architectural practice for over a decade), it will be the wager of this study to demonstrate, in turn, that Drexler's provocation had a rather different, and certainly more subtle, critical agenda than has been attributed to it. While questioning the lasting efficacy of the modernist paradigm upon which the museum's aesthetic had been founded, the exhibition was not proposing a romantic turn to the past.[4]

1 *The Architecture of the Ecole des Beaux-Arts* was on show at MOMA from October 29, 1975, through January 4, 1976. Comprised primarily of student drawings, the exhibition also included images of Henri Labrouste's Bibliothèque Sainte-Geneviève, Charles Garnier's Paris Opéra, along with selected French and American Beaux-Arts buildings.
2 That the exhibition project dated back to 1967 is confirmed in correspondence between Arthur Drexler and Richard Chafee. On December 1, 1967, Drexler responded to a letter from Chafee, noting: "The museum's trustees have approved, in principle, a Beaux-Arts exhibition." Exhibition files, Department of Architecture and Design, Museum of Modern Art, New York. [Henceforth "Exhibition files."]
3 For a foundational document see the exhibition catalog, Alfred Barr, Henry-Russell Hitchcock, Philip Johnson, and Lewis Mumford, *Modern Architecture—International Exhibition* (New York: Museum of Modern Art and W. W. Norton and Co., 1932).

4 For Drexler's response to the historicist reception see Michael Kimmelman, "The New Museum of Modern Art: Interview with Arthur Drexler," in *Art News*, 83:5 (1984), 66; and Arthur Drexler in "Forum: The Beaux-Arts Exhibition," *Oppositions*, 8 (Spring 1977); reprinted in K. Michael Hays (ed.), *Oppositions Reader* (New York: Princeton Architectural Press, 1998): 686–7.
5 See Manfredo Tafuri, "The Ashes of Jefferson," [1976] trans. Pellegrino d'Acierno and Robert Connolly, in *The Sphere and the Labyrinth: Avant-Gardes and Architecture from Piranesi to the 1970's* (Cambridge, Mass.: MIT Press, 1987), 291–303; and Robert A. M. Stern, "Gray Architecture as Post-Modernism, or, Up and Down from Orthodoxy," [1976] in K. Michael Hays (ed.), *Architecture | Theory | since 1968* (Cambridge, Mass.: MIT Press, 1998), 242–5.
6 On the notion of "postmodernization," a rereading of Fredric Jameson's notion of postmodernism, see Michael Hardt and Antonio Negri, *Empire* (Cambridge, Mass.: Harvard University Press, 2000).
7 See Charles Jencks, *The Language of Postmodern Architecture* (New York: Rizzoli, 1977). Beyond architecture and architectural history, this became a reference for theorists from Fredric Jameson to Andreas Huyssen and beyond.

Arthur Drexler and the Postmodern Turn

This is not to suggest that *The Architecture of the Ecole des Beaux-Arts* was not an important event in the history of postmodernism in architecture. Indeed, along with Drexler's almost equally notorious exhibition of 1979, *Transformations in Modern Architecture*, it was symptomatic of the replacement of a supposedly coherent set of modernist codes and their determinate references by a set of knowingly ambiguous, allusive (and elusive) and decidedly unstable or multivalent ones. This turn from modernist certainties to postmodern instabilities was famously prefigured by Robert Venturi's *Complexity and Contradiction in Architecture*, a 1966 publication sponsored by Drexler as the first in a series of Museum of Modern Art Papers on Architecture. Moreover, the shift from considerations of functionalism and abstraction to debates on structuralism, semiology, and meaning—heralded by the publication of Charles Jencks's and George Baird's 1969 anthology, *Meaning in Architecture*—had by 1975 given rise to the contours of the most polemical debate of the decade: the "Grays" versus the "Whites."[5] Drexler's musings on an architecture coming after modernism were, as we shall see, in close dialog with this polemical duality, but his position needs to be distinguished from both the populist pluralism of Venturi and the Grays as well as from the autonomous formalism of the Whites. Rather than occupying a position along this Gray/White axis of integration into versus withdrawal from the semantic structures of commercialization, Drexler's work in the 1970s can be read as demonstrating another response: it traced the impact on the discipline of historical forces driving "postmodernization."[6]

Drexler's response to the transformation of a modernist industrial paradigm into a postmodern, post-industrial one also remains far from explained with reference to the mainstream understanding of American architecture's semantic turn as codified by a critic like Charles Jencks. Indeed, the widespread reception of Jencks's *The Language of Post-Modern Architecture*, which became something of a touchstone in the 1980s, foreclosed other more nuanced and complex readings of the discipline's reaction to its historical condition both within and beyond its disciplinary parameters.[7] If questions concerning language, communication, and meaning *were* central to Drexler's thinking, for him these topoi remained bound up with technological and informatic counterparts. Unlike the disinterestedness and simple pleasures of formal play or parody articulated by Jencks, and unlike his delirious and apolitical reading of pluralism, Drexler would come to different (and more contestatory) conclusions regarding the social and political as well as aesthetic ramifications of the instabilities of meaning central to both architectural and artificial languages. To him, furthermore, as director of MoMA's department of architecture and design, there were institutional questions at stake in this *post*-modern turn, questions regarding the viability of MoMA's foundational codes. But we are getting ahead of ourselves, for little of this would seem to be evident in an installation of spectacular nineteenth-century architectural watercolors.

Shortly after *The Architecture of the Ecole des Beaux-Arts* opened, Drexler staged the first of two symposia on the exhibition under the rubric "Retrieving the Nineteenth Century." He invited Henry Russell-Hitchcock and Vincent Scully along with three younger historians involved with the exhibition—Richard Chafee, Neil Levine, and David van Zanten—to speak on topics including "The Politics of Teaching Architecture," "The Theory of Composition," "The Uses of the Past," and "The Idea of Architectural Legibility."[8] In a characteristically evasive manner, Drexler introduced the event by pointing to a nostalgic, even utopian gesture staged by Suzanne Stephens and Susanne Torre, who had produced buttons for the occasion reading "Bring back the Bauhaus."[9] If, on the one hand, Drexler nodded affirmatively toward that modernist institution, he went on to suggest that "on the other hand one does have the feeling that one would like to keep moving and take a look at what the future might hold." While Drexler remained rightfully suspicious of futurological projections, he recognized the imperative to investigate the impact of contemporary historical forces on the discipline, "an operation," he explained, "that at the moment might require some sort of *detour*. The detour," he continued, "is provoked by a condition we have inherited from the '60s and from the still earlier demise of the Bauhaus."[10]

The second symposia took place the following week. It was organized and moderated by Anthony Vidler, who regarded MoMA's presentation of this spectacular array of Beaux-Arts renderings as something of an "auto-critical act" on the part of that institution.[11] Rejecting the "neat reversal" of dialectical opposites—modernism and the Beaux-Arts academy—the session was vectored around a reassessment of modernism and modernist historiography. Topics included "Form and Polemics of the Modern Movement's Attack on the Academic City" and "The Re-assessment of Beaux-Arts Urban Aesthetics and the Future of Modern Urbanism."[12] Speakers included Colin Rowe, Carl Schorske, and George Baird.

Drexler had preemptively introduced Vidler's symposia as "the second installment of our human psychodrama." There would be many subsequent installments to this psychodrama as his attempted *detour* through the Beaux-Arts was captured within the ongoing battle of the Grays versus the Whites, or, more specifically, through the discursive and institutional politics of the Institute for Architecture and Urban Studies (IAUS). Immediately after the show closed, the IAUS held a forum, the proceedings of which were published in *Oppositions* 8, a special issue edited by Vidler as a critical response to the show. The Institute even staged its own Beaux-Arts exhibition in January 1977, *Princeton's Beaux-Arts and Its New Academicism: From Labatut to the Program of Geddes*, in which it recast the school's contemporary legacy from the perspective of an ongoing Beaux-Arts pedagogy. An accompanying forum was

---

8 Undated document entitled "Retrieving the Nineteenth Century," Exhibition files.
9 This was noted by many reviewers but the instigators were only named in "Drawing from the Famed Ecole des Beaux-Arts," *Interiors* (January 1976), 12.
10 Transcribed from sound recordings of the Beaux-Arts symposium, November 11, 1975. Archives of the Museum of Modern Art. [Henceforth "Sound recordings."] Unless otherwise noted, all citations during my discussion of the symposia are from this source or the recordings of the following week.
11 Anthony Vidler, "Academicism: Modernism," *Oppositions*, 8 (Spring 1977), 2.
12 "Retrieving the Nineteenth Century," Exhibition files.
13 *Five Architects: Eisenman, Graves, Gwathmy, Hejduk, Meier* (New York: Museum of Modern Art, Oxford University Press, 1975).
14 Cited in Franz Schulze, *Philip Johnson: Life and Work* (New York: Alfred A. Knopf, 1994), 330. On the foundation of the Institute see also Peter Lemos, "The Triumph of the Quill," in *The Village Voice*, May 3, 1983, 98–9.
15 Tafuri, "The Ashes of Jefferson," 298.

published in *Oppositions* 9. Drexler had perhaps anticipated that his exhibition would operate to further destabilize a now orthodox late modernism. Certainly he was aware that the show's spectacular images would prove entirely seductive to a public audience. Yet he had not foreseen the extent to which his detour would be captured within the problematic of architectural semantics. This reception was, however, far from surprising, for Drexler had operated as a key mediator in the Gray/White debate during the late 1960s. If, on the one hand, he had published Venturi's *Complexity and Contradiction in Architecture*, on the other hand he was involved with the CASE meeting of 1969 that launched the careers of Peter Eisenman, Michael Graves, Charles Gwathmey, John Hejduk, and Richard Meier, aka the New York Five, and which formed the basis of the 1972 MoMA publication *Five Architects*.[13] Drexler had also been central to the foundation, in 1967, of the IAUS as an independent forum for architectural discourse, a "halfway house," in Eisenman's terms, between academe and the profession.[14] Drexler was in fact not only a founding member, but also served for a number of years as the chairman of the Board of Trustees.

By 1975, however, Drexler had all but withdrawn from Institute activities, his position replaced by his predecessor at MoMA, Philip Johnson. Drexler's invocation of the Beaux-Arts at that time was read as firmly on the side of the Grays, a perception confirmed by his solicitation of Scully—a key spokesperson of "inclusivism"—for the first symposium. This was countered, of course, by Vidler's invitation of Rowe, key spokesperson of the New York Five. Yet if both parties deployed the show as a fulcrum with which to disarticulate their positions with respect to the impasse of late modernism (an impasse visible in the failure of modernist codes to signify within the late capitalist context), this apparent polarization remained caught in a dialectical opposition through a common project of recuperating semantics. For "both camps," as Manfredo Tafuri explained in "The Ashes of Jefferson," "the theme of 'resemanticization' is central; only the instruments employed to reach such an objective vary."[15]

Although *The Architecture of the Ecole des Beaux-Arts* was commenting on the semantic exhaustion of late-modernism, Drexler's exhibition was not proposing that architecture speak again through legible codes. If

Fig. 1 Installation view of *The Architecture of the Ecole des Beaux-Arts*, Museum of Modern Art, New York, October 29, 1975 through January 4, 1976

modernist aesthetic codes had ceased to function in a meaningful way, their replacement or rearticulation with historicist forms was not Drexler's response to historical forces then impacting designers. According to him: "It would be misleading to suggest that it was the intention of the authors or of this museum to induce a revival of Beaux-Arts architecture, which would be absurd."[16]

At one point during the second MOMA symposium, Drexler interrupted a discussion about moral convictions to make a parenthetical remark about modernism's temporality. Modern architecture, he explained with reference to Ludwig Mies van der Rohe, entailed a desire to "escape time… to make something that simply eluded further development, further evolution." Noting that one could not "write a history of modern architecture without really having a considerable background in theology," he explained that modernism's "messianic fervor" was bent on "bring[ing] history to an end" or to "bring[ing] paradise to earth."[17] When Vidler retorted, "I think Colin's right in saying that the anti-urban ethic within the Modern Movement is fundamentally Marxist, and that the city of capital was to be destroyed," Drexler responded by insisting that the modernist ethic was, rather, a drive to produce "a prototype made ready for infinite replication around the world."[18] It would soon become clear that it was something about the social and technological implications of this mode of repetition, and the subsequent eclipse of this paradigm by information technology, that was burdening Drexler.

When the 500-page catalog finally appeared in 1977, Drexler's contribution, "Engineer's Architecture: Truth and Its Consequences," offered some clarification to his almost entirely opaque earlier remarks. Surely one of the strangest texts to offer thoughts on nineteenth-century architecture and its offspring, "Engineer's Architecture" addressed the implications of modern architecture's "engineering style." Articulating a dystopic inversion of the enlightenment faith in technology, Drexler characterized modern architecture's quest for a unified, purified aesthetic in alarming terms. "In pursuit of the absolute," he declared, "we wish to exalt the act of building while devaluing its contingent forms, and the bewildering freedom contingency implies." Engineering, he continued,

> was the purification of architecture necessary for the *final solution*—the solution to the problem of existence in historical time. "Objectivity" (*die neue Sachlichkeit*) begins by sorting out conflicting demands, but its aim is to end the conflict by producing the definitive building. Should that

16 Arthur Drexler, MIT Press Author questionnaire, dated March 2, 1977. Exhibition files.
17 Sound recordings, 11/18/1975. Neil Levine has demonstrated that Wright's work provided a counter-example for Drexler, an architecture in which history did not come to an end. See Levine, "Frank Lloyd Wright: Architect," in *JSAH*, 53 (September 1994), 345. On the Judeo-Christian provenance of Drexler's notion of freedom see Allan Greenberg, "Thoughts on Freedom and Imitation," in *Architectural Design*, 58:9/10 (1988), 29–44.
18 Sound recordings, 11/18/1975. See also Drexler, "Engineer's Architecture: Truth and Its Consequences," in Arthur Drexler (ed.), *The Architecture of the Ecole des Beaux-Arts* (New York: Museum of Modern Art, 1977), 14.
19 Drexler, "Engineer's Architecture," 14.
20 Drexler, "Engineer's Architecture," 59.
21 Drexler, "Engineer's Architecture," 14.
22 Drexler, "Engineer's Architecture," 15.
23 Drexler, "Engineer's Architecture," 59.
24 Arthur Drexler, "Preface," *The Architecture of the Ecole des Beaux-Arts* (New York: Museum of Modern Art, 1975), 3.
25 Drexler, "Engineer's Architecture," 51.
26 Drexler, "Engineer's Architecture," 43.

happen not style merely but the historical process must come to an end.[19]

Eradicating conflict and contingency, Drexler saw the victory of a rationalist modernism as an apocalyptic elimination of difference, literally (through rhetorical exaggeration) as a fascist homogenization. Yet even during such a melancholic appraisal, he would not make the gesture of damning modernism per se, only this reductive tendency.

"Reductionist philosophies of architecture do not have a mandate from heaven," Drexler argued, indicating that there might be an alternative.[20] In place of those high modernist values he proposed to embrace that which had been devalued: contingency "and the bewildering freedom contingency implies." Putting his show into dialog with Venturi and the Grays, Drexler also disarticulated his reading of contingent and nondeterminate strategies from that with which they might easily be conflated, "a taste for contradiction as an end in itself."[21] Regarding such a dialectical inversion of the "engineering style" as another trap, he identified "the characteristic problem for modern architecture in its post-Miesian phase: it acknowledges freedom by seeking to embody divergent possibilities (which it chooses to see as contradictions), but it has not yet dared to relinquish the reductionist imperative of the engineering style."[22]

Beyond a philosophical or even populist embrace of pluralism, the project of renewing or rearticulating "freedom and necessity" was for Drexler motivated by a contemporary development: a new potential for the discipline had arisen on account of the indeterminacy operating within new technological systems. "Already it is possible to suggest," he argued, somewhat optimistically, "if only with evidence from outside the realm of architecture, that the dominant utilitarian view of existence is being challenged from within its own technological disciplines." Against the "historical revivalism architects fear," Drexler posited the aim of his Beaux-Arts show as staging, if somewhat allegorically, "a non-reductive interpretation of technology itself."[23] Counterintuitively, the Beaux-Arts was to be "retrieved" in order to point to the potentials of a new mode of eclecticism, one recast as a liberal pluralism on account of affinities with non-deterministic logics and enabled by a transformative coupling of aesthetics and new technology.

In the preface to the catalog Drexler offered a small clue to his puzzling remarks. After invoking "Walter Gropius's alarming phrase… 'total architecture,'" and the modernist belief in "redemption through design—*good* design," he contrasted modernist certainties with "the kind of freedom achieved by Italian design in the '60s [which] replaced moral imperatives with irony and humor, but not with new convictions."[24] His aside, a reference to the work of groups such as Superstudio and Archizoom, was not incidental. Their work offered a model of contemporary practice premised neither on form following function nor (in some cases) on semantic legibility, and it presented a set of strategies that sought prospects for a radical dismantling of determinist relations. If such work had failed, in Drexler's assessment, to articulate new convictions, the manner in which it forged lines of flight from modernist codes was nevertheless instructive. Commenting on historically specific social, technological, and even economic transformations, it identified how, or even where, postmodern architecture might pursue an ethical vocation.

This "kind of freedom" was put in direct dialog with modernism for, as Drexler understood it, modernism had been motivated by dreams not only of aesthetic but also of social restraint. The virtues of prohibitions, such as that on ornament, thus had to be radically reconsidered. With reference to Loos's famous essay of 1908, "Ornament und Verbrechen," he argued that "the modern prohibition against ornament perversely equates it with crime or law breaking," and in so doing "conceals a deeper but familiar meaning: freedom is sin."[25] Implicit in the prohibition, its counter-image, was recognition of a space of freedom connected to "dangerous play." But what Drexler recognized was that play, especially formal play, did not by itself provide an escape route since certain transformations operated all too easily within the very logic of the present system. Continuing, he pointed to the theme of his next blockbuster exhibition, *Transformations*: "Ornament can be suppressed, but if thrown out it returns with a vengeance, seeking to convert all form into ornamental play." It was on account of such a return of suppressed ornament (as distinctive from, say, a critical retrieval or radical transformation) that a degraded form of difference had emerged. As he explained: "Having denied to architecture its fictive body, we limit ourselves to such complications of truth as can be forced from structure and surface, or from the unwarranted enlargement of the insignificant," a situation giving rise to "virtuoso displays of technique" that were "divorced from problems of value."[26]

In *Transformations* the viewer entered passageways saturated by black-and-white photographs. Captured within an image-dense environment, they were encircled by a dizzying proliferation of curtain walls and expressionistic structural forms organized as multiple small bits of information. Wallpapered onto faceted surfaces in the galleries, the buildings were not individually framed or captioned but rather "classified" into four groups: sculptural form, structural technique, regional vernacular, and selections of elements figured as repetitive "fragments," such as windows, colonnades, roofs, detachable parts, etc. The center gallery contained backlit color transparencies of mirror-glass buildings set into a darkly colored background. This use of photographs, Drexler noted, indicating a connection to his earlier show, would be akin to the "large fancy renderings" of the Beaux-Arts.[27] He explained of contemporary curtain walls, moreover: "glass cladding systems have been so refined as to communicate almost nothing."[28]

While much adverse criticism focused on the purely photographic nature of the show, Drexler insisted that his preference would have been to continue the saturation of photographs: "If I hadn't run out of money," he remarked, "there would have been more pictures on the ceiling."[29] For Drexler both the photographic format and the installation's organization were relevant to this presentation of late modernism. "I'm not myself a believer in the half-truth that the medium is the message," he explained with a nod to McLuhanism, "but everyone must have seen that the medium influences the form that the message can take." Beyond the capacity of the book, magazine or even newspaper, this exhibition would, by contrast, "surround you with images and put you in a different relation to them," it would present "far more images simultaneously than you can ever absorb in any other way, including, for that matter, one might observe, multiple projection slide shows."[30]

Drexler's installation strategy had three main effects: first it referenced, even mimicked, the dissolution of a previously totalized system of design into a fragmented array of parts. "When systems fail," he explained of modernism, "when unifying thought and diagrams no longer seem adequate for the task set for them, attention shifts as one sinks beneath the waves and reaches for the life belt or a raft or a stick of wood. Attention shifts to fragments, to some isolated element useful in design."[31] In a 1977 typescript he had noted that these fragments "provide motifs which may be separated from the whole and easily manipulated…. Carried far enough, this approach to design can generate its own mode of organization."[32] In the catalog he expanded on this effect, positing that such manipulation of motifs produces an entropic force that operated through a process of exaggeration:

If the structural elements of a particularly striking

---

27 Arthur Drexler in Arthur Drexler and Andrew MacNair, "Response: Arthur Drexler on *Transformations*," *Skyline* (Summer 1979), 6. Directed by Arthur Drexler, *Transformations in Modern Architecture* was on show at MoMA from February 21 through April 24, 1979.
28 Arthur Drexler, *Transformations in Modern Architecture* (New York: Museum of Modern Art, 1979), 12.
29 Drexler, "Response," 6.
30 Arthur Drexler, sound recordings of lecture on *Transformations in Modern Architecture*, held at MoMA, April 10, 1979. Archives of the Museum of Modern Art. [Henceforth "Lecture on *Transformations*."]
31 Drexler, Lecture on *Transformations*.
32 Arthur Drexler, typescript dated March 24, 1977, 4. Exhibition files.
33 Drexler, *Transformations*, 12.
34 Drexler, "Response," 6.
35 Drexler, "Response," 6.
36 Typescript copy of wall text. Exhibition files.

work are too thin or too fat, the first wave of imitations will make them thinner of fatter; the second wave will try to do the same with all remaining elements. This process, perhaps unconscious, exerts a centrifugal force on coherent systems of design and ultimately reduces them to parodies.[33]

The galleries confronted the visitor with a grotesque array of such exaggerations, modernist elements taken out of their function within a system of coherent codes and grossly distorted in desperate attempts at individual expression. Presenting late modern architecture as a series of bad copies, *Transformations* thus demonstrated a decline.

Second, and related to the first, this organization of fragments allowed new connections to be made. "It's rather like an intelligence test," Drexler remarked. "What do these two pictures have in common? [...] And that question infuriates architects. 'My work has nothing in common with Joe's and Jim's. Obviously unique, I have invented this all by myself.'"[34] Drexler soon offered concrete references:

I think it is very interesting to stand in one place and to see SOM's BNA skyscraper, which is pure frame, if nothing else, on one wall at the beginning of the section that deals with structure and, at the end of the section that deals with sculptural form, buildings by Michael Graves and Peter Eisenman and Richard Meier.... The fact that there is some connection between SOM and this exalted group of architects is something that perhaps even they themselves have never thought of.[35]

Thematizing the knowing breakdown of his own categorizations, Drexler's opening wall text had also pointed out similarities amongst supposedly polarized practices: "more often than we might have supposed, they co-exist comfortably and even begin to merge, despite the intensity with which contending factions proclaim their uniqueness."[36] While many were angered by the abrupt juxtaposition of "high-end" work with degraded vernacular derivations, this adjacency served to foreground the purely formal nature of any connections as well as the mode of circulation of codes. In "narrowing the comparisons to similarities in aesthetic

Fig. 2 Installation view of *Transformations in Modern Architecture*, Museum of Modern Art, New York, February 21 through April 24, 1979

choice," Drexler explained sardonically, attention was focused on "the borrowing of formal ideas customary to architecture."[37]

Third, and far less evidently, the exhibition demonstrated the failure of late modern buildings to communicate about either their function or, we might stress, their fiction. Modernist forms, Drexler stated, "have had to be justified according to determinist doctrines which the forms themselves contradict."[38] *Transformations*' opening wall text had obliquely addressed this paradox when it informed the viewer that:

> Architectural fictions, the play of unnecessary forms with which the historical style sought to transcend necessity, were rejected as unworthy…. What we now reject is the idea that fictions have to be disguised. How architectural truths and fictions transform each other constitutes a large part of recent history, and is the subject of this exhibition.[39]

If comprising the subject of *Transformations*, any lesson arising remained far from self-evident, for Drexler's commentary pointed only to the failure of any residual fictional investigations in the work on display. A few further clues were, however, offered in the catalog.

In distinction to the unwitting formal paradoxes arising from modernism's determinist claims, Drexler's essay noted three contemporary tendencies: first, a critical discourse regarding the "structure of meaning" (i.e., Eisenman and *Oppositions*); second, the turn to "meaning" and historicization as a means of dispelling "the odor of 'good taste'" (the semantic investigations of the Grays); and, third, conceptual or experimental, even fictional work cast as social criticism.[40] "Abundant opportunities to build in the sixties, despite faltering convictions, perhaps helped to deflect purely theoretical studies toward social criticism cast as architectural jokes," he explained of the latter category.

> We live overwhelmed by machines: therefore why not walking machine-cities on mechanical legs, of science-fiction comic-strip provenance, as in the entertaining drawings of the English group Archigram? And existential nausea ought to have its architectural mode, so why not the surreal perspectives of "utility grids" covering the earth, as in the Antonioniesque productions of the Italian group Superstudio? Deliberately ambiguous, these and similar studies—especially those accompanied by left-wing political expectations—owe much of their charm to uncertainty. Since they cannot be serious they must be jokes, unless they are meant to be warnings.[41]

Read as knowing if ultimately dystopic engagements with

---

[37] Drexler, *Transformations*, 9.
[38] Drexler, *Transformations*, 3.
[39] Typescript copy of wall text. This was reiterated in the MOMA press release of February 21, 1979.
[40] In this Drexler is following the three categories formulated by Emilio Ambasz in 1972: conformist (design as autonomous); reformist (pop and semantics); and contestatory (radical). See Emilio Ambasz (ed.), *Italy: The New Domestic Landscape; Achievements and Problems of Italian Design* (New York: Museum of Modern Art, 1972).
[41] Drexler, *Transformations*, 6.
[42] Drexler, *Transformations*, 6.
[43] Reyner Banham, "MOMA's Architectural Mystery Tour," *AIA Journal*, 69:7 (June 1980), 56–7.
[44] Banham, "MOMA's Architectural Mystery Tour," 56.
[45] Kenneth Frampton, "Blow Up," *Skyline* (April 1979), 6.
[46] Barbaralee Diamonstein, "Pushing Future Directions in Modern Design," *Art News* (March 1977), 44.

the historical condition of the 1960s and early '70s, such experimental work had embraced ambiguity and uncertainty. That Drexler had strong reservations about the political efficacy of such practices, particularly regarding their ability to generate new "values," was evident from the passages cited above. Alienation, he went on to argue, had been summoned by radical architects "as a tactic of subversion for political ends." Far from provoking revolution, such tactics, according to Drexler, would now simply "postpone revolution by increasing the tolerance for alienation." Exhibiting a particularly Tafurian melancholy, Drexler regarded the work as perhaps the last realm of radical practice, while at the same time fundamentally impotent in the face of capitalism's ongoing capacity to resolve all contradictions.[42]

In his review, "MoMA's Architectural Mystery Tour," Reyner Banham recounted the "genuine bafflement" aroused by *Transformations* and the sense of anticipation that the tardy catalog would offer some clarification as to its intent and discursive coordinates. If the book managed to clarify the onslaught "a bit"—since "one can read the text and digest the illustrations at one's own speed and in greater comfort"—there was also something about Drexler's approach that "refuses to come to a point or a conclusion. What one now sees," Banham correctly surmised, "is that this not coming to a point is programmatic—it may even be what the show was all about."[43] Pointing to Drexler's suggestion that modernism "has been against interpretation, preferring the self-evident fitness of things," Banham noted, in the first instance, the irony of presenting a selection of buildings that could no longer speak for themselves. "Practically every building," he wrote, "comes to us trailing banners of interpretation, be it by Peter Eisenman, Charles Jencks, myself, Peter Cook, Alan Colquhoun, Allan Temko, Philip Johnson, Ada Louise [Huxtable], Edgar Kaufmann, Oscar Newman—or even Arthur Drexler!" But he went on to praise the curator for retrieving important work of the recent past, and in so doing betrayed his understanding that the show was ultimately premised on quality. Even Banham misrecognized the irony of its intentionally discursive "muddle."[44]

Reviewing the exhibition for *Skyline*, Kenneth Frampton identified its melancholic tone. Drexler, he argued, had been "forced by history to finally acknowledge the dominance of the value-free positivism over which it has always been the liberal curator's duty to draw a redeeming mask." The curator, he continued, perceptively, had been "anguished by his own remorse at the loss of the ideal object." Frampton opened his critical review, entitled "Blow Up," with a wry remark regarding historical pressures, pressures that were indeed on Drexler's mind. "While Frank Lloyd Wright was understandably distressed by his reading of Victor Hugo's prophecy that the printed word would kill architecture," Frampton noted, "he seems to have had little intimation of how reproduction in general would eventually reduce architecture to irrelevancy or, as Abraham Moles put it at a much later date, to a condition in which the monuments of Europe would be 'worn away by Kodaks.'" Frampton identified two reproduction technologies informing the "spectral profile" of late modernism: building production and photographic reproduction. Yet his invocation of Moles, an information theorist, pointed to a further generation of technology that was indeed haunting, or even *killing* architecture. He acknowledged this when arguing that Drexler had "opted for the 'admass' strategy of photographic overkill, for the television approach of 'socking it to them,' that is, for a theoretically and ultimately infinite exhibition."[45]

That Drexler might have knowingly mobilized such as assault of images over any materialist conception of the architectural object was rejected by Frampton as capitulation to spectacle. The visitor, Frampton recounted,

> is bombarded by a welter of images that he surely cannot assimilate, and the relatively scant curatorial information provided gives only the most cursory indication of how the material is to be interpreted or evaluated. Instead we are confronted with Eliot's strategy of distraction: "to be distracted from distraction by distraction."

To his mind the exhibition simply acted to disorient the viewer in its saturated, even postmodern media space, a space without legibility or a coherent narrative. Yet while Frampton disagreed with the show's premises, the fact that architecture was already fully captured within the "consciousness industry" of admass culture *was* Drexler's point. "The design issues we are faced with today," Drexler had explained while preparing the show, "are the design of systems that influence the way we live."[46] Immersed within an expansive system of media and information networks, the contemporary subject, in Drexler's assessment, could not escape this technological milieu and it was therefore an imperative to find strategies of working, even of designing, within it.

If the semiotic reception of his earlier Beaux-Arts exhibition had seen only the surface, and the modernist reception had focused on the loss of rational structure, Drexler had been fascinated by the indeterminate relation between the two systems. Noting that the history of modern architecture had "evolve[d] in the context of scientific determinism," he argued that one could equally trace "the history of the architect's attitude toward freedom and necessity,"[47] to his mind the site of ethical, even political struggle. (At a formal level this is how he read the disarticulation of structure and cladding in Henri Labrouste's Bibliothèque Sainte-Geneviève.) Yet the space between freedom and necessity, that space of play, of decisions, and of actions, did not, as demonstrated in *Transformations*, on its own accord prompt architects to rethink the ethical dimensions of their work. Moreover, if questions raised by his Beaux-Arts "revival"—issues of pedagogy, morality, fiction, revolution and the end of modernism—remained important subtexts for his investigation of contemporary practice in *Transformations*, they had perhaps been even more carefully nuanced following reactions to the former show. Drexler's aim, as Levine has recently argued, was to supplement this melancholic duo with exhibitions on key modernist figures such as Frank Lloyd Wright (and I would add Mies van der Rohe), whose work he believed would demonstrate earlier, and positive, instances of modern architecture's capacity to forge relations between freedom and necessity.[48] But the stakes had also changed. What Drexler understood was that the discipline now had to take into account the implications of a new generation of technology.

Prefacing *The Design Collection: Selected Objects* of 1970, Drexler told a post-apocalyptic tale of an archaeological excavation of MoMA's design collection that, in retrospect, seems relevant here. At the center of his story was a crisis in the "20th century category, the 'functional.'" If the collected objects were, on the one hand, to be read as useful, Drexler explained that "the variety of forms deemed functionally appropriate to serve a single purpose, as in the design of chairs, would suggest that human beings were remarkably flexible and, moreover, were eager to assume the shapes dictated by their functional objects." With reference to objects exceeding their practical function or use-value, he noted that the archaeologist might conclude that "the appearance of a chair—or indeed any other object—conferred some special distinction on its owner." A second order exchange-value had overtaken the primacy and legibility of use-value, a situation exacerbated by the object's suspension within the museum. Drexler continued his tale with a parody of the divide between modernist objects composed of geometric figures—as though the

47 Drexler, "Engineer's Architecture," 52–3.
48 See Levine, "Frank Lloyd Wright: Architect."
49 Arthur Drexler, "Preface," *The Design Collection: Selected Objects* (New York: Museum of Modern Art, 1970).

"figures themselves possessed a peculiar potency"—and those derived from nature, including "the wave patterns of liquids, the contours of vegetables." If these formal oppositions preoccupied this civilization (and, we might note, returned to prominence in the blobs versus boxes opposition of the 1990s), "the more astute archaeologist" would recognize that by the third quarter of the century there was "a deliberate rejection of design and technique alike."[49]

Referencing the "curious brown 'anti-object'" on the facing page—a urethane foam armchair designed by Gunnar Anderson in 1964—the archaeologist might offer a very preliminary assessment of "what stresses and disillusionment may have led to this reversal" in the certainties of form. They might do so, Drexler speculated, by noting a connection to "the heightening of aesthetic and technical ingenuity in the design of computers and other instruments of superefficiency—a class of objects feared as much as it was admired." The very next page of the catalog was an installation view of the Architecture and Design galleries that offered a further clue to his remarks. Along with the museum's usual lineup of modernist design, from Mies van der Rohe's Barcelona chair (1929) to the Self-Aligning Ball Bearing (1934), and Alvar Aalto's molded plywood armchair (1934), was to be found the control panel (or circuit board) for IBM 305, Random Access Memory Accounting Machine of 1956.

Drexler had introduced the RAMAC circuit board into the museum's collection in 1958 and presented it as the final stage of technological-aesthetic development in an exhibition that year, *Twentieth Century Design from the Collection*. This was the first time the collection had been

Fig. 3 Installation view of the Architecture and Design Galleries, Museum of Modern Art, New York, c. 1970

exhibited as such and the RAMAC circuit board appeared as the very last image in the catalog in a category, "The New Machine Art." Drexler explained that it demonstrated a paradigm shift:

> Since the end of World War II, electronics has altered our conception of how things need to be shaped in order to work, and of how they may be related to each other. Geometric machine art suggested by its finite shapes the direct action of push and pull: the new machines are incomprehensible unless one knows about the existence of invisible forces.... Perhaps the most striking characteristic of the new machine aesthetic is its dematerialization of finite shapes into diagrammatic relationships. Examples are the printed electric circuits, which replace three-dimensional objects with groups of patterns printed on a flat surface. Such patterns can hardly be said to have precise boundaries, or to be complete in themselves.[50]

He explained, furthermore, that artists and designers were increasingly "concerned with the philosophical concepts underlying technology."

Between 1959 and 1970 the RAMAC circuit board continued to haunt Drexler's consideration of the impact of this new generation of machines. As early as a 1959 symposium, "Design as Commentary," he was interrogated over the status of this emblematic object. Responding to the question "is it design?" he explained:

> It symbolizes the changing sense of what constitutes an object, the move from the finite geometry of the '20s and '30s which seemed to mark the ultimate development of the machine, to what has happened since the war with the development of electronics: the dematerialization of objects, the reduction to parts.[51]

He tried to clarify the nature of this formal shift by way of a parallel transformation from the Barcelona chair to Harry Bertoia's wire chair. When the other commentators remained unconvinced, and repeatedly challenged the idea that the circuit board had an aesthetic, Drexler finally conceded that beyond aesthetics was the question of technology itself. "Technology dominates most of what we do," he argued, "It would seem the logical place to look for hints of what is happening in ideas." If new technologies had raised the question "what actually constitutes an object?" a "new image," he explained, is "beginning to form, largely through electronics."[52] While Drexler never expanded on those ideas in any detail, he pointed again and again to this dematerialization effected by electronics. Coming at the question from yet another angle, the moderator asked why the RAMAC was

[50] Arthur Drexler and Greta Daniel, *Introduction to Twentieth Century Design from the Collection of the Museum of Modern Art, New York* (New York: Museum of Modern Art, 1959), 94.
[51] Arthur Drexler, "Design as Commentary," *Industrial Design* (February 1959), 54–65: 64.
[52] Drexler, "Design as Commentary," 64.
[53] Arthur Drexler, cited in A. Ferebee, "Technology Yes, Industrial Design, Maybe," *Industrial Design*, 10 (June 1963), 72–4: 73.
[54] Harriet Morrison, "Inside the Control Box," *Herald Tribune*, March 10, 1965. Clipping in MoMA Public Information Scrapbook, on microfilm at the Archives of American Art.

Fig. 4 Page from "Design as Commentary," *Industrial Design* (February 1959)

Fig. 5 Standard Oil Plants from "Technology Yes. Industrial Design, Maybe," *Industrial Design* (June 1963)

not shown in its entirety. Briefly evading the question with the response that it "was just physically impossible," Drexler eventually queried in return: "What *is* the whole of RAMAC?" "This is what I mean about the new concept of what constitutes an object. It isn't just the three consoles that make RAMAC. Its all the other machines that work with it, that make it possible to do the operation that RAMAC can do."

In 1963 Drexler was again interviewed on his decision to exhibit "the RAMAC computer's brilliantly colored wire assembly as an object in itself." Questioned, in this instance, about his use of the term "dematerialization," Drexler insisted that it was a historical phenomenon emerging in the late twentieth century. He then pointed to the telephone, imagining its potential dissolution: "This is a finite object, but suppose instead of a dial I had a series of buttons on my desk, and instead of a mouthpiece, a receiver set into the tip of the desk? If this were done, would you still call the telephone a single object?"[53] Reduced to a system of parts, many of which were beyond the control of the traditional designer, the object had ceased to be confinable within the limits of a cohesive, unified body. As such, Drexler optimistically proposed, they might escape capitulation to the "economic complex in which things are made," those market-driven determinants of the IBM computer or Braun phonograph's modernist external forms. And with respect to addressing the subject immersed within this technological milieu, Drexler explained that "Art and technology are aspects of the effort to understand and organize experience…. To insist on their opposition," he continued, noting the human subject's radical imbrication in this condition, "is to ignore logic, metaphysics, psychoanalysis, and electroencephalography." It seems important to stress that Drexler recognized that those historical forces had profoundly impacted the human subject. A short note titled "Inside the Control Box" conveyed his discussions on transformations in man-made objects as they affected the museum. After detailing expansions into systems of control, the imaging of outer space, disposable objects, and the turn to an aesthetics of process, Drexler had offered the insight that such "objects" were not only symptomatic of "the world in which they occur," but that that this technology "tells each of us something about ourselves."[54]

Drexler explained at one point in the 1963 interview that he "was planning an exhibition which will try to show technology and design in relation to the whole culture—not just marketing." "Spread around him on his desk," the critic reported, were "photos of oil cracking plants and gas storage systems." Pointing to the Standard

Oil refinery in Aruba, Drexler commented, "This whole structure is a diagram of process." Was it architecture? Drexler thought "Yes. But I think you have to change the idea of architecture."[55]

The following year MoMA presented *Twentieth Century Engineering*, regarded by many critics as a problematic aestheticization of technology. Donald Judd, for instance, argued that MoMA had simply fallen back onto a codified paradigm of elegance.[56] If the structures were selected for their aesthetic resonances, it was not only elegance that was at stake for Drexler but rather the manner or even realm in which they articulated aesthetics and technology. (We will return to this shortly.) The exhibition presented, in the first instance, structures by modern architects Drexler continued to admire, such as Wright's 1939 Johnson Wax Administration building as well as Mies's 860 Lakeshore Drive Apartments of 1951, and the Chicago Convention Hall of 1954. Second was experimental structures by engineers, including folded plate concrete structures of Felix Candella and Pier Luigi Nervi, geodesic domes of Buckminster Fuller, and inflatable structures by Frei Otto, all of which were making their way into the imagination of architects and onto the pages of magazines like *Architectural Design* and *Archigram*. Also

55 Drexler in "Technology Yes, Industrial Design, Maybe," 74. See also Arthur Drexler, "Interview with Arthur Drexler," *Interiors*, 135:4 (November 1965), 155–6.
56 Donald Judd, "Month in Review," *Arts Magazine* (October 1964), 60–4.
57 Arthur Drexler, "Visionary Architecture," *Arts and Architecture*, 78:1 (January 1961), 11.
58 Drexler, "Visionary Architecture," 11. See also John Fowler, "Opinion: Visionary Architecture," in *Architectural Design* (May 1961), 181–2.
59 Drexler, "Visionary Architecture," 28.

Fig. 6 Installation view of *Visionary Architecture*, Museum of Modern Art, New York, September 29 through December 4, 1960

included were experimental structures by architects, such as George Nelson's U.S. Exhibition Pavilion (Moscow, 1959), Louis Kahn and Anne Tyng's 1955 *City Tower* project, and Victor Lundy's inflatable Atomic Energy Commission exhibition building of 1960.

Earlier in 1960 Drexler had exhibited Michael Webb's Furniture Manufacturer's Showroom in *Visionary Architecture*. It was a project that incorporated the process-oriented logic, and even the formal qualities, of oil refinery plants into its "bowelist" aesthetic and it appeared alongside a remarkable line-up of *fictions* of technology. In addition to modernist work (by Hans Poelzig, Eric Mendelsohn, El Lissitsky, and, again, Mies and Wright), this prescient exhibition of experimental work also included: Fuller's *Partial Enclosure of Manhattan Island* of 1960; William Katavalos's *Chemical Architecture* of 1960; Paolo Soleri's *Theological Center of Biotechnic City* of 1959; Kiyonori Kikutake's *Marine City* of 1960; and Noriaki Kurokawa's *Agricultural City* of 1959, among others. Such work, it is important to note, appeared not as an isolated aberration in Drexler's curatorial selections but as ongoing counter-narratives to the institution's presentation of a more mainstream trajectory of modernism. Kahn and Tyng's *City Tower* was presented in *Visionary Architecture* prior to *Twentieth Century Engineering*, and Frederick Kiesler's *Endless House* of 1949–60 (then under construction for exhibition at MoMA) was later to be included in *Transformations*.

It was in this context that Drexler first offered something like a theory of fiction, casting visionary strategies as a "second history of architecture that parallels the real one." For the architect, he argued, "ideal projects afford the sole occasions when he can rebuild the world as he knows it ought to be."[57] But it was not just ideal or unbuilt projects that qualified as visionary. "When ideal projects are inspired by criticism of the existing structure of society," Drexler explained of their radical intent, "they may bring forth ideas that make history. These projects may be called visionary."[58] That such work, "private" as the fictions might have been, was understood to have an impact was indicated by Drexler:

> Visionary projects, like Plato's ideal forms, cast their shadows over into the real world of experience, expense, and frustration. If we could learn what they have to teach, we might exchange irrelevant rationalizations for more useful critical standards. Vision and reality might then coincide.[59]

Drexler's reference to platonic forms and their shadows was perhaps unfortunate when one considers the relation between "vision and reality" the curator described. The visionary images, if situated in a separate realm from reality, were cast as akin to a virtual plane that might be actualized in the present, not, as with Plato's ideal forms manifesting (through a passage of realization) as degraded copies. Moreover, as Gilles Deleuze has argued in his reading of Henri Bergson, the creative evolution operating in the passage of actualization has transformative and differentiating capacities.[60] For Drexler, these visionary strategies in fact harbored a type of utopian ideal. While not taking the form of the totalizing plans of modernist utopias, they remained for him strategies of producing concepts of a better world that might have an effect. This trajectory of experimental practice has, as I have argued elsewhere, recently been recuperated in service of a paternity to contemporary experimentations with new technology. But this recuperation, if at times interesting, has often been at the expense of the critical and utopian ideals of its purported forefathers and has elided experimental work's political cast.[61]

In 1970, the RAMAC circuit board was exhibited again in a show of *Recent Acquisitions* co-curated by Drexler and Emilio Ambasz, then Curator of Design. Following their common interest in process-oriented experimental work, *Recent Acquisitions* included a number of "soft" chairs such as Gaetano Pesce's 1969 Up-1 chair sold compressed in a vacuum vinyl container. "Opening of the sealed container," we are told in the press release, "allows the chair, made of stretch fabric over injected urethane, to automatically expand." For *Recent Acquisitions* the museum purchased Raimund Abraham's drawings for *Universal City*, dating from 1964–67, and attempted to add Haus Rucker Co.'s Environmental Control Helmet to the collection. Upon Drexler's recommendation, the 1969 Sacco chair, a soft leather form filled with polystrene beads, furnished Kynaston McShine's *Information* show of 1970, an exhibition avowedly responding to a culture "considerably altered by communications systems such as television and film, and by increased mobility."[62]

Drexler's interest in the social and aesthetic potentials of post-industrial technology intersected with many of Ambasz's own, and the young curator would have brought him in contact with additional institutional and political stakes raised by this transformation.[63] Both believed that the indeterminacy facilitated by such technologies would, in principle, offer a space not just of a pernicious assimilation into the socioeconomic system

---

60 See Michael Hardt, *Gilles Deleuze: An Apprenticeship in Philosophy* (Minneapolis: University of Minnesota Press, 1993).
61 See Felicity D. Scott, "Involuntary Prisoners of Architecture," in *October*, 106 (Fall 2003), 75–101.
62 Kynaston L. McShine (ed.), *Information* (New York: Museum of Modern Art, 1970), 2.
63 See, for instance, Emilio Ambasz, "The University of Design and Development," and "The Designs of Freedom," in *Perspecta*, 13/14 (1971), 360–1 and 363–5.
64 Emilio Ambasz, cited in Andrea Oppenheimer Dean, "Arthur Drexler Remembered by Colleagues and Architects," *Architecture* (March 1987), 36.
65 Ambasz, cited in "Arthur Drexler Remembered," 36.
66 Drexler, Lecture on *Transformations*.
67 Michael Kimmelman, "The New Museum of Modern Art: Interview with Arthur Drexler," *Art News*, 83:5 (1984), 66. See also Levine, "Frank Lloyd Wright," in which he traces Drexler's reading of Wright as a counter-narrative to such "end of history" tropes.
68 Drexler, "Engineer's Architecture," 51.

but also of a mode of active, critical participation. (Ambasz later recalled in an obituary that he thought "that Arthur understood and shared my passions for what I was doing."[64]) It was through Ambasz's 1972 exhibition, *Italy: The New Domestic Landscape*, that not only Italian design but in particular the Architettura Radicale of Superstudio and others, which strangely haunted both the Beaux-Arts show and *Transformations*, would become familiar to MoMA. Yet unlike Ambasz, whose work was increasingly vectored towards both theoretical discourse and interventions into the means of production, the latter manifested most provocatively in *The Taxi Project* of 1976, Drexler would insist on potentials within the realm of aesthetics. Ambasz recalled that Drexler

> saw architecture as a high art, as an act of imagination. His idea was that knowledge comes after images, and he therefore had a lingering distrust of ideology. For him the supreme misfortune occurred when the idea arrived before the image.[65]

But that image, to extend Drexler's lesson, was to be loaded; it was not to take the form of a poor copy or degraded iteration of an already failed system but rather to be a virtual plane operating as ethico-political interventions into current conditions. Its production as an aesthetic object, moreover, carried with it the burden and challenges of its historical moment, for it was only through such specificity that it might in turn impact that condition.

What are we to make, then, of Drexler's melancholic reading of late modernism? His struggle both with modernism and with new technologies seems, if in retrospect naïve, nevertheless to offer a cautionary tale. Drexler acknowledged, in the first instance, that architecture was "of course a conservative, validating operation." "If one wishes to generate a revolution," he conceded, "there are better techniques than those that owe their existence to architecture."[66] But if Drexler was aware of architecture's relation to the social, aesthetic, technological, and political norms operating within capitalism, this did not mean that he concurred either with the position of celebration (Grays) or with that of withdrawal (Whites). He also avoided falling into the trap of moralizing about architecture's imbrication within these fields. If implicitly flawed or inept as the locus of ethico-political intervention, this did not mean such ideals should be jettisoned; the discipline remained for Drexler a site of "visionary" conceptualization of alternatives; that is, it retained an ethical vocation.

In a 1984 interview, Drexler alluded to prospects for architecture: "History doesn't come to an end. Something will happen, but not on command."[67] If modern architecture had to him become "impoverished," and had failed to continue in its task of forging knowing relations between aesthetics and technology, he indicated that this situation did not represent an irreversible impasse. For just as modern architects had engaged mechanical technology with such ideals in mind, contemporary architects could continue to harness and to radicalize the transformative prospects opened up by new technologies—notably computers and the open-ended and dispersed systems through and within which they operated. If the discipline's turn to semantics at the end of the 1960s was, polemically, a move away from then prevalent scientific and technological investigations, what Drexler recognized were additional potentials remaining in the technological counterparts of the linguistic turn that had either been all too quickly forgotten or that were yet to be adequately articulated.

It became important then to distinguish a radical pluralist paradigm from what Drexler termed the "arbitrary complexity" of the Grays, a complexity staged as the embrace of pluralism and ecclecticism in opposition to the "arbitrary simplicity" of both high modernism and the Whites. But any critical embrace of complexity, and particularly of the uncertainty and indeterminacy facilitated by new technology, would not imply that anything goes but that architects assume responsibility for their decisions and for their actions, that they make ethical decisions with respect to the language of their expression. To avoid the desublimation of ornament as he had wryly presented it in *Transformations*—a desublimation manifest in the drive to pseudo-differentiation—Drexler proposed "valuing the connection between ornament and freedom, and providing for it the moral space, so to speak, in which the free will can play."[68] While he never adequately described what form this might take, it seems that for him such a re-valuation would have been located somehow at the intersection of fiction and technology, where architects could pursue ethical and political agendas and could do so through formal and aesthetic experimentation.

An ethical response to postmodernism—terms used by Drexler in his catalog essay—would thus, we might posit following the implications of Drexler's investigations, have to include the formulation of a historically specific criticality to form and a non-servile virtuosity with respect to new technologies, and it would have to refuse both the conservative rejection and the inadequately theorized adoption of new technological potentials. Despite its vanguard character, the uncritical adoption of new technology for design has the potential of operating, like historicism, as a form of conservatism, as in the return to an uncritical formalism evident in post-critical and post-theoretical streams of contemporary practice. For neither attribute to architecture, and particularly to architectural form, significant scope beyond occupying and lightly reforming extant possibilities of the discipline's role—social, theoretical, political, ethical, or otherwise.[69] If we are to continue to extend Drexler's lessons to issues haunting our own period, it

---

[69] See Drexler, "Engineer's Architecture," 15.

[70] These sorts of claims were heard repeatedly from the post-critical camp at a conference on the state of contemporary architecture, Columbia University, April 18–19, 2003.

might be argued that the discipline's response to technological development remain not in a dialectic of the rejection or celebration of the new but, rather, that engagement with technology continue to open out onto ethical questions and political demands, no matter how difficult this might have become in light of the legacy of modernist idealism. It is not enough to claim, as was heard in the late sixties and as we are hearing again today, that such questions are not the task of architecture, that the architect's task is "just" to make architecture.[70] The challenge to the discipline, to its institutions and to its aesthetic codes that stands as a potential legacy of Drexler's paradoxical musings might be summarized as follows: how to conceive an architecture that forges moments of radical (not pseudo-) differentiation, and hence transformations, within a highly codified and iterative system; and how to operate within the existing administrative and commercial system while finding space to open onto ethical questions adequate to the contemporary social, geopolitical, and technological milieu.

Acknowledgements
This work has benefited from many people to whom I would like to extend my gratitude, including K. Michael Hays, Mark Wigley, George Baird, Neil Levine, and Laura Kurgan. I want particularly to thank Anne Dixon, Pierre Adler, Michelle Elligot and Terrence Riley at MoMA for kindly and expertly facilitating my archival research. Aspects of this article were first presented at Cornell University in 2001 in *The Seventies: The Formation of Contemporary Architectural Discourse* (organized by George Baird, K. Michael Hays, and Val Wark).

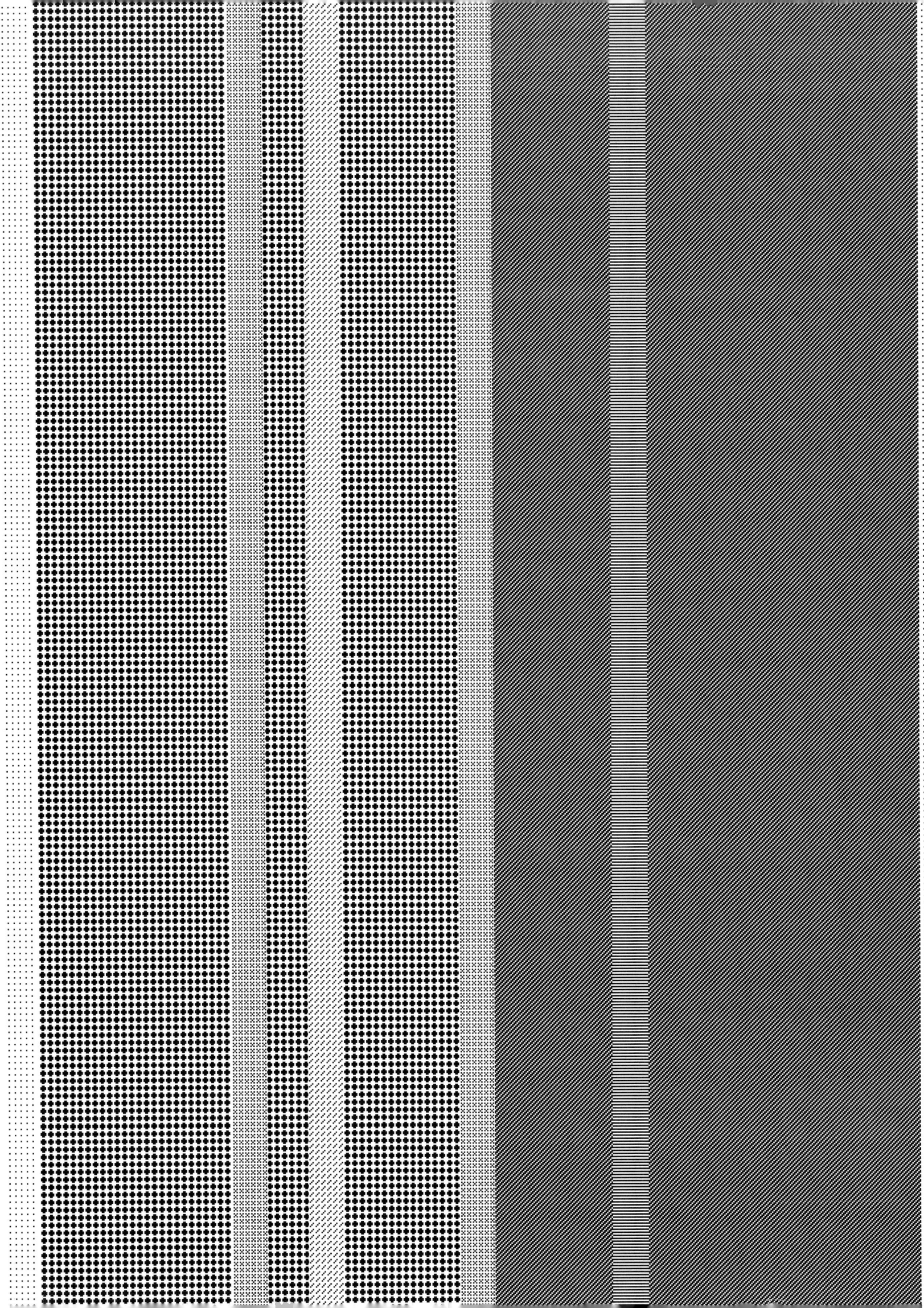